Beckett on screen

Manchester University Press

Beckett on screen
The television plays

JONATHAN BIGNELL

Manchester University Press
Manchester and New York
distributed in the United States exclusively
by Palgrave Macmillan

Copyright © Jonathan Bignell 2009

The right of Jonathan Bignell to be identified as the author
of this work has been asserted by him in accordance with
the Copyright, Designs and Patents Act 1988.

Published by Manchester University Press
Oxford Road, Manchester M13 9NR, UK
and Room 400, 175 Fifth Avenue, New York, NY 10010, USA
www.manchesteruniversitypress.co.uk

Distributed in the United States exclusively by
Palgrave Macmillan, 175 Fifth Avenue,
New York, NY 10010, USA

Distributed in Canada exclusively by
UBC Press, University of British Columbia, 2029 West Mall,
Vancouver, BC, Canada V6T 1Z2

British Library Cataloguing-in-Publication Data is available

Library of Congress Cataloging-in-Publication Data is available

ISBN 978 0 7190 6421 0 paperback

First published by Manchester University Press in hardback 2009

This paperback edition first published 2012

The publisher has no responsibility for the persistence or accuracy of URLs for any
external or third-party internet websites referred to in this book, and does not guarantee
that any content on such websites is, or will remain, accurate or appropriate.

Printed by Lightning Source

Contents

Acknowledgements	page vii
Introduction	1

1 Production
Introduction	17
Television and video aesthetics	18
The significance of film in *Beckett on Film: Play*	31
Studios, sound-stages and theatre	37
Monochrome and colour	41
Sound, music and voice: dissociated conventions	44

2 Broadcasting contexts
Introduction	52
Television forms	53
Drama, arts and video art	57
Avant gardes in the cinema	66
Public Service Broadcasting and the value of Beckett	76
Television, plays and DVDs: *Beckett on Film*	82

3 Institutions and authorship
Introduction	88
Staging authorship	90
Beckett and conventions of television authorship	99
Collaboration and networking	105
Authenticity, identity and performance	111
Beckettian 'signatures' in *Film*	114
Posthumous reverence	119

4 Intertexts
  Introduction — 125
  Beckett among the modernists — 128
  Film and silent cinema — 133
  Picture planes and performance spaces — 138
  Learning to see — 151
  Viewer and viewed — 159

5 Evaluations
  Introduction — 164
  Broadcasting and conceptions of audience — 165
  Beckett and television criticism — 168
  The place of the viewer — 172
  Schedules and audiences — 176
  Reviewers and commentators — 184
  The reception of *Film*: author, director and star — 190
  Audience, form and the politics of television drama — 195

6 Afterword: the lessons of history — 202

Bibliography — 209

Index — 223

Acknowledgements

I would like to record the contribution of some of the people who encouraged my initial interest and enthusiasm for Beckett's work many years ago, especially Peter Coulson and Iain Wright. In more recent times, I have benefited from the wisdom and experience of Michael Bott, Mary Bryden, Daniela Caselli, Julian Garforth, James Knowlson, Anna McMullan and John Pilling, each of whom I encountered first at the University of Reading where the different contexts of teaching graduate students, participating in research seminars and learning about the Samuel Beckett Archive have been very helpful to the development of my own ideas. Conversations with actors and television directors have added valuable insights to my work, and I would especially like to thank Walter Asmus in this regard. I am equally grateful to the staff of the BBC Written Archives Centre in Reading, England, for providing access to original BBC documents and assisting me on this project as well as several others. Unfortunately it has not been possible to include illustrations from television productions in this book. While the principles of 'fair dealing' extend to academic use of photographic stills in the USA, under British law it is still necessary to clear copyrights and pay high fees to rights owners, and I hope readers will understand and sympathise.

This book is intended as a contribution to academic work on the history and theory of television drama, as well as being a study of the presentation of Beckett's dramatic work on television and in *Film*. I am grateful to the many television academics I have worked with, who are too numerous to name but some of whose work is discussed in this book. The Centre for Television Drama Studies at the University of Reading, and the research programmes funded by the Arts and Humanities Research Council that I have led there, have provided vigorous contexts in which to test ideas, and I am grateful for the support which my colleagues and the funding body have given me. The research on which this book is based was carried out largely while working at the University of Reading, and I would like to thank my colleagues in the Department of Film, Theatre and Television for the remarkable fellowship and the culture of excellence for which the Department is justly renowned. Some of the initial work for the book was done in my previous post at Royal Holloway, University of London, and I am also grateful for the intense and fruitful experience there that had a significant influence on my approach to television in the context of media arts. I gratefully acknowledge the assistance of a research award from The Leverhulme Trust which released me from teaching duties during the period when I conducted archival research on the BBC television productions of Beckett's dramas and began the drafting of the book. The discussions I had with Christina Adamou during the writing of her PhD thesis on Beckett's television dramas have contributed greatly to the clarification of my approach to the material I have written about here, and similarly, work by Alastair Hird for an MA by Research and PhD research by Katherine Weiss and David Foster have assisted me in developing my approach to Beckett's work. I am also grateful for encouragement and suggestions made by participants in the seminars run by the Beckett International Foundation at the University of Reading, including some of the people already named here. I have published some of the ideas in this book in earlier articles and essays, each of which is listed in the bibliography of this book, and I am grateful for the opportunity to present preliminary versions of material discussed here, and also to Manchester University Press for enabling me to develop this research project in book form. Early versions of parts of this book were presented at conferences organised by the Society for Cinema Studies, the journal *Screen*, postgraduates at Royal Holloway, University of London, the University of New South Wales and the Beckett International Foundation. I am grateful to the organisers of these events and to the delegates whose questions and comments have assisted in developing my ideas. Extracts from Samuel Beckett's unpublished manuscripts, *Eh Joe*, *Ghost Trio*, and *...but the clouds...*, and from his letter to the BBC of 27 November 1976, are reproduced by kind permission of the Estate of Samuel Beckett c/o Rosica Colin Limited, London. Finally, I would like once again to thank Lib Taylor for her encouragement, support and love throughout the lengthy process of completing this book.

Introduction

This book primarily addresses Samuel Beckett's television dramas broadcast in Britain, from *Eh Joe* in 1966 to *Quad* in 1982. The broadcasting of Beckett's theatre work on British television has a long history that runs parallel to his writing specifically for the television medium. For this reason the book includes comparative discussion of some broadcasts of television adaptations of theatre plays written by Beckett, including the *Beckett on Film* series of adaptations of each of his theatre plays, which were made for Channel 4 and the Irish channel RTE and first screened in Britain in 2001. The book also discusses the versions of his television plays produced and broadcast in the 1980s in Germany, where conditions of production in a context of Public Service Broadcasting connect with those at the BBC and exemplify Beckett's European significance as a writer for television. Despite the main focus on television in this study, there is an extended analysis of Beckett's only cinema work, *Film* (1964, 1979) made for the cinema in two different versions. The film was originally conceived as a television drama (Knowlson 1996: 451), was first made shortly before Beckett's earliest foray into television and provides an opportunity to assess thematic, formal and audience reception issues that reflect on the television plays. These audio-visual texts are considered in relation to the evolving critical discourses about television and film, and the historical conditions of production and reception at the time the dramas were made. The television plays are analysed in relation to television production practices, broadcasting contexts, institutional constraints, the significance of authorship in television, intertextual meanings deriving from film, radio, theatre, television and visual art, and audience reception and critical commentary. In addition to critical analysis of the television plays as broadcast, the project emphasises the significance of their production and reception in the television culture in which they were made and watched. This book argues that the concerns of television theory fruitfully reshape the understandings of Beckett's television work that are in circulation in the discourses of Beckett scholarship. My aim is therefore to contribute to the academic analysis of television drama, which has so far paid little attention to Beckett's television work, and also to debates and dialogues in Beckett studies by offering a critical, historical and cultural framework for the television plays and Beckett's work in related media.

The book thus diverges significantly from much of the existing academic writing on Beckett's television and film work by centring its approach less on interpretive analysis of the plays as texts than on their aesthetic and institutional relationship with the history and criticism of British television drama and other audio-visual forms. Although the chapters include close analysis of the meanings of selected sequences from the television plays, and interpretive discussion of whole plays or groups of plays, there is an existing body of detailed analysis of this kind that readers can already consult, represented most recently and most usefully by Graley Herren's 2007 study. In this respect, the book aims to move away from the hitherto dominant critical discourses around Beckett's television work which approach it in textual and authorial terms. Of Beckett's twenty-nine shorter dramas, five are for television, one for film, and seven for radio, but critical interest in this media work has been limited as compared to Beckett's prose and theatre writing. The inaccessibility (until recently) of the works in their audio or audio-visual forms is one reason for this, while another reason is the background of most Beckett commentators in literary or theatre studies. By drawing attention to the aesthetics and contexts of the television medium in this book, I hope to invigorate the study of Beckett's plays for television and introduce them to a broader audience and readership.

The second critical context for this book is its argument throughout that an analysis of Beckett's television dramas is important to the discipline of Television Studies because that analysis provides a location to think through two dominant but often opposed traditions of critical work on television drama (Bignell *et al.* 2000a). The first of these is a tradition concerned with the aesthetics and signification of the audio-visual text, where authorship and formal decisions are often interpreted in political terms as either progressive or reactionary, innovative or generically conformist. The single television play lends itself to the focus in earlier academic work about television on the programme text as a unit, since this accommodates issues of authorship and literary quality, the assumption that the programme is the basic unit of production and reception, and the ability to critique and compare representations for their ideological content and structural principles (Cooke 2003: 98–103). The emphasis was on questions of coherence, aesthetic unity, commitment, message and authorial style. Debates on realisms were a key focus, relegating work like Beckett's, which did not easily fit into versions of realism, to a minor role. Single plays by, for example, the British television playwright David Mercer, in which questions of fantasy were explored, began to seem less significant than they probably were at the time of their broadcast. Beckett's plays eschew the conventions of television realisms, and it is not surprising that developing critical discourses of this kind neglected to mention them.

A second critical tradition is represented by the work of critics like Raymond Williams (1974) or John Ellis (1982), for whom the single television play was much less amenable than popular series drama to their interest in the textual flow of television programmes across a period of viewing, and the viewer's experience of a flow of meanings within, between and across programmes. The free-standing single drama was necessarily one of a kind, so while these approaches to television drama shared with the first critical tradition a concern with commitment and ideological critique, the programmes discussed were popular, generic productions familiar to viewers and encountered by large audiences week after week. Informed by a Cultural Studies agenda that sought to critique the constitution of 'ordinary' television like soap opera, sport and police drama, the proponents of this critical tradition worked on television's contribution to cultural politics more than adopting a 'literary' focus on the dissection of single programmes. With small audiences and little claim to engage with the quotidian experiences of everyday life or the conventions and routines of popular genres, Beckett's television plays made little impression on this cultural study of television either.

The question of whether Beckett's television plays are single 'literary' dramas or part of a larger series is relevant to this problem of their relationships with television genres and customary modes of address to the audience. In writing about the plays it would be usual to cite the titles of individual Beckett dramas as if they were single, independent works. But some of them were in effect episodes in a series with its own title and production system. Inasmuch as some of the plays were made for broadcasting under a collective title (as the *Shades* programme was for *The Lively Arts* series in 1977, containing three Beckett plays, and the *Beckett on Film* productions were), this requires a decision about whether to italicise the titles of the series in which each play appears, as *Arena* or *Beckett on Film*, for example, and thus not differentiate them from individual plays like *Ghost Trio* or *Play*. Throughout the book I have italicised play titles and also used italics for their containing series. This convention respects the conventions of Beckett criticism where plays are italicised as individual works, but it contradicts the conventions of television scholarship where series titles are italicised but individual episodes within them are given in roman typeface and placed in inverted commas. The technical issue of citing television programmes in this book points explicitly to the question of how they belong to the conventional routines of their medium and is therefore much more significant than the trivial issue of the choice between italics and quotation marks suggests. The

Beckett on Film season exhibits this difficulty in several ways. These were separate films involving different teams of people, but they are grouped under a collective title and were shown in the manner of an irregular series on television. In the cinema, the films were also grouped together under a common title even though in cinema exhibition this collective showing is extremely unusual. The key questions of interrelationship, independence, specificity of medium, shared mode of address and, potentially, coherence of audience are each raised in practical terms by this question of citation. This book focuses on the question of the plays' identity within the aesthetic and institutional conventions of their media, which opens up new lines of interpretation and debate.

A recent critical tradition in Television Studies begins from a concern for the audience, regarded either as constructed, positioned and constituted by a text, or as agents of interpretation whose pleasures, resistances and interpretive strategies are of greater interest than the textual forms which enable these responses. Feminist work on television, emerging at the beginning of the 1980s, was a key driving force in this new emphasis on audiences, and targeted either those drama forms which were seen to be addressed to women (notably soap opera) or modes of viewing deemed particular to the domestic environment and women's viewing routines. This work, claiming the political importance of the study of representations of and for the feminine, neglected British television drama in the form of the single play (see Brunsdon *et al.* 1997 for example) and entirely ignores Beckett's television and film work. As the study of actual audiences developed to include work on viewers of situation comedy, police drama, hospital drama and other kinds of fiction, its political interest in how audiences responded to programmes representing institutions like the family or the law confirmed generic series formats as the customary objects of analysis. Beckett's television work seems to stand outside of a history and practice of politically engaged writing within the single play, where politics was understood as the public sphere of employment, government and state institutions. His work also looked unconnected with the more extended political concerns of the drama series, which dealt with the power relations and hierarchies of the family or the workplace. So Beckett's work was apparently innocent of the consistent concern for television theorists and for some British television drama writers to connect with, empower and energise the audience as political agents.

This book does not seek to redeem Beckett's television plays for either of these dominant critical traditions. Instead, it contextualises the plays and shows how they participate in British and more broadly European television aesthetics and histories. Beckett's work in television has many significant characteristics which enable it to become a locus for theoretical discussions of television textuality, because of its concern with framing, composition, and relations between image and sound, for example. Beckett's television plays also provide an interesting occasion for work on television's relationship with its audiences, and the role of commissioning, scheduling and advertising in relation to the debates and contradictions that run though the notion of Public Service Broadcasting in the United Kingdom. How decisions to make a Beckett play for television were made, and how such a play would be offered to an audience, are subjects that are discussed extensively in this book in relation to discourses about the value of television and of Beckett's work, especially since existing discourses have had little to say about them.

For someone like myself whose research has focused largely on television drama in the academic field of Television Studies, the political risk in writing about Beckett's television plays is that the citation of Beckett functions as a marker that points to a conservative tendency in academic criticism to form a canon of 'great works'. This canon-forming activity is based around the primacy of the author, literary-critical evaluations of 'quality' based in the organic unity of texts, and the exclusion of politics from critical criteria for judgement. Both academics (Murdoch 1980) and television professionals themselves (for example, McGrath 1977, 1981) have long argued against this set of evaluative criteria. Writing about Beckett can appear to be 'conservative' because his television plays are not engaged in any obvious way either with popular television entertainment forms or with the 'committed' writing for television that seeks to politicise its audience. Furthermore, Beckett's reputation as a theatrical and literary *auteur* makes any claim for his significance in television seem to rest on his status in other media. This implicitly devalues his television work as secondary to his literary or theatrical output, and devalues television as only being of worth when it imports cultural value from outside. But this book begins from the premise that the citation of someone who crossed the boundary between the television and theatre institutions of production, and between working as a creative writer and a theorist of the arts, is a politically productive challenge to the discourses of Television Studies. The focus on Beckett's work enables this book to develop a productive dialogue between, and question the separation of, high and popular cultures, 'committed' and 'conservative' agendas, realist and modernist forms, and political and pedagogical theories of broadcasting.

A parallel issue arises in relation to historiography in Television Studies. For this book argues that a cultural materialist analysis of Beckett's television work illuminates what is at stake in the changing traditions of television drama. Rather than discussing the plays in a decontextualised and ahistoric framework, this book aims to locate their production, their aesthetic strategies and their reception in relation to preceding, concurrent and successive television forms, both of drama and of related programme types such as arts programmes, and also in relation to film and visual art. These contexts shape the place that Beckett's work for television has in histories of television and especially of television drama. The activity of framing Beckett's television plays in these ways raises the interesting issue of the unitary nature of the 'Beckett' thus constructed. Citations of Beckett's work do not have the same meaning in each of the moments in the history of television that I have differentiated in the chapters that follow. Focusing on Beckett's work against these different backgrounds relies on a notion of television history that has significant and inevitable inclusions and exclusions. The primary background I have discussed is the changing fortunes of the prestigious single television play in the 1960s and 1970s, but even author-centred scholarship on this television form (see Brandt 1981 for example) passed over Beckett, implicitly placing his dramas at the margins of the field. More recent currents of work on British television drama would include popular forms such as adventure drama or situation comedy (see Bignell and Lacey 2005 for example) that would make Beckett's work look even less central.

By focusing on Beckett's television plays I am implicitly arguing that they exceed the norms of the single play form and should be regarded as more than typical: as an instance of a possible and in some ways preferable kind of formally innovative television play. However, as the history of British television proceeded through the 1960s to the present, Beckett's television work and adaptations of his theatre plays became increasingly exceptional rather than typical, increasingly marginal rather than high-profile, so that my discussion needs to shift in the ways that it places Beckett's work in comparison and contrast with dominant or alternative traditions. That is one reason why the second predominant background against which I discuss his work is that of arts programming. There is little written on this television genre (see Walker 1993 for example), but its relatively robust persistence in the British television landscape provides a further diachronic background against which both BBC and Channel 4 screenings of Beckett's drama can be understood. Inasmuch as the focus on Beckett connotes both the representativeness of his television work in standing for a wider field of forms and possibilities, and also a necessary non-representativeness because of its marginality in existing accounts, questions of which methodological and historical frame to adopt necessarily arise. But these theoretical problems are attendant on any selective study (see Bignell 2000) and to draw attention to their purchase in studies of both Beckett and television these reflections on methodology are explored and discussed at intervals across this book.

A significant proportion of the scholarship in this study is based in original archival research. The book draws on archival research on BBC documents and publications that record the production history of Beckett's television dramas, and the reception of the plays by British television audiences. The book also refers to manuscript and draft versions of Beckett's television plays, and Beckett's notes on their production process, that are held in the University of Reading's archives. The minutiae of these production and reception histories provide a fascinating array of data that are in general little known, and a significant proportion of the book is devoted to explaining and discussing the significance of this production history within television institutions (most particularly the BBC). So the book aims to contribute to scholarship on Beckett's television work by placing the plays within the culture of television production and reception that enabled and informed them. The interpretive and theoretical methodologies that have characterised existing publications on Beckett's television plays depend on readings of the audio-visual texts in their broadcast form and the written screenplays with which the programmes have occasional problematic relationships. But the book argues that these programmes and the interpretations that can be made of them are vitally shaped and conditioned by the specific histories and institutional and technological contexts that gave rise to the dramas as television programmes.

Beckett's authorship must be understood in relation to a complex network of negotiations, collaborations, institutional contexts, aesthetic forms and histories, and patterns of scheduling, broadcast form and audience reception. I draw on methodologies within the discipline of Television Studies that emphasise institutional frameworks, professional relationships, technological modes of production, and concerns to measure and evaluate reception by actual viewers, because these factors shaped the creation and significance of the plays in the British broadcasting landscape. The book therefore provides new perspectives on the relationships between Beckett's television dramas and the cultural forms in British television from the 1960s to the early twenty-first century and also illuminates the cultural history and forms of British television drama in general. For instance, a significant and little-explored issue within Television Studies is the role of formally experimental and avant-garde television drama in a broader context of Modernism in television, film, radio, theatre, literature and the visual arts (Caughie 2000). This book connects the forms and contexts of Beckett's television plays with Modernism and the avant-garde in television and touches on British television drama's relationships with literary and cinematic Modernism. The plays, and *Film* too, look strikingly anachronistic in relation to the contexts in which I place them, and this issue is significant to the argument threading through this study that innovation and experiment are resolutely historical, sometimes by means of the recapitulation of surpassed and supposedly outmoded aesthetic choices and modes of address to the audience. Slow, visually sparse and largely disconnected from their contemporary comparators, Beckett's television and film works announce their innovative status by a paradoxical invocation of past traditions. Like Modernist work in other media, Beckett's screenplays look forward by looking back, acquiring both a seriousness of purpose and a reflexive consciousness of their place in media history that problematised them for their viewers.

Work on data collected by BBC Audience Research can reveal how the plays were received, and references to journalistic reviews and other sources assist in this process. By addressing each stage in the making of television drama, from production and broadcast through to reception by the first and subsequent audiences, and the critical evaluation of television plays by professional reviewers and academics, the book is able to evaluate the significance of, for example, public service commitments and audience research, since for the BBC a concern for positive audience response was played off against the broadcasting institution's sense of responsibility to disseminate the work of a 'great writer'. Questions of cultural politics, aesthetics and value, and historical developments in the ethos of British broadcasting, are addressed via the study of Beckett's television work. Beckett's television dramas were almost all broadcast in Britain under the auspices of arts series, and my research at the BBC Written Archives Centre has shown how the assumptions about audiences for arts programming affected the presentation and scheduling of the plays. This approach complements existing studies of audience response to television in the field of Television Studies, which have focused on popular and generic television drama and its viewers. Similarly, the reception of *Film* is analysed through the documentation provided by its creators, reviewers and academic critics, revealing how the different frames of reference brought to the film by different audiences constructed its meaning in different ways.

This book could have been organised into chapters which analyse Beckett's television plays one at a time, in chronological order of broadcast, with comparative discussion of television adaptations of Beckett's theatre work and *Film*. This was a tempting organisational structure when I was planning the project, and there was also some pressure from academics in the field of Beckett Studies to adopt this scheme. However, it is vital to the theoretical and methodological principles and arguments outlined briefly above that this book is not organised in this way. The book focuses instead on theoretical, contextual and historical issues across the plays as a group. Thus it goes beyond the critical orthodoxy in Beckett Studies of detailed textual criticism, and incorporates and contextualises this work in the much broader critical frameworks of Television Studies. Across the twenty years or so in which I have worked (sporadically, and rarely for the purposes of publication) on Beckett's television dramas, I have sometimes felt that there is a territorial dispute between the largely literary tradition of Beckett Studies and the discipline of Television Studies whose heritage of close analysis of audio-visual material co-exists with cultural, historical and reception-oriented concerns. A significant critical principle actualised in this book is that an unwillingness to acknowledge the value of alternative approaches and a certain proprietary protectiveness of Beckett's work impacts on the analysis of Beckett's television dramas with the effect of marginalising it. As I have suggested above, this book argues that both Beckett Studies and Television Studies too can be invigorated by the approach taken here.

The first chapter focuses on the significance of the technologies used in making the five dramas written by Beckett for British television and also discusses television adaptations of Beckett's theatre plays. Each of the plays was recorded in a television studio, and work on the aesthetics of television requires attention to questions of scenic design which are concretely determined by the possibilities of the studio space in which they were shot. The plays were not transmitted live, but Beckett's insistence on long takes, with little post-production editing, associates them both with continuous theatre performance and early live television drama. As production technologies changed, edited 'cinematic' narrative increasingly supplanted this 'theatrical' form in British television, opening up forms of social realism associated with filmed realist cinema, social realism in post-1956 British theatre, and television and film documentary. Production technologies for Beckett's work partially determined its cultural significance by associating it with a particular avant-garde tradition, and with a history of 'literary' or 'theatrical' television and radio drama, and by distancing it from critical realist television drama shot on film in exterior locations. This makes Beckett's television work look both anachronistic and experimental at the same time. As Laura Mulvey (2007: 1) has recently noted, the term 'experimental' is imprecise and is 'necessarily an evocative rather than a definitive term in the context of television aesthetics, but it enables the designation of ways in which practitioners have pushed at the medium's conventions and boundaries, expanding its vocabulary and investigating its specifity'. The discussion of the aesthetic significance of studio production and the plays' uses of film recording technology in the television studio are evaluated in this context of simultaneous anachronism and innovation.

The second chapter considers the broadcasting contexts in which Beckett's television plays were made and shown. Beckett's dramas for British television were screened not in the customary scheduling positions and drama series of their time but in arts programming slots on BBC2, and this militated against considering them in relation to work by an emerging canon of television writers. So while Beckett's television plays lend themselves to the critical approaches developed to discuss authored drama (rather than generic series drama), their production background, scheduling and promotion separated them from the canon of authored dramas being developed by critics of the time. The chapter's discussion of archival sources places the scheduling and promotional contexts of the plays in comparison with and contrast to other television drama forms. For example, *Eh Joe* (1966) was scheduled as a one-off event, whose timeslot was not regularly used for drama, whereas the *Lively Arts* broadcast of three Beckett plays in 1977 was part of a regularly scheduled series organised around the work of living contemporary writers working mainly in literature or theatre. While the chapter concentrates on television broadcasting contexts, mention is made of BBC radio, which was for a long time committed to broadcasting original experimental drama in the Third Programme (later Radio 3), including plays for radio by Beckett. The chapter also connects Beckett's television work with avant-garde (especially European) cinema. The aesthetics of performance and the dissociation of image and sound are discussed in these contexts, and the directorial strategies used by Beckett and his collaborators and the significance of casting are also analysed. As a kind of drama that was distinctly different from what surrounded it in the schedules of its time, Beckett's television work was detached from the customary temporal flow of broadcasting, so while there are connections with a variety of television contexts that are discussed in the chapter, Beckett's plays work both with and against television cultures and draw attention to their distinctiveness.

The third chapter addresses the institutional frameworks through which Beckett gained access to television personnel, and what his authorship meant to them. In television and film production, conventional working practices often remove control over production decisions from the author, and directorial decisions are powerfully influenced by the demands of the broadcasting institution and its perception of the desires and competencies of the audience. These pressures were largely absent in the production of Beckett's plays, however, and this institutional culture needs to be explained. Many of the personnel with whom Beckett worked were experienced in a particular form of authored television drama which has since been sidelined by developments in technology, institutional politics and academic television criticism. This chapter traces the role of the authorial signature in Beckett's television work. He had a reputation (as does his estate after his death) for being a prescriptive and precise director of his own texts, where stage-direction, set design, lighting cues and costumes are all carefully described. Some of the programmes referred to in the chapter were directed by Beckett himself, with technical and directorial assistance, or directed by others either in his presence or after extensive consultation with him. Beckett's authorship is evaluated in relation to the particular conflicts and divergent assumptions around authorship in television institutions.

The fourth chapter contains the most sustained work on the intertextual relationships between Beckett's television drama and other work by him and by others. Authored television drama has been important to the legitimation of television against charges of triviality, and Beckett's fame as a stage dramatist made the broadcast of his work significant. This association with discourses of 'quality' is discussed in the chapter in relation to matters of visual design, music and literary reference in the television plays, which link them to other media. Television drama has been conceived as quality programming, marked by authorial creativity, and became a site for exploring the specificity of the medium. But one form of specificity drew, paradoxically, on theatrical experimentation so that the television studio could function like the 'black box' of the modern stage, and studio plays could allow some of the experiments in contemporary, anti-naturalist theatre to be screened. The broadcast of Beckett's work amid BBC2 arts programming places it in this context; it occurred after his first theatre work and developed alongside productions of his theatre plays. The chapter addresses the relationship between uses of visual space in Beckett's television plays and *Film* and his theatrical works. Questions of performance relating to 'theatricality' are also important to similarities and differences between the television versions of theatre plays and the television plays themselves, and this chapter is the one which deals most fully with adaptations of theatre including the recent Channel 4/RTE *Beckett on Film* season. It also refers to Beckett's novels and prose essays on painting and other topics to discuss visual space, framing and spectatorship, and relates these to the television work. Formal and compositional issues together with aesthetic and philosophical theories of vision are considered in relation to theories of visual meaning in Television Studies discourses. The chapter involves discussion of the prevalent motif identified by Beckett critics of increasing formal simplicity or minimalism in his theatre, prose and media works, and it argues that Beckett's persistence with the unfamiliar and problematic television medium was a way of moving towards a purity of visual form through the spatial and abstract qualities of the television image, and its manipulability by technological means. But that apparent purity is in fact constituted by allusion, adaptation and reworking of themes, forms and motifs from texts outside of television (such as visual art), and the chapter proposes that this paradox is a key characteristic of how Beckett's television dramas work. Invoking these televisual and extra-televisual frameworks makes the plays an important contribution to theoretical work on the conceptualisation of television's visual space and the relationships of television with film and other media.

The fifth chapter discusses the formation of and critical response to a canon of British television drama in terms of an opposition between critical realism and aesthetic modernism. Critics' responses to Beckett's work in the 1970s, for example, reflected the critical debate of the time over the politics of naturalistic versus avant-garde form. British television drama from the 1960s onwards has moved away from theatricality and Modernist experimentation towards elaborations of cinematic naturalism. This latter form was seen as relevant, contemporary and politically progressive. Beckett's television plays are situated within a complex dialectic of critical discourses around the aesthetics and politics of television drama, and part of this debate concerns the address to the television audience. This chapter connects critical work on Beckett's television plays with discursive models of how television audiences are imagined by authors, critics and television institutions, since assumptions about audiences affected the presentation and scheduling of Beckett's television plays. Archival research on audience data collected by the BBC reveals how the plays were received, and thus the chapter complements existing academic studies of audience response to television which have focused on popular television drama. The sixth, concluding chapter is an afterword that reflects on the arguments advanced in this project and returns to the issues raised here about their relationship with critical traditions in Beckett scholarship and in Television Studies. It suggests how some of boundaries of this project might be opened up in future work and locates the contribution of this book to the historiography of Beckett's oeuvre as part of the historiography of television.

1

Production

Introduction

This chapter examines the significance of the production technologies used in making the five dramas written by Beckett for television and compares and contrasts these production technologies with those used in realising *Film* and television adaptations of theatre texts by Beckett. The British television plays were recorded in television studios and were shot on film, with the exception of *Eh Joe* (1966), which was a videotape production. The German productions of Beckett's plays in the 1980s were also made on videotape. The plays were not transmitted live, but Beckett's insistence on long takes, with little post-production editing, associates them both with the continuous time of theatre performance and with the live broadcast of drama on television, which was the established means of making television drama in Britain until the late 1950s. When videotape editing and film cameras were introduced in drama production from the early 1960s, edited 'cinematic' narrative increasingly supplanted 'theatrical' form, and filmed social realist television drama gained a high public and critical profile. Filmed television drama had formal and thematic similarities with realist New Wave cinema, the social engagement of post-1956 British theatre, and television and film documentary. Production technologies for Beckett's work partially determined its cultural significance by separating it from this emergent nexus and associating it with an avant-garde tradition in television and a history of 'literary' or 'theatrical' television and radio drama. This chapter explores and evaluates the aesthetic significance of the filmed and videotaped studio production of Beckett's television plays in this range of contexts.

Some awareness of developments in television technology is needed in order to understand the significance of the television forms in Beckett's television plays. Each of the plays was recorded in a studio, resulting in a high-quality videotape or film for later broadcast. There are few examples in existing scholarship that examine Beckett's television plays in the light of their use of particular technical resources (see Homan 1992), though there are several analyses that focus on the 'essentials' of vision and sound in the medium. Linda Ben-Zvi's essay (1985) on *All That Fall*, *Film* and *Ghost Trio* is one of the few examples in its period of scholarship which stress the significance of their medium of transmission. Nevertheless, the works are still considered independently of other dramas in their respective media, and the essay pays little attention to their institutional and social contexts. Catherine Russell (1989) describes the television plays as 'videotapes' rather than broadcasts, which are to be understood via analogies with Lacanian models of language and subjectivity. Russell's analysis of the formal relations between sequences of each play, and relationships between the plays, maps Lacanian insights onto particular moments and sequences. While the audio-visual forms and textures of the plays are important to Russell, her essay is not concerned with the plays' situation in the medium of television as a cultural form. It is this specific relationship between aesthetics, technology and production practice that forms the core of this chapter.

Television and video aesthetics

Since television drama inherited theatre's and literature's mantle of quality and authorial creativity (often via radio drama), it offered, paradoxically, an opportunity to consider the essential aesthetic of the medium. The Langham Group, working at the BBC in 1958–60, for example, were interested in the connections between the aesthetics of television and of avant-garde film (see

Cooke 2003: 53–4). On one hand, by using single-camera shooting and takes of unusually long duration, for example, television could explore the anti-conventional forms being developed in European art cinema by the New Wave directors in France. On the other, the use of video feedback (pointing the electronic studio camera at its own video monitor, producing strobing patterns of interference), overlay of one camera's shot on top of another, and split-screen for example, offered television-specific visual effects that could be integrated in a range of ways into fantasy, science fiction and avant-garde productions. The Langham Group's experiments occurred just as television drama moved away from a focus on adaptations of stage drama or literature, favouring instead the work of dramatists writing specifically for television like Alun Owen or Clive Exton (Hill 2007: 25). So although the Group's notable productions included, for example, *Torrents of Spring* and *Mario* in 1959, based loosely on short stories, their work looked anomalous both because of its experimental visual design and because of its conservative tendency to perpetuate a 'literary' television drama rather than a specifically televisual one. That kind of experimentation did not last long as an organised initiative, but it enabled BBC producer–directors like James MacTaggart and writers like Troy Kennedy Martin to make television plays that cut visual sequences to music scores and used montages of still images in plays in the early 1960s that contrast strongly with naturalistic forms of storytelling. The aesthetic of Beckett's *Eh Joe* draws on this strand of television production practice and takes some of its innovations in studio drama to an exceptional extreme.

Eh Joe was written in 1965, and begins with a wide shot of a set representing a room with door, windows and a simple bed. Joe examines the room and checks that its door and window are sealed and curtained, before sitting on the bed. A female voice, V, speaks to him accusingly as the camera moves across the set towards him and frames him in an increasingly tight series of close-ups, until at the end of the play only Joe's face can be seen. As Stan Gontarsky (1983: 425) and others have pointed out, the fact that the play begins in a room connects it to the earlier *Film*

(1964) which is also substantially set in a simple city apartment. Beckett's script for *Eh Joe* refers to the opening sequence as a 'pursuit' (Beckett 1986: 361), and this also connects it to *Film*'s pursuit of the male figure O by E, the camera's point of view, which ultimately confronts O and is revealed to be the gaze of a man who exactly resembles O, an apparent double. The figure seeking refuge alone in a room is also reminiscent of many of Beckett's dramatic and prose works, for example the novel *Molloy* (1959) and the short play *Rockaby* (1982, see Beckett 1986). The enclosed space has also often been regarded as a representation of the mind, yet it is significant to note its connections with the room of naturalistic theatre and the rooms in which many of the studio television dramas of the 1960s took place. While the relationship of these motifs to Beckett's prose and drama are revealing in biographical and intratextual terms, they reveal little about how the space and tone of *Eh Joe* work as television.

The original manuscript and typescript versions of *Eh Joe* describe the opening sequence in which Joe checks the windows and door of his room as comprising separate shots connected by cuts: the direction 'Cut to' introduces each action on the set (Beckett undated b, c, e). The original structure using cuts would have brought the camera into the room in a series of leaps across space, and positioned it as a close witness of Joe's actions, anticipating its closing in on him in the later part of the play. But when the opening sequence is shot as a single long take, as it is in both the 1966 British and 1988 German versions as broadcast, the camera seems removed from the space, at the edge of the set, leaving Joe a certain freedom from it as he moves around the room. This freedom is then cut short when the camera begins its series of moves towards him, breaking the play into two quite distinct parts. Long takes produce the impression of temporal continuity, and allow the camera to follow characters in a space with which they interact. The aim of using the long take is usually to reveal character and the relationship between characters and environment, where that environment may also include their dealings with other characters. The long take suggests a generosity with time in which there is the opportunity to consider what can be seen, thus handing interpretive authority to the audience. The extended look at the character places pressure on that character by enforcing the viewer's concentration on the detail of how he or she acts and reacts across a sustained passage of action. At the same time, the use of long shot where the camera takes in a wide field of vision shows the character moving in a spatial context, and this is seen at the opening of *Eh Joe* and in Beckett's subsequent television work. Long shot permits the camera to have a physical and emotional distance from the character, so that an analytical and critical understanding can be gained by revealing body movements, gesture, costume and so on, and the action is embedded in the represented world. This is a distinctly different visual system from the use of rapid alternations of shot–reverse–shot and close-up, which cut up space, person, body and relationships between characters, and determine how the viewer can perceive action. Rapid cutting and extensive close-up can be analytical in that they segment and select, presenting directorial interpretations of character and action, but the long-take long shot allows the viewer to make sense of space and character in a different way, similar to a Brechtian notion that the audience can choose where to look and has to work to bring frameworks of interpretation to the images they see. This visual style empowers the audience and draws on the theatrical convention of space energised by action that privileges performance and is designed for it, whereas segmented shooting and close-up seem more filmic since there is no 'dead space' that can open up additional meanings.

The visible space at the opening of *Eh Joe* is in long shot and contains unusually large set elements such as over-long curtains and large bare walls that are much taller than they would be in any conventionally 'real' room. Joe's movements in checking the room are also large-scale gestures. This concern with size contrasts strongly with the later restriction of camera movement to small incremental steps, and the focus on Joe's restricted range of gestures and facial expressions which are observed in increasingly concentrated close-up. The exaggerated movement of the opening connects with silent cinema, pantomime and puppet theatre, while the restricted movement of the second part of the play has much more in common with television representations of psychological states using close camera shots and an acting style developed in cinema and television in the days of live broadcasting in the 1950s and before. The large theatrical movement and the open theatrical set in the first half as distinct from the restricted framing and limited expression of the second half represent a shift in the representational codes of the play and necessitate different responses from the audience. Indeed, the expectations on the audience's part of what kind of drama this is must change radically. The first part might lead the viewer to believe that this is a non-naturalistic, theatrical drama in which the action must be read through a symbolic code rather than a naturalistic or psychological one. By contrast, the second part conforms more easily to the conventions for the television representation of internal states and emotions through largely non-verbal codes and the assumption of the revelation of psychology through minimal gestural movement. In television, this emphasis on small but significant gesture and expression, often without directive shaping by dialogue, was refined especially by the Method acting styles of actors like Paul Newman, who began their screen careers in live studio drama on American television (see Bignell 1996). But this American tradition remained marginal to the British practice, at least until the late 1960s, for television plays to be driven by speech rather than movement or gesture. So for British audiences of this BBC production of *Eh Joe*, the contrasting styles of theatricality in the first part of the play and close-ups suggesting wordless psychological revelation in the second would raise questions of categorisation and interpretation.

The play invites the audience to consider it as the representation of Joe's guilt over the death of his beloved, since the female voice, V, castigates Joe for his apparent neglect of a woman who is later said to have killed herself. Voice, in this reading, would be the voice of his own conscience. Jack MacGowran's performance as Joe in the BBC's 1966 production certainly fulfils Beckett's stage direction (1986: 362) that the face should represent a 'mounting tension of listening'. On one hand, the low lighting and strong shadow of both the BBC and the later German SDR productions (see Kalb 1989: 109) produce an increased focus on the minute detail of Joe's face and are used to connote dramatic intensity and psychological complexity. At the same time, the strong shadows cast by the lighting make it more difficult for the viewer to determine the interpretation of Joe's expressions. In contrast to the opinion of John Fletcher and John Spurling (1985: 95), television conventions of close-up and lighting increase rather than reduce the play's ambiguity. The play was recorded at a time when the visual detail in the image was nowhere near as clear as it would be today, since the video cameras used had less tonal depth and capacity for contrast than film cameras. The television image on BBC2 was broadcast using 625 lines of visual information, while BBC1 and ITV used only 405 lines, but the strong shadow and low lighting in the video production of *Eh Joe* did not exploit this greater picture quality. These technical and production factors add to the play's problematic invocation of different and ambiguous schemas of interpretation.

Furthermore, the ambiguity about how to read Joe's facial expression and its relationship to Voice's words is enhanced by the duration of the camera shot that moves increasingly closer to his face. Historically, television drama has used gradually shorter camera shots, and a brief comparison between *Eh Joe*'s average lengths of shot and those of some other dramas made in comparable ways at different dates can illuminate just how different *Eh Joe* is from television norms. The whole play is one long take, uninterrupted by cutting away to another camera or by editing that would introduce time ellipses into the narrative. The play's duration is eighteen minutes. Thus, although the shot is divided into steps whereby the camera moves physically across the set and then stops, only to resume movement again, it is experienced by the audience as a single sequence of extraordinary duration. In the second part of the play, the camera's position moves from the approximate centre of the set in a series of nine movements towards Joe, and the duration of the periods when the camera is still varies since these periods of stillness correspond to Voice's words, which take varying lengths of time to deliver.

Taken as a whole, the periods of camera stillness average a little less than two minutes each. Even if these periods of stillness had been made as a series of separate shots to be edited together, their length individually would be much longer than shots in other dramas, even those of much earlier date. As a brief comparison, Lez Cooke (2003: 47) has calculated the average shot length in Alun Owen's 1960 studio-recorded play *Lena, O My Lena* in the ABC company's *Armchair Theatre* strand, coming up with a figure of 12.5 seconds. The viewer would have experienced the shots as less long than that since the camera was often in motion around the set and offered zooms in and away from the actors and set components within individual shots. So the rough figure of two minutes of still image in *Eh Joe* is very much longer than the norms of the period, and also feels much longer because of the lack of change in camera focus or directional alignment. In fact an average shot length of two minutes is the same figure as for a live 1938 BBC costume drama production, *Clive of India*, at a time when techniques of directing drama on television were still in their infancy (Jacobs 2000: 52–3) and shot lengths were very long by today's standards. The effect of such lengthy periods of camera stillness is to offer nothing else for the audience to see than the close-ups on Joe's face, and thus to focus visual attention on them. While attention to sound becomes more significant for this reason, since Voice is speaking while the camera is still, the opportunity to look for interpretations of Joe's face through Jack MacGowran's generally understated performance leaves plenty of room for hypotheses, alternatives and uncertainties.

Looking at *Eh Joe*'s structure and the peculiarity of its camera-work provides some evidence for considering the play as an instance of explicitly reflexive television that draws attention to its means of technological and formal articulation. This has been argued by specialists in Beckett criticism, though generally from an essentialist and author-centred perspective, and has been said of his later television work as well. Enoch Brater's (1985, see also Brater 1987: 74–110) precise descriptions of Beckett's television later plays *Nacht und Träume* and *Quad* lead to a fascinating series of displacements between language and image, authorial 'message' and medium, but tend towards a formalist and essentialist conception of television. Of *Nacht und Träume*, Brater (1985: 51) concludes that: 'Writing with the basic material of television, video images, Beckett makes us sense the verbal potential of all that he renders so palpably visual ... The video image says more precisely because it says less, and in saying less it says everything in the way this medium can be made to say it.' Brater's argument is premised on the value given to Beckett's alleged search for a 'poetics' of television: an essence of the communication principles of the medium. Beckett's paring down of dramatic form, his gradual reduction of verbal and spatial textures, and concentration on geometrical, mathematical forms and music, are regarded as Modernist experiments in medium-specificity. For Brater, 'writing' with images produces the verbal polysemia of the visual icon. The television image's plenitude comes from its stark spareness as an articulation, and this reduction to an essence paradoxically reveals the shared generic qualities of all audio-visual forms. Brater's argument positions the plays firmly as meta-commentary on their medium, as avant-garde works that have more in common with video art (like the works of Bruce Nauman, himself strongly influenced by Beckett) than with broadcast drama. The plays produced for television in Germany were shot on video, so that Brater's argument connects with other theoretical discussions of video as the 'essential' technology that underlies television aesthetics (see Chapter 4). I am not arguing that Brater's point is wrong, but simply that the reflexive and experimental qualities of *Eh Joe* need to be understood in a broader television context. The use of the long take and still camera both mark the play as exceptional in its own time and link it anachronistically to a long history of developments in editing rhythms that connect it with much earlier drama broadcasts. If *Eh Joe* is medium-specific and reflexive, it is so by virtue of television drama's ongoing struggle to assimilate to and differentiate itself from other media and to develop rhetorical strategies and production techniques for studio drama.

Recording *Eh Joe* in one long take was a considerable feat, but there were advantages as well as disadvantages in the technique from a production point of view. A long and detailed memo of May 1964 (BBC WAC T5/2239/7) from the BBC's television recording engineers explained the process of assembly editing and dubbing sound on the Ampex and RCA videotape that the BBC used at this time. The expensive Ampex tape was very cumbersome and lacked the facility to pause the tape during a recording. It had a tape life of only 60 plays, and high internal charges were levied by BBC technical departments for editing time and tape storage. This made it preferable to shoot on video in long takes 'as if live', to avoid any editing of tape sequences after the shoot, and to avoid keeping taped performances for later broadcast and instead to immediately re-use the tape for another programme. Because tape could not be cued up to a precise start point (it took ten seconds for the picture to appear after starting to play it) it was impossible to make precise edits by playing a tape on one player and recording the desired sequences from it on another (the practice of assembly editing). Editors had to physically cut the tape, but tape with physical cuts was impossible to re-use and it was recommended that programmes needing numerous edits were shot on 35mm film instead. The internal BBC charge for using a tape in 1964 was £28 per hour, plus £60 per hour if the tape was physically cut. If a tape was kept in store for more than six months an internal charge of £60 per hour's worth of tape was levied against the producer's budget. Because of these high costs, until the mid-1960s the recording of programmes was done in continuous tranches of time like live performances wherever possible, and when mistakes were made scenes would be performed again after winding the tape back to a previous start point, rather than editing the mistakes out. With Beckett's characteristic long takes, as in *Eh Joe*, there was no need to make numerous edits within the play as a whole, and so no need to physically cut the videotape or to assemble separately-shot sequences together. While this meant that Jack MacGowran would have been forced to repeat his performance if a mistake was made, the technical strictures of using videotape suited Beckett's play rather than causing production difficulties. It is a testament to the BBC's sense of *Eh Joe*'s importance that the other major problem with tape – namely the desirability of reusing it and wiping programmes made on it rather than keeping them – was avoided and the play survives to this day. This contrasts with popular mass-audience programmes of the time that were routinely wiped, such as the long-running science fiction drama *Doctor Who*, of which more than one hundred 25-minute episodes from the mid-1960s have been lost because their tapes were wiped and re-used. All of Beckett's later plays for television in Britain were made on film, at greater expense but with more certainty of preservation. Making *Eh Joe* on videotape has a range of meanings and contexts; and among them, its status as television rather than cinema or theatre produces interesting tensions between its dramatic form, its technologies of production and the ways it can be interpreted.

The ontology of liveness as a property of television, perhaps an essential one, is also signalled by the duration of *Eh Joe*'s long take, and its grainy videotape look as opposed to film's relative luminance. Tape was used sparingly until the mid-1960s, and this has created a lasting assumption that the medium's 'essence' is determined by its possibility to relay events and performances live, or to recreate an experience for the viewer that simulates a live broadcast. This essentialism is perpetuated by television's customary broadcast of news, sports events, or national occasions at or close to the time of their occurrence, and the concomitant aim for the medium to connect with the lived temporality of the audience. In theoretical terms, this emphasis on liveness corresponds to an inclination to consider television semiotically as a medium of denotation: a medium that presents, shows and witnesses, rather than re-presents, tells or narrates (Heath and Skirrow 1977). However, at the same time the use of such semiotic methodologies in film and television studies has directed attention away from features of the media that are specific to them because of these methodologies' principle of comparing visual representations with verbal language. For example, the notion that tense in film and television is always present (because the image is present on the screen to the spectator) whatever the narrative temporality being represented, is based on the denotation that derives from the photographic basis of the film and television media. By contrast, literature describes action rather than presenting it. Temporality in Beckett's plays is very often significant, since they deal with experiences that are remembered, re-told or re-enacted, often inaccurately or with differences between each version, and they stage the characters' attempts to reinvoke or resurrect a lost and beloved person. In this respect, they exploit the tensions between tenses in television as a broadcast medium and the assumed temporality of its programming. This argument is the basis of Graley Herren's recent study of Beckett's screen work, which suggests that the dramas work with Henri Bergson's (1912) theory of perception. Bergson argues that 'the present is always already memory, the past masquerading as the present. Thus, in exploiting television's capacity to make the dead seem "live," Beckett is only reiterating the function of perception itself, which always already serves as a memory machine' (Herren 2007: 13).

While it may be an exaggeration to assert that television is without tense, it is certainly plausible to argue that tense and temporality are subject to a potential suspension and ambivalence in television that are distinctively different from either the theatrical or literary mode of signification. This difference can be extended into the difference between film and television as a result of their different means of image production, as Jane Feuer (1983: 13) points out by quoting Herbert Zettl (1978): 'While in film each frame is actually a static image, the television image is continually moving, very much in the manner of the Bergsonian *durée*. The scanning beam is constantly trying to complete an always incomplete image. Even if the image on the screen seems at rest, it is structurally in motion. Each television frame is always in a state of becoming. While the film frame is a concrete record of the past, the television frame (when live) is a reflection of the living, constantly changing present.' The temporality of television is not fundamentally that of the static photographic frame but instead a fluid and temporally unfinished sequence. This differentiates television from film for some theorists attempting to define the essence of the medium, such as Richard

Deinst (1994: 20, see also Fry 1993): 'A televisual image has to be established and sustained onscreen moment by moment. With transmission, images and sets of images pass the time and fill out the current: in this sense television is always "live". On film, on the other hand, the image appears in a here-and-now necessarily separate from the then-and-there of its production.' The transmission of television as a broadcast medium produces an assumption of its collective simultaneous presence to each of a programme's viewers, whether the programme was recorded live or not. The integration of television into the routines of daily life depends fundamentally on its existence in time, at the specific time of its broadcast, and this has been exploited in different ways by the production and the dramatic forms of Beckett's television plays.

There is an ambivalent temporality produced in the relationship between image and voice in Beckett's plays, since there is potentially a temporal separation between the two. Voice implies the presence of a speaker, and easily if not definitively establishes a temporal moment of enunciation in relation to which a past and a future may be constructed in the discourse that is enounced. Although the visual image on screen may be present to the viewer, it can be difficult or impossible to establish whether the image represents a past, a present or a future in narrative terms. The same questions arise with theatre, but are inflected distinctively in television because voice and image are broadcast to the spectator from another place. Television and other broadcast media (particularly radio) are also associated with representations of the present, despite the necessary delay involved in the production and transmission of a text, and the possibility of preservation and repetition at a different time from the time of making. During the production of Beckett's *Quad* in the studios of the German television company Süddeutscher Rundfunk (SDR) in 1981, the temporalities of video production in the studio led to a significant change to the pre-production screenplay. The play consisted of a single long take from a video camera mounted on a crane, shooting statically down into a lighted area in which four robed figures move around the sides and diagonally crossing lines of a rectangle marked out on the floor. During the taping, Beckett, who was present, reviewed the sequence in the studio gallery where the camera output was being recorded and displayed on monitor screens. The vision mixing gallery of a television studio is a separate space from the performance area, and the live output of electronic cameras, usually three or four of them, is displayed on small monitors arranged in a row, usually in black-and-white, with a further colour monitor screen showing the director's choice of shot from among the possibilities offered by each camera for each moment of the programme. The role of the director, working with the vision mixer, is to instruct the camera operators what to shoot and then to select from the shots offered by each camera to create a single sequence of shots that will comprise the programme. What Beckett would have seen in the gallery at Stuttgart, then, would have been the 'master' monitor in colour, together with monitors ranged alongside it where the output of the single camera used in the production would also have been visible.

The colour master image needed to be checked to make sure that its tonal contrasts would register adequately on black-and-white television sets (the process of 'grading'). Beckett happened to see the performance in monochrome and remarked that the drama seemed to belong to a more distant fictional time than the implied present of the action seen in colour. As a result, a second iteration of the play was shot with the colour signal removed from the input into the recording machines, with the performers' movement slowed down, and with different music. This second version of the performance became a second part of the play as a whole, which was titled in German *Quadrat I & II*. Here the temporality of recording on tape permitted the performance of the original screenplay, which had been shot in one take as if live, to be reviewed after a brief interval. The interval between recording and reviewing permitted the creation of a second version of the performance, its taping in one further take as if live, and the assembly of the two versions together into a single work. The change of pace and the change from colour to monochrome permitted the connotation of distance in time to be produced, and thus there are several different temporalities being exploited at the levels of the production process, the aesthetic forms of the play in its completed form, and in its range of possible interpretations. *Quad* can become a play 'about' time because of the manipulations of time and the uses of recording and reviewing technologies that the television studio made possible.

The significance of film in *Beckett on Film: Play*

Beckett's British television plays after *Eh Joe* in 1966 were shot on 35-mm cinema film cameras in a large studio (a soundstage), and this combination of resources has important effects on their aesthetic and institutional meanings. In the 1960s and 1970s drama was normally shot on video in the studio, with film resources used for short sequences set in outside locations or for special effects. The granting of film resources to Beckett's studio plays was expensive and represents the privilege granted to his work. This is especially the case since the film cameras were used in studio settings, where video would be the normal technology used. Furthermore, the long takes in Beckett's television plays contrasted with the increasing tendency through the 1960s and 1970s to adopt 'cinematic' editing conventions based on montage where sequences would be cut together to juxtapose alternate points of view. The introduction of lightweight 16-mm film cameras (as opposed to the bulky 35-mm cameras used to film Beckett's work) into television drama, deriving from documentary and news, reinforced the sense that exterior shooting on film, 'documenting' a realistic social environment, was the cutting edge of television fiction. Dramas such as *Up the Junction* (1965) and *Cathy Come Home* (1966), by the director/producer team of Ken Loach and Tony Garnett, for example, were always in a minority but have been canonised by Television Studies and in popular memory. They were social realist works (about working class women and homelessness in the two examples above) which also shared formal and political concerns with European cinema, post-1956 British theatre, and television and film documentary. Beckett's work, recorded in the studio, in long takes 'as if live', contrasts strongly with this trend, which contributes to its relative neglect by academic critics of television and by historians of British broadcasting. The filmed studio productions of Beckett's ...*but the clouds*..., *Ghost Trio* and the film adaptation of *Not I* in 1977 are considered in Chapter 3 in relation to their place within BBC drama production contexts and personnel, developing this institutional context further. But to consider the television video aesthetic discussed so far and the possibilities of film in more detail, it is illuminating to move much closer to the present and the *Beckett on Film* productions of 2001, notably *Play*.

The filmed *Beckett on Film* plays fall between the two stools of being faithful to the texts as Beckett's estate insisted and being accessible to the audience. In order to make them suitable for cinema screening and television broadcast the producers made them more 'cinematic': they were shot on film cameras (rather than video) for greater colour density, contrast and depth of field. Nevertheless they were shot in large studios, like the television plays of an earlier era. In contrast to the often bare staging of Dublin's The Gate Theatre for its Beckett season, on which the films were based, the film directors tended to fill in the empty space in their studios with props and settings, thus removing some of the abstraction of the theatre texts as written and as usually performed. This kind of adaptation for the assumed demands of another medium is exactly what Beckett himself disliked. For example, in a letter of 23 March Beckett wrote to his friend the theatre director Alan Schneider, referring to the filming of the Schiller Theatre stage production of *Waiting for Godot* in Berlin in 1975 (Harmon 1998: 324): 'Berlin wasn't too bad in the end. We were nearly there. There will be a film of a performance, purely documentary, no *adaphatroce*' [dreadful adaptation]. None of the *Beckett on Film* plays were written for television or for cinema; they are theatre plays adapted into another medium. While Beckett would accept a 'documentary' recording of a stage performance, he was usually opposed to reconfiguring theatre plays for broadcast or cinema exhibition unless he approved detailed plans for the production or had a major role in the adaptation and direction himself.

The theatre version of *Play* consists of three heads, of two women and a man (W1, W2 and M), protruding from three large urns positioned facing the audience. As a single light illuminates each head, by turns the figures recount the garbled story of a love-triangle, seemingly compelled by the light to speak as if in perpetual atonement for the betrayal that the affair might represent. *Play* has been discussed as a self-conscious reference to the conventions of theatre, both because of its title and its emphasis on the positioning of the audience and the performers (McMullan 1993: 17–25) as speakers and witnesses. Anthony Minghella's direction of the *Beckett on Film* version (2001) foregrounds the play's references to Dante's account of the torments of sinners in the underworld by placing M, W1 and W2 among a large assemblage of other urns seen in wide shot, and this broadens the framework of intertextual reference beyond theatre to literature. The language of *Play* is infused with cliché, and in the theatre version speech is demanded by the operation of the light instead of being produced by an internal need or desire on the part of the speaker. The language the characters use repeatedly fails to grasp the essence of the event recounted over and over by them. Yet the visual dimensions of performance, particularly the expression and vocal tone of the actors, are similarly withdrawn from definitive signification because of their comparative inexpressivity, immobility and restricted visibility in the urns. So the inadequacy of language to summon the apparently originary 'real story' that connects them is paralleled by the inadequacy of the codes of gesture and expression to render it. The camera in the *Beckett on Film* production fulfils the functions of the light in the theatrical version, yet because it occupies the role of a point of view in cinema or television, it also draws attention to the parallel between the camera and an observing eye such as that represented by the camera, E, in Beckett's *Film*. In the theorisation of identification in cinema (often extended to television), the two identifications described by Christian Metz (1982) are first the identification with the cinematic apparatus, and second the identification with human figures on the screen.

Inasmuch as the camera in the *Beckett on Film* version of *Play* seems to force the characters to speak, this connects the camera and the audience together and draws on the conventional identification between the spectator and the camera in cinema and television. However, the fragmentary nature of the piece, its repetitions, the performance style and visual appearance of the performers, and the attention drawn to the medium of recording all conspire to withdraw the second conventional identification between the spectator and the character. The look of the camera and of the spectator are made surprisingly active, rather than being effaced or passive, and the role of the look as in itself an action or performance becomes equally as significant as, if not more so than, the performance and activity of the actors. Far from being a 'documentary' record of a stage performance, the film version renders the camera an agent and not a witness.

The performance was created as a single work and has been shown in cinema exhibition. It was shot on a sound-stage similar to that used in the production of feature films. Its actors, Alan Rickman, Kristen Scott Thomas and Juliet Stevenson, are also familiar from British cinema. Yet the use of a studio set, and the financing of the film by Channel 4 and the Irish national broadcaster RTE connect the drama to television institutions and exhibition. Although a wide-screen image was recorded, this is a frame size now common in television drama programmes with high production values, and is created by electronic image processing rather than the use of specifically cinematic film stock. Interruptions to the dialogue are provided by apparently skipping frames such as might happen in an ill-adjusted film projector, revealing the frame borders and manufacturer's stamp etched into the film stock. Again, however, these apparent marks of the filmic are post-production effects and not the result of the operation of the camera itself, or of a projector. This production of *Play*, then, situates itself between television and film, and the text itself contains allusions both to theatre and to literature. As Paul Lawley (1984) has argued, the structure of the dialogue follows a fugue or canon pattern, with repeats, and so also makes links between drama and music, diminishing the significance of individual words in favour of a series of patterns and repetitions.

The visual structure of the Channel 4 version corresponds in some ways to the conventions of cinematic and television drama form. The play begins with a wide establishing shot, then moves to alternations of close-up determined by which performer is speaking. Yet the cuts between camera angles and close-ups are not in themselves expressive of a pace and rhythm of drama directed by the dialogue, since there is no unfolding narrative progression or moment of crisis that is especially significant to the movement of the story. The alternation of shots is disconnected from the story and creates pace and rhythm on its own, thus departing from the television convention of using the camera to communicate a story that seems independent of the camera's agency. As McMullan (1993: 21) argued of the theatre version, 'strategies of representation, rather than producing knowledge, truth and enlightenment, are revealed as arbitrary mechanisms of discipline and control'. As Lawley points out (1984: 27–31), the story told by the characters revolves around sex, desire and betrayal, yet although the language of the text includes many clichéd references relating to the body and to bodily action, the absence of the performers' bodies further reduces the depth and significance of bodiliness in the play. McMullan argues (1993: 24) that desire 'which at first seems to drive the cycles of narration and perception, is increasingly erased, leaving simply a chain of empty signifiers.' In the theatre version of *Play*, the repetition of the dialogue can be regarded as an allusion to the simultaneous repeatability of performances as versions of an original text, and also to the unrepeatability of performance since each occasion of performance will be different. Anthony Minghella's production for *Beckett on Film* recasts this idea in cinematic and televisual terms. Films and television dramas are made by performing a number of takes of the same sequence of the text. The film or television programme is then the product of a series of repetitions of specific sequences, and each sequence which does not make it into the final cut will be absent and discarded. Furthermore, television programmes are repeated, and films are shown in repeat screenings. The production of the *Beckett on Film* version of *Play* from a series of disconnected repetitions, and the repeatability of the programme itself once completed, are alluded to by Anthony Minghella's direction. In *Play* the represented action gives way to brief foregrounding of the leader strip at the start of a roll of film, which would not normally be seen in a cinema showing or in a television broadcast of a film and is there to allow the projectionist to thread the film up before starting to show it. At various points during the action the frame jumps and a blank white screen can be seen, as if pieces of film have been inexpertly edited together. The presence of the leader strip and of cut marks in the completed drama draw attention not only to the materiality of the film's physical base but also to the notion of the cinematic, in comparison with and contrast to the televisual and the theatrical. Making, showing and repeating become ways of both linking and separating cinema from television and from theatre.

The repetitions in *Play* may be an allusion to the repeated performances of theatre. They may also allude to the possibility of storing and replaying television sequences, thus shifting their relationship to the time of their production and reception, and potentially dissociating them from being fixed in a temporal moment. In contrast to much of the theoretical work on television which determines its identity by reference to its live broadcasting, the French philosopher Jean-François Lyotard (1991: 49–50) argues that television puts an end to the here and now, in the sense that digital television technology is able to reconstitute, reproduce and repeat the encounter with an object of perception: 'After they have been put into digital form, these items of data can be synthesised anywhere and anytime to produce identical chromatic or acoustic products (simulacra) … The whole idea of an "initial" perception, of what since Kant has been called an "aesthetic", an empirical or transcendental mode whereby the mind is affected by a "matter" which it does not fully control, which happens to it here and now – this whole idea seems completely out of date.' The possibility of storing data in a digital form that is not degraded by storage, copying or reproduction means that the association between data and a temporal moment is disrupted. For Lyotard, television inaugurates an epoch of the simulacrum. Beckett's television plays contain numerous instances of repetition of particular moments or of whole sequences. Repetition is necessarily a comment on the manipulation of time, both announcing the potential repeatability that videotape or film storage of sound and image can achieve, yet also alluding to the liveness that has characterised television and the live performance of theatre. The *Beckett on Film* version of *Play* in particular, with its post-production digital effects, some which simulate the materiality of film projection and some of which create a 'virtual' setting photo-realistically, opens up the question of medium specificity and reflexivity while also deferring it and complicating it because of its allusions to multiple media of performance, recording and exhibition.

Studios, sound-stages and theatre

Until the late 1950s, British television drama was theatrical in form, focusing on the performance of actors observed by a relatively static camera in relatively lengthy shots, in a space whose dynamics derived from the theatre stage. Indeed, many of the dramas broadcast in these years were excerpts from, adaptations of, or restagings in the studio of theatre performances, and were necessarily live because of the impossibility of pre-recording until the availability of magnetic tape. British television drama of this kind, especially single plays, appears to belong to a vanished literary and theatrical tradition. This is an accurate characterisation inasmuch as early television drama consisted often of extracts from theatre works. In the 1960s and 1970s, when most of Beckett's television plays were being screened by the BBC, the weekly anthology slots in which much television drama was shown still bore titles like *First Night* and *Theatre 625*, which immediately associated them with theatre. The perceived emphases on language and text and on authorship, which theatricality appeared to bring with it, led to significant reaction against this history and these critical concerns, with consequent effects on perceptions of Beckett's work. Beckett's television work similarly connects with experiments using theatre's 'black box' or 'empty space' for anti-naturalist drama, and the inclusion of his work amid BBC2 arts programming (as was the case with *Ghost Trio* and *…but the clouds…* for example) signals these connections. As I have argued elsewhere (Bignell 2001–2), Beckett's television plays draw on aesthetic forms and production practices, and demand modes of viewing from their audience, that associate them with theatre and with early television drama.

However, I also argued that Beckett's television aesthetic aims at the same time for a mode of dramatic realisation that is particular to television, in the context of experiments in medium-specific television drama and storytelling. As Jason Jacobs (1998) has shown, inasmuch as it is possible to reconstruct early live television drama programmes of the 1930s to the 1950s (since very few filmed recordings of these plays exist), a range of strategies were employed by the producers and directors of early television drama that either associated it with the more rapid and dynamic relationships between time and space in cinema or were self-consciously experimental strategies aimed at discovering a television aesthetic that was specifically different from both theatre and cinema. According to Jacobs (1998: 50), 'it was a performance already considerably mediated by adaptation, studio organisation, camera set-ups, telecine film inserts and captions. In other words, there is evidence that some early television drama was far more *segmented* than previous writers have given it credit for. The real aesthetic advantage of television is therefore not simply its ability to faithfully relay a continuous performance in real time; on the contrary, it is primarily television's ability to mediate this performance in new and exciting ways, different but similar to the techniques of film, radio and theatre.' The television form of Beckett's drama does not simply and anachronistically reproduce the conventions and conditions of early live television drama. Instead, it reproduces the conventionally accepted wisdom, after the event, about what that early live drama was like, at the same time as Beckett returned to pseudo-theatrical pseudo-live recording of the plays in order to explore the possibilities of the television medium. Anachronism is a thus a critical and reflexive strategy, which matches the plays' thematic concerns with memory, repetition and the slow pacing of action in screen time.

Ghost Trio and *...but the clouds...* were shot in 1977 at the BBC's Ealing film studios, in a highly unionised culture and with an industrialised division of tasks. Beckett compared the arrangements unfavourably with those at SDR in Germany (Knowlson 1996: 632), where the crew seemed more committed to their work, but the context of this situation was in part that drama producers were pressuring the BBC to grant them location filming rather than studio production. Exterior filming was the favoured method for creative teams who considered themselves innovative and politically engaged, so that studio facilities and staff were in danger of being underemployed and were regarded as overmanned. Many studio drama productions, especially in anthology series where the production schedule left little time for directorial finesse and experimentation, gave little leeway for direction that did not match the standard conventions of using wide shots of the set and closer two-shots (with two people in the frame) of main characters, alternating with close-up in a very conventionalised system of getting shots to capture the performances and shots for dramatic emphasis. As W. Stephen Gilbert (1980: 43) summarises, the studio was 'entrenched in the tradition of naturalism and all the political implications of how naturalism works as a broadcast code. For the studios are not manned by drama specialists ... The accumulated habits of creating a "look" in the studio are difficult to dislodge.' The BBC's Ealing film studio where Beckett's plays were made was in some ways an exception to this, however, since Ealing offered sound-stages where film cameras could be used in large enclosed sets. The BBC's Film Group, based at Ealing, made plays in the studio but used vision and sound technologies deriving from cinema. The recordings of *Ghost Trio* and *...but the clouds...* that were made at Ealing for inclusion in the *Lively Arts* programme *Shades* (1977) therefore mix cinematic and television technologies and production processes, and are one-off 'studio films' shown on television. As I have argued already in this chapter, the technical specificities of different media, and their connotations for production personnel as well as audiences, are mixed in Beckett's dramas for television in ways that encourage critical reflection on these questions of specificity.

Beckett's dramas for television are devised in a way that plays on the assumptions of the audience about previous television formats that were and are inaccurately remembered. Beckett's theatrical television form is an allusion to a past that did not exist in any simple way as a contrast to the television present at the time his television plays were made. The situation is very similar to that of Beckett's *Film*, in which silent movies are alluded to, and audience assumptions and expectations about them are triggered, yet as I have argued elsewhere (Bignell 1999), *Film* is also far from a recreation or simulation of a historic silent movie. What is shared between Beckett's television dramas and the early live television studio drama of the 1940s and 1950s is the comparative lengthiness of shots and the significance of reframing using camera movement within shots. The shot length of British television drama in the 1960s and 1970s was considerably longer than that of cinema. However, in the television studio it was common to change the composition of a shot, the tightness of its framing and the relationships between performer, co-performers and set by physically moving the camera closer to or further from the action, or by zooming into or out of the action. In other words, pace and dynamism were created by camera movement rather than by cutting. It is this technique of camera movement that Beckett self-consciously uses, whether by zooming in slow and deliberate steps in *Eh Joe*, for example, or by moving the wheeled dolly on which the camera is mounted across the acting area as in *Ghost Trio*. The length of shots in Beckett's dramas is nevertheless much greater than the average for British television drama in any decade after the Second World War, and the camera movement is much slower. Since the dramas almost always concern only one visible performer, the dynamic movement made possible by panning between speakers, by zooming in or out to include or exclude one performer from a group present on the stage, and by physically moving the camera around the several figures present on the set, is extremely rare. Overall, Beckett's television dramas, whether written specifically for television or adapted for television studio production, alluded to the aesthetic of television studio production, yet they neither reproduce its characteristic qualities nor counter them by developing an aesthetic that is, for example, more cinematic or more theatrical than the historical record of early live television drama demonstrates.

Monochrome and colour

Production methods on Beckett's television plays were unusual in their relationships between image and sound and in the technology used to realise them. By the end of the 1960s programmes were being made and usually broadcast in colour, so making and screening Beckett's television plays in monochrome after this date is therefore unusual and significant. The unit costs of producing a single play like Beckett's, as opposed to a serial or series, are proportionately high and are less recoverable from the overseas sales and repeated use of the same actors and sets which apply to television series. The use of black and white film for the plays added to the unfavourable economics of making short single dramas because of the largely correct assumption on the part of television producers and executives that audiences would demand colour programmes once colour receivers became generally available in the late 1960s. To make Beckett's plays at all, and especially if they were in monochrome, was hardly likely to encourage audiences to watch them for their visual pleasure. *Eh Joe* was made in 1966, just as colour was about to arrive, and the *Lively Arts* broadcast of *Ghost Trio*, *Not I* and *...but the clouds...* under the title *Shades* in 1977 used colour film for its discussion feature enfolding the plays but monochrome film for the plays themselves. Even in 1982, the broadcast of *Quad* began with colour in the first part but moved to monochrome for the second part.

Ghost Trio opens with a wide shot of a set with a window,

door, bed and a stool on which a dishevelled figure (F) sits. An unseen voice, V, introduces the viewer to the shapes and components of the set before F makes a series of moves around the room, appears to hear music that is present on the soundtrack, and looks through the door to find a boy who seems to indicate wordlessly that an expected visitor will not arrive. Right at the start of the play, V draws attention to the fact that the visual images are all in shades of grey, thus remarking implicitly on the unusual fact that the play is recorded in monochrome. The title of *Ghost Trio* clearly alludes to the notion of death, and the paradoxical life after death that a ghost represents, offering an internal significance for the greyness inasmuch as it might connote ghostliness. But with further relation to television specifically, the phenomenon of shadowed edges around the edges of shapes within the picture (caused by inaccurate aerial positioning or weather effects) is called 'ghosting' and is particularly noticeable in monochrome pictures and in images with strong contrasts of dark and light, like those in *Ghost Trio*. The grey that is used for all of the images in the play is also the colour that a television screen takes on when it is switched off. So as well as the multiple connotations of greys and monochrome as signifiers within V's monologue and the play's visual action, setting up relays and patterns of connotation around death, ghostliness, and a kind of forlorn and exhausted tone, monochrome has material significance in relation to the choices of television mise-en-scène and the meaning of monochrome for producers and audiences at the time of production.

Colour television in Britain was first broadcast in 1967, on the BBC2 channel. By 1977, much of the viewing audience was watching television in colour habitually, and the use of monochrome was most common in repeated programmes from the past, and occasional news footage. Their lack of colour distinguishes Beckett's television plays after *Eh Joe* from the programmes surrounding them in the schedules of the time and has connotations of the past. Most significant among these connotations is the allusion to the tradition of monochrome studio drama in the 1950s and early 1960s, exemplified by *Armchair Theatre*, *The*

Wednesday Play and other strands of anthology drama on television. The plays broadcast in *Shades* would have been perceived in 1977 as anachronistic in form and realisation. This in itself produces another kind of ghostliness, whereby the productions are dislocated from the temporality of television's present at the time of their broadcast, and offer frameworks for interpretation that link them to earlier 'dead' modes of television drama production, though ambivalently.

Quad was shot in colour at the SDR studios, and at least in its use of colour in the first part of the play it conformed to the conventions of colour transmission. Since the play consisted of non-narrative, wordless movement without voice-over or any expressive camera movement, it diverged from the conventions of television drama and looked more like a piece of contemporary dance staged for the camera. The play presents a square of lines on the studio floor, with diagonal lines connecting their corners, and the entire piece is shot from one overhead camera position. The performers appear one at a time from the unlit surrounding space, and move in criss-crossing patterns around the square and its diagonals, before disappearing again into darkness. The shrouded figures, of indeterminate sex, each avoid the centre of the square when they approach it, before resuming their paths along the lines. Patterns of movement and the question of why the figures move as they do are left open to interpretation, and there is no dialogue or voice-over to frame the action. Some of the systems of colour that could have provided further patterning, and thus systems of signification if not narrative or story, were abandoned because of problems during production. Beckett's original screenplay aimed to use systematic attributions of different coloured light for each of the four performers, to identify them in this way in parallel and counterpoint to their differently coloured costumes. But these uses of the ceiling lights in the studio, fitted with coloured gels, were unworkable in practice. The camera operator Jim Lewis said (in Fehsenfeld 1982: 360) that the intended combination of lights for each player produced 'an indefinite shade of orange'. In the play the four performers enter the lighted area of the rectangle from an unlit space right at the edge of the frame, and their entrance and exit were to be highlighted by colour as the light matching each performer came on as they entered. Lewis explained that 'the frequency of light going on and off with the entrance and exit of each player proved too distracting and had to be abandoned'. In *Quad* then, a broader use of production technologies for studio recording was envisaged, adding colour as a signifying system for the first part of the play and within this creating a systematised set of colour cues attached to the appearance and movement of the performers. But these additional resources that made the play at least assimilable into production conventions for the colour broadcasting of the time led to difficulties rather than opportunities. That kind of multiplication of connotations and signifiers, unlike the reference to media other than television and television's own history in the monochrome plays, was regarded by Beckett and his production team as inappropriate. So while *Quad* is at least visually consonant with contemporary colour broadcasting, its dramatic form multiplies interpretive questions in a similar way to the monochrome plays by refusing other television drama conventions of dialogue, narration, storyline and alternation of points of view.

Sound, music and voice: dissociated conventions

In *Eh Joe*, Joe may or may not be aware of the camera that is moving towards him. He reacts to the Voice that is associated with it, but may or may not see it and does not seem to see it even when he looks towards it. This makes the play much less mechanical and more ambiguous in meaning than *Film*, which is probably why Martin Esslin (1991: 83) could describe it as showing 'astonishing ... mastery of the medium', whereas John Fletcher (1978: 99) called it a 'rare lapse of taste'. Esslin (1987: 68) argued that television's 'video-recording techniques and less complex technical structure, allowed [Beckett] to take almost complete control of the production process, even when he was not officially credited as the director'. In the 1966 BBC version of the play (where Beckett was present but not officially directing), but not in the 1988 German version where Beckett was more closely involved, a light comes on above Joe's head whenever Voice speaks, resulting in a slight change in the appearance of Joe's face. This links the voice with a visual agency and with the camera, reducing the separation between sound and image and reinforcing the notion of control over Joe, in a similar way to how a light seems to determine and control the characters' speech in *Play* in its stage version. But it also backs up the suggestion in the text that the voice is not coming from Joe's mind: 'You know that penny farthing hell you call your mind … That's where you think this is coming from, don't you' (Beckett 1984: 202) and 'Look up, Joe, look up, we're watching you' (203). Beckett revised the latter line to 'Look up, Joe, look up, we're looking down' (Beckett undated d) before changing it back to the published version, linking the voice to the light coming from above. Similarly, the manuscript version of *Ghost Trio* describes the overhead shot of Figure's pallet bed saying 'Close-up of pallet object of a special gaze' (Beckett undated f), suggesting again that the notion of looking down from above has a special status that is not linked to the camera shots from other points of view and potentially fracturing the univocal agency of the voice in the play. By the time of *Ghost Trio* the play is not preoccupied by the oppressive relationship of voice to character whereby the two of them are locked in a struggle for mastery over perception. From *Film* to *Eh Joe* and finally to *Ghost Trio*, the relationship that comes to dominate the dramas is the relation between the voice and the viewer. In *Eh Joe* and *Ghost Trio*, the main character looks up towards the camera and smiles, suggesting a final mastery over the threat it represents and concluding each play. In later work, however, the voice more clearly addresses the viewer, and cameras become static witnesses rather than protagonists.

Whereas voice-over, for example in television documentary, is conventionally a dominant discourse anchoring the meaning of images and determining their tone, the personalisation of Voice in *Eh Joe* and her dialogic relationship with Joe disallow the possibility that the voice frames the truth of the image. Yet Voice has a directive power, not only in the viewer's interpretation of Joe's reactions but also in setting up the story of the dead woman who is invisible both to Joe and to the viewer. Since Joe is male and Voice is female, it is not straightforward to understand Voice as a representation of Joe's conscience or personality. Yet there remains the possibility mentioned by Stan Gontarski (1983: 427) that, following a Jungian reading, Voice could be regarded as an alter ego and thus an internal other to Joe. So it is unclear whether Voice is in Joe's mind, whether Voice is Joe's alternative personality, and whether Voice's statements are true. The vituperative tone and teasing or goading of Joe most evident in the repeated refrain 'Eh Joe?' make it clear that Voice is in no way neutral, and this reduces the strength of an interpretation of Voice as an objective narrator.

Indeed, Voice's narration is explicitly a command to visualise a narrative, since particularly towards the end of her narration the words 'remember' and 'imagine' occur frequently. An alternative narrative composed of memory images is solicited by Voice for both Joe and the viewer, and Voice takes on the narrative and authorial control that would in other circumstances be the property of the television apparatus of camera, mise-en-scène and characters. The story of the dead woman is an absent television narrative potentiality that stands between Voice and Joe, and between the viewer and the play. While television as a medium centres on the seeing of distant events, the recording of events that can be replayed in the present, and in its public service functions has the potential to investigate and redress traumatic incidents (in documentary, for example), all of these resonances are introduced by the story of the dead woman but remain visually absent from the play. It is striking that the visualisation of the play alludes to a potentially dramatic incident for television representation yet bars this visualisation from the audience in favour of a relatively static visual scheme and a reduction in dramatic tone and narrative tension (Gontarski 1983: 431). As Vivien Mercier (1977: 133) has pointed out, the text of the play refers on numerous occasions to eyes, yet the primary access to the significance of the story which Voice tells is the expressivity of Joe's eyes and they do not make clear the meanings of the story for him or for the viewer. The play refuses television possibilities such as inserted flashback sequences, or telling the story with voice-over using a sequence of inserted still images, a technique that was used in one television adaptation of *Krapp's Last Tape* and was recommended as a non-naturalistic dramatic form by the avant-garde television playwright John McGrath (1977) and used in his own drama *Diary of a Young Man* (1964). The refusal to open out the action to include visual representations of the remembered story makes the second part of the play unusual and claustrophobic, and it goes against audience expectations for the drama of the time.

The original draft of the play, as Stan Gontarski points out (1983: 430), contained a voice telling her own story, but Beckett revised this two weeks later to allow the interpretation that Voice is inside Joe's head, and that the dead woman is inside Voice's story as a separate character. But the question of whether Voice is imagined by Joe is made more complex by Beckett's response to the question when asked it. He said 'she really whispers in him. He hears her' (in Kalb 1989: 103). The focus on Joe's reaction is enabled not only by the gradual close-up towards him but also by the significant intervals between camera movements in which attention must rest solely on Joe's face. It is very unconventional to position the camera directly in front of the performer, and to move it by incremental steps into close-up without cutaways to other shots. Particularly in the 1960s when cameras were cumbersome and heavy, it was unusual to use a long tracking movement into close-up. There would normally be cutaways to alternative angles on the performer, returning to the original camera once movement across the set had been completed. Whereas in *Film* the camera is relatively mobile, either tracking, panning or being moved along its track by camera operators, the television plays often fix the camera in a single position or move it slowly through a series of simple dolly movements, focusing instead on the ability of the lens to alter the size of the frame through variations on the close-up. The relationship between camera movement and Voice is also problematic. The camera moves only in pauses between Voice's utterances. It is not clear, therefore, whether the camera moves because Voice has completed one sequence of speech or whether a camera movement provides the occasion for Voice to begin speaking again. In either case, however, the connotation of interrogation is provided both by Voice's tone and language in speaking to Joe and by the increasing close-up provided by camera movement. The significance of interrogation and judgement are also reinforced by the frequent biblical allusions and religious references in Voice's speech.

The social situation of television codes it in terms of witness (Ellis 2000). Television bears witness to events in social life, recording public, political, ceremonial and sporting occasions. It bears witness to the ordinariness of people's lives in the genre of documentary. It witnesses performance, and in the 1960s this was still often theatrical and light entertainment performance staged for the camera in the television studio. *Eh Joe* is structured around the witnessing of Joe's reactions to a story which appears to concern him. Voice is a witness to the story of the dead woman and testifies to this knowledge, confronting Joe with it. The audience bears witness to the interrogation of Joe, and the increasing close-ups draw the viewer into this encounter. Beckett's characters either tell their own story or have it told to them by means of an external agency such as a tape recorder, or through a voice-over separated from the action. Voice-over usually signifies retrospection or reflection by a character, as it does for example in Dennis Potter's acclaimed serial *The Singing Detective* (1986). But there are few occasions where voice-over is directly addressed to a character. *Eh Joe* not only stages these forms of bearing witness, but does so using television forms that raise questions for the audience about their relationship to what is seen and heard. The concentration, abstraction and intrusiveness of *Eh Joe* foreground the delegation of the television medium as a surrogate witness for the audience.

Ghost Trio's single character, Figure, holds a cassette recorder in his hands and at intervals the soundtrack introduces phrases from Schubert's 'Ghost Sonata', one of the intertexts that might explain the play's title. The volume of the music in *Ghost Trio* increases slightly as the camera moves towards the cassette player and diminishes slightly when the camera moves away from it. It seems that the music is diegetic and has a visible source. However, Figure does not operate the controls of the cassette player and there is no visual evidence that the machine is operating. The use of music in the play defies the conventions of both diegetic and non-diegetic music in television, since diegetic music is signified as such by the visible presence of a functioning playback device or some other evidence of its source. Non-diegetic music, on the other hand, is conventionally used as a cue to tone and narrative turning-points by being laid over the beginnings and endings of shots and subordinated to dialogue or voice-over. Neither of these possibilities are clearly fixed in *Ghost Trio*. The significance of the cassette player as a source of sound is indicated in the holograph of the play (Beckett undated f) by the fact that Beckett drew a diagram of it consisting of a rectangle with an inner rectangle containing two circles (the operating knobs). Its visible form was therefore indicated prominently and explicitly, but in schematic and diagrammatic terms rather than by specifying, for example, a model name or brand. The first production of the play for *Shades* in 1977 included a close-up from above of the cassette player sitting on the stool, a small grey rectangle on the larger rectangle of the seat, reinforcing the cassette player's role as a teasing sign rather than a material prop with realist and functional attributes. The shot was omitted in the later SDR production of *Geister Trio* in 1988. These points demonstrate further how vision and sound would seem to work together to determine the reality of the space and the source of the music, but also deprive the viewer of this security of meaning. The music in *Ghost Trio* and *Nacht und Träume* substitutes for the visual or vocal expression of emotion by the characters and draws attention to the expectation that there is an emotional tone and significance to the action, but the plays fragment this emotional level into the constituent visual and aural components that would normally express it in a unified and structured way.

Related dissociations of sound and image and refusals of television convention occur in *... but the clouds ....* In the play, a male voice-over, V, recounts how he used to sit at night thinking of an absent lover, would get up and walk the surrounding roads and then return to waiting again, hoping for the loved woman to appear to him. Visually, the play begins with a hunched and barely visible figure of a man, M, then shows the figure dressed in nightwear and later in coat and hat moving into and out of a lighted circle. Finally the shadowy image of a woman, W, appears mouthing words spoken by the voice, words that are a few lines of Yeats's poem 'The Tower' in which the title phrase occurs. The immobility of M makes it more difficult for the television viewer to attribute the voice to him, and the dislocation of voice-over from action in television is a conventional means of separating the voice from the action in time, thus raising further questions about whether M and V might be the same person at different times, one seen, one heard. The image of M dissolves into that of W in a parallel movement where one appears as the other disappears. The figure of W is always facing in the opposite direction to M, and the viewer never sees M and W together. At the end of the play V speaks W's words as she mouths the lines of Yeats's poem. Here again, there is a disjunction between voice and image, an ambivalent temporality that gestures towards the security of voice-over as a contemporary recounting of action visually represented and occurring in the past. But those gestures to the conventions of voice-over are supplemented by the question of whether V is actually conjuring up both M and W in the moment of enunciation, in the present of the play. The times and signifying hierarchies of speech and image are rendered unstable.

These problems of interpretation are part of the larger ambiguity that this chapter has drawn out by referring in detail to a few of Beckett's television works, and clearly there are shared emphases among the plays that characterise their dialogues with conventions of camera style, sound, space and music. The sense of the plays as a corpus with shared concerns and interpretive problems is exacerbated, rather than simplified, when they are addressed in relation to television histories and production conventions and when they are related to cinema or theatre. Furthermore, the implication of this chapter is that the plays can be fruitfully understood as one-off dramas and at the same time grouped as a series. Chapter 3 extends the questions of context and critical framework explored here by addressing the broadcasting contexts that gave rise to the plays' commissioning and had important effects on how they were produced and received.

2

Broadcasting contexts

Introduction

Beckett's plays for British television were not screened in drama anthology series on the mass audience channels BBC1 or ITV, but in arts programming slots on BBC2, and this militated against considering them in relation to work by an emerging canon of television writers. So while Beckett's television plays lend themselves to being considered in the dominant critical discourses around authored drama, the fact that they were not screened in drama anthology slots separates them from the canon being developed by critics of the time. Archival work discussed in this chapter places the different scheduling and trailing contexts of the plays in comparison and contrast to other television drama forms. For example, *Eh Joe* (1966) was scheduled as a one-off event, whose timeslot was not regularly planned for drama, whereas the *Lively Arts* broadcast of three Beckett plays under the title *Shades* (1977) was part of a regularly scheduled series organised around the work of living contemporary writers working mainly in literature or theatre. While this chapter concentrates on television broadcasting contexts, comparisons and contrasts will be made with BBC radio, which was for a long time committed to broadcasting original experimental drama in the Third Programme (later Radio 3), and with avant-garde (especially European) cinema and video art. Eckart Voigts-Virchow (1998) is one of the few writers about Beckett's television work who positions the plays in a critical and historical context centring on broadcast television. His approach is similar to my own in this book, though he neglects the tradition of avant-garde television drama and its connections with work in radio, which I regard as important legitimating contexts for the plays. Voigts-Virchow (1998: 227) contends that 'the stone age of TV production is exactly where Beckett's television locates its aesthetic strategies as a perennial offence to the medium's surface gloss.' It is true that 'Beckett's television plays are part of a high modernist avant-garde left behind in a remote cage of the post-modernist TV zoo' (1998: 245) because of their anachronistic forms and their difference from the programming around them. But by tracing the specific aesthetic moments, institutional relationships and cultural significance of the plays in detail, this conclusion can be historicised and explained to show how it could be that the plays were made at all and why they are significant. This chapter discusses these informing histories and relationships in order to assess both what a study of Beckett's television work might offer to Television Studies, and especially television historiography, and why that encounter has been missed so far.

Television forms

There are a number of forms in television drama. The anthology series written by a multitude of writers consists of self-contained narratives and one-off characters, where any individual play may belong to a different genre from the last (as in *The Wednesday Play* and *Play for Today* anthologies in the 1960s and 1970s). The only play by Beckett presented in an anthology slot was the television version of *Krapp's Last Tape*, made for *Thirty Minute Theatre* (1965–73) and broadcast on 29 November 1972 on the BBC2 channel (subsequently repeated on 17 December 1982) from 10.30 to 11.00 pm. The play was directed by Donald McWhinnie and featured Patrick Magee as Krapp. Its spatially limited setting in Krapp's room and its focus on reminiscence and regret suited the expectations for this studio-shot series of plays, some written specially for television and others, like Beckett's play, adapted from theatre productions. The dramatist Alun Owen, for example, who had written for *Thirty Minute*

Theatre himself, believed: 'The 30 minute play is to the short story what the longer play is to the novel. Television is not suited to the epic ... television is ideal for the small cast in a confined space, capturing a small moment in time' (in Davis 1967: 8). As Chapter 1 has explained, however, this kind of studio drama in which performance and character psychology are foregrounded became increasingly uncommon. A few dramatists persisted with it as the drama form most suited to television's supposed intimate relation with the viewer and its relatively small image size for home viewing. Among these was Alan Plater (Edmands and Hewitt 1968: 9), a distinguished writer of studio-shot plays, who argued: 'The thing that works best on television is a face talking – whether it's in a play or with newsreel cameras or anything – just a face talking, just a face looking. Eyes and a mouth.' The attention to a single figure, shot with emphasis on the close-up in long takes observing a performer's face and body, was what both *Eh Joe* and *Krapp* were offering.

But this form was precisely what dramatists who regarded themselves as cutting-edge in the 1960s and 1970s attacked as a mythology of television that came from its close relationships with theatre forms, and the presence of theatre personnel behind and in front of the camera. The producer and writer Troy Kennedy Martin (1964: 25), for example, who came to prominence in the mid-1960s with his work on the contemporary police drama *Z Cars*, argued that the emphasis on close-ups of 'faces talking and faces reacting' displayed 'a deep rooted belief that the close-up of an actor's face somehow reacts subjectively on the viewer'. Rejecting the claims of intimacy and connection with the viewer that this supposedly theatrical and naturalist studio drama of the close-up made, dramatists and producers opted instead for series and serial drama which aimed to involve the viewer with continuity of theme, setting and character across a number of episodes, alongside an attempt to eschew the close-up in favour of 'cinematic' wide shots and real locations outside the studio. The form of the episodic series consists of largely self-contained narratives, belonging to the same genre, with regular characters and settings linking one episode to the next. Narratives are initiated and resolved in each episode. In contrast to the series form, the episodic serial has an ongoing story for a number of episodes, with recurrent characters and settings, moving towards a conclusion over a number of weeks or months. Serials consist of a developing story divided into several parts, and television soap opera is a special case of the serial form where the end of the story is infinitely deferred. Television fiction is now rarely seen in the form of single one-off programmes and is increasingly made in episodic forms resembling the serial. The increased competition between channels for audiences was the primary driver of this change.

Before the beginning of the BBC's competition with commercial ITV television in 1955, original drama for television was regarded as an attractive draw for audiences. But once BBC became more concerned with ratings when ITV appeared, it was immediately evident that light entertainment drew the largest audiences. For drama, the response was to group single plays in anthology strands, and to focus increasingly on the production of series. None of Beckett's plays for television were broadcast in drama series, and over the years from *Eh Joe* in 1966 to *Quad* in 1982, the screening of his work looked increasingly anomalous as anthology strands such as *The Wednesday Play* and *Play for Today* became the dominant vehicles within BBC schedules for original dramas, and by the mid-1980s even these anthologies disappeared and series and serials became the norm. The year before *Eh Joe* was broadcast, 1965, was the first full year of production for the BBC's *Wednesday Play*. In that year, 33 new plays were presented, written by 27 writers, and all but one of the plays were written specifically for television. Dennis Potter wrote four of them, demonstrating the opportunity offered by the series to new writers (Cooke 2003: 68). The first four months of 1965 saw three plays on controversial subject matter. *Fable* was produced by James MacTaggart, directed by Christopher Morahan and written by John Hopkins. It was set in a near future where a black majority population exercised power over a white minority. Although it was intended as a parable about apartheid, it was understood by many viewers as a warning about black immigration, then becoming a matter of public debate. John Hopkins also wrote *Horror of Darkness*, directed by Anthony Page (who directed the BBC film version of Beckett's *Not I* in 1975) and produced by James MacTaggart. It demonstrated the anxiety and fear felt by homosexual men in a Britain where homosexual acts were still illegal. A third play, *Three Clear Sundays*, produced again by James MacTaggart and directed by Ken Loach, written by the convicted murderer James O'Connor, demonstrated the inhumanity and potential miscarriages of justice produced by capital punishment.

The engagement of these dramas with contemporary social issues, and the association of the anthology strands in which they appeared with those issues, contrasts strongly with the kinds of drama Beckett produced. Each of the plays, like Tony Garnett's and Ken Loach's *Up the Junction* (1965) and its contribution to public understanding of abortion, aimed to contribute to public political debates. The law changed on some of these issues shortly after the plays were broadcast, though not necessarily as a direct result. Capital punishment was suspended in 1965, homosexuality between consenting adults in private environments became legal in 1967, and abortion laws were relaxed in 1968. These television dramas were written by predominantly young television playwrights, influenced by the debates around television form going on at the time and by the experiments in theatrical form occurring in theatre. Their politics was that of the New Left, and the rising generation of university-educated men (and a few women) who were beginning to occupy positions of influence in broadcasting as well as in other spheres of British cultural and political life. The plays of the 1960s and 1970s surrounding Beckett's screen work were sometimes shot in the studio using conventional multi-camera techniques, but were edited and directed to foreground the narrative flexibility, rapid pace and rhythm of editing in cinema. Two implications should be noted. On one hand, Beckett's work was granted a particular privilege as a kind of drama that was offered to the audience as a special event, different from the emergent drama culture of the period, and on the other hand, its formal experimentation and its demands on the viewer tended to marginalise the plays outside of the production and reception contexts that were becoming increasingly formalised and disciplined for both programme-makers and audiences.

Drama, arts and video art

Beckett's plays for television, and the plays adapted from his theatre work, were made for broadcast rather than as one-off gallery works, but they were increasingly made at the edges of the culture of television drama production or for arts series that did not usually commission drama. *Eh Joe*, for example, was outside the normal seasonal planning and scheduling of British television, inasmuch as it was the only new play on BBC2 in summer 1966 that was not part of an anthology series. This part of the year was the 'low season' for drama with the schedule full of repeats from the previous season (BBC WAC T5/782/3). The twelve *Wednesday Plays* of summer 1966 were all repeats, as were the nine plays in the science fiction anthology *Out of the Unknown*, for example. The BBC was slow in setting up recording and transmission dates for *Eh Joe*, which eventually emerged on BBC2 at 10.20 pm on Monday 4 July 1966, directed by Alan Gibson. The play was not shown in a regular slot of any kind, with no corresponding programme on the Mondays preceding or following it. While broadsheet newspapers like *The Times* drew attention to *Eh Joe* on the day of broadcast, they made little attempt to associate it with other contemporary television drama programmes. The *Radio Times* billing (30 June 1966) for the play noted: '*Eh Joe?* [sic] was written specifically for television by Samuel Beckett, the Irishman long resident in France whose plays – *Waiting for Godot, Endgame, Krapp's Last Tape* – have formed an important part of the post-war theatre revolution.' The billing noted connections between the performers in the play and both television and theatre productions: 'The distinguished Irish actor Jack MacGowran has for long been a close personal friend of the author, and he has become (with Patrick Magee) one of the principal interpreters of his work. He is also one of drama's most skilled pantomimists, as evidenced by his recent television performance as the jockey turned Trappist monk in *Silent Song*. Sian Phillips, the voice of Joe's past, has been seen recently in the West End theatre in *The Night of the Iguana* and *Man and Superman*.' So *Eh Joe* was exceptional as television drama in terms of its scheduling and was offered to the audience through its attribution to an important theatre writer and its actors' connections with notable performances on stage and screen. It was not offered in conformity with the scheduling practices and promotional discourses of contemporary television drama. The connection of *Eh Joe* with theatre was to be reinforced at its original broadcast by a spoken credit for Sian Phillips over the closing titles, advertising her role in Shaw's play at London's Vaudeville Theatre (BBC WAC T5/1296/1).

A similar context obtained when Beckett's next original work for television was presented in 1977. Tristram Powell produced the *Shades* programme containing three Beckett dramas for the BBC2 arts series *The Lively Arts*, and when it was announced in the *Radio Times* (16–22 April 1977: 19), the billing subtitled the programme 'A Samuel Beckett Première'. The *Radio Times* advertised *Shades* in a short accompanying feature article that described Beckett as 'one of the most famous and secretive of playwrights' and emphasised his personal involvement in the production. It noted that 'the bleak poetry of his vision has had its passionate admirers and detractors', but Beckett's status was indicated by a mention of his Nobel Prize in 1969. This claim for Beckett's literary status and a sense that the 'poetry' needed some supporting interpretation was confirmed by the inclusion in the *Shades* programme of commentary by Martin Esslin, described as 'an authority on modern theatre and, until recently, Head of BBC Radio Drama'. The programme's high-cultural status was significant and clearly contrasted with the competing programme on BBC1, an episode of the American drama about slavery, *Roots*, which made a great impact in terms of press coverage and attracted large audiences. Beckett had the special status of a theatre *auteur*, and was regarded as a unique 'brand' whose cachet the BBC was keen to reflect on itself.

Beckett's other British television plays were all presented under the auspices of *Arena*, BBC2's flagship arts programme, and this is highly significant for their institutional status and their address to their audience. For the majority of television viewers, arts television programmes are their primary access to the arts (Walker 1993). This has the effect of ensuring continuity of television coverage of the arts, but it also reinforces the ghettoisation of arts programmes and the divisions between an assumed minority audience of informed viewers and an ignorant majority. The bridge between the audience and the art is most often the personality, whether a television personality acting as presenter such as Huw Wheldon on *Monitor*, Humphrey Burton on *Aquarius* and Melvyn Bragg on *The South Bank Show*, or the personality of the artist proposed as the source and explanatory context for the work. There is a long and distinguished tradition of these kinds of programme, including in the 1960s *Monitor* (BBC), *Tempo* (ITV), *New Tempo* (ITV) and *Omnibus* (BBC). In the 1970s the key programmes were *Aquarius* (ITV) *Arena* (BBC) and *The South Bank Show* (ITV), and some of them continued into the 1980s, including *Arena*. It was not surprising that Melvyn Bragg was chosen to lead the presentation of *The Lively Arts: Shades* and to act as interviewer of Martin Esslin about Beckett's life and work in the programme since Beckett's *Ghost Trio*, *...but the clouds...* and *Not I* appeared there as artworks that were felt to need intermediary figures between them and the audience. Television arts programming was acting as an exhibition medium for Beckett's work in a general sense, and as a commissioner of original arts work since *Ghost Trio* and *...but the clouds...* were written for the programme, and the film of *Not I* had already been made for BBC use. As the presenter of the programme, Melvyn Bragg brought an already distinguished reputation as a cultural commentator and public intellectual that suited both the presumed difficulty and prestige of Beckett's work and also promised that he would be an accessible and reliable conduit for its understanding by the audience.

Thus television arts programmes, in the case of *Shades* and more generally, have an exhibiting and curatorial function as an alternative museum or gallery. The television medium can be used simply to relay pre-existing work (by broadcasting a theatrical performance of a Beckett play, for example) or as a medium of artistic exploration in itself, as has been argued of Beckett's dramas written for television. In either case, programme producers need to decide whether they wish to concentrate on artists as creative individuals or on the works they create. This affects the choice and relationship of the contributing voices, interviewees or experts who may appear in the programme, since the contributions of artists could take precedence over those of critics or historians of art, or alternatively commentators could evaluate and critique artists' work as well as introducing or explicating it. The role of presenters and explanatory or contextual material, and the scheduling of arts programmes, also take into account the presumed purpose of programmes and their intended or expected audiences. In the British broadcasting context, programmes have each of two functions to varying extents. They celebrate the arts by exhibiting and featuring artistic work, but they also critique and evaluate the arts. Since aesthetic knowledge and the authority to impose aesthetic standards are in Britain associated with the upper middle class, the broadcasting of arts programmes and the representation of the arts are imbued with assumptions about class, especially the class of the audience. In recognition of this, and also as a strategy to combat assumptions about the relationship between arts material and the class of the audience, British arts programming has given significant attention to both popular culture and elite culture within the same programme strand or within a single episode of an arts series. Television as a medium is regarded as the most accessible and central broadcasting medium, yet despite this, and also because of it, television is at the margins of cultural authority. Television itself is not regarded as an arts medium, and in general programme producers include artists as contributors rather than, for example, commissioning artists to make programmes themselves. The requirement to give attention and concentration to programmes such as the BBC arts programmes in which Beckett's plays for television were screened is at odds with the conventional representations in popular and academic discourse of the inattentive, grazing viewer.

Television has presented the arts since its earliest days, but an elite group of presenters, producers and sometimes directors have led the development of arts programming. The contributors featured in arts programmes as well as those who have made them tend to belong to a powerful sector of the British establishment and some of them have gone on to become significant political figures and leaders of broadcasting institutions. The most lauded arts programme made by BBC was *Monitor*, presented by Huw Wheldon who had worked for the Arts Council from the mid-1940s to 1951 and organised some of the concerts in the 1951 Festival of Britain. He became Managing Director of the BBC in 1969. Some *Monitor* programmes were commissioned from young directors such as John Schlesinger, John Boorman and Ken Russell, each of whom subsequently became leading figures of the British film industry. Sir Kenneth Clark, a leading art historian until his death in 1983, was important in the founding of ITV, as chairman of the Independent Television Authority, and made arts programmes for ATV in the late 1950s as well as the lavish, popular and well-regarded 13-part series *Civilisation* for BBC2 (1969). The series was commissioned by David Attenborough, Controller of BBC2 and a television presenter and producer. *Arena*, under whose title Beckett's theatre plays were presented in their television versions, was edited by Alan Yentob from 1975 to 1985. Yentob joined the BBC in 1968 and, after working on *Arena*, he rose to become head of Music and Arts. In 1987 he was appointed Controller of BBC2 and in 1993 became Controller of BBC1. Melvyn Bragg, presenter of *Shades* for *The Lively Arts*, was recruited in 1977 by Nick Elliott, head of Features at London Weekend Television to present *The South Bank Show* on ITV. Bragg had worked as a writer and editor on *Monitor* and had also established himself as a novelist by the time he appeared in *Shades*, so his role as a recognised cultural commentator was already secure. He and Esslin (former head of BBC Radio Drama) were both part of an elite with long and distinguished careers in broadcasting that were appropriate for the presentation of Beckett and his work, which were viewed as similarly established, significant and serious.

The BBC had been presenting Beckett's radio plays for many years by the time his television work was broadcast, and some of the key producers and performers worked on both radio and television broadcasts of Beckett's dramas. Many of the thematic concerns of the television plays, especially with memory, mourning and loss, are also shared by Beckett's earlier radio work as the BBC's pre-broadcast introductions to them show. *All That Fall* was directed by Donald McWhinnie and broadcast on the Third Programme on 13 January 1957, featuring Patrick Magee. The BBC's synopsis noted: 'The theme is of the inadequacy of life and death, in an atmosphere of decay.' The French version of *Endgame*, *Fin de Partie*, was broadcast on 2 May 1957, produced by Michael Bakewell, using the same cast as the Royal Court Theatre's world première of the play three weeks previously, including Jean Martin and Roger Blin, with Jacques Brunius as a narrator. *Embers* was broadcast on 24 June 1959, directed by McWhinnie, with Magee and Jack MacGowran. Beckett's version of the French New Wave writer Robert Pinget's *The Old Tune (La Manivelle)*, described by BBC as 'A conversation piece written for the Third Programme' was produced by Barbara Bray and broadcast on 23 August 1960, with Beckett's collaborators Magee and MacGowran appearing again. It was BBC Radio that first presented *Endgame* on 22 May 1962, in a version adapted and produced by Bakewell and a cast that included Maurice Denham and Donald Wolfit. *Words and Music*, with music by John Beckett, was produced by Bakewell and featured Magee and Felix Felton. Its first Third Programme broadcast was on 13 November 1962, and the *Radio Times* introduced the play with the explanation: 'Croak, an aged tyrant, has two servants, Words and Music. He shouts out at them themes – "love", "age", etc., which they attempt to portray, and which sharpen his memories of a woman once loved whose face he cannot escape.' *Cascando*, directed by McWhinnie with Magee as Voice and Denys Hawthorne as Opener, was first broadcast on 6 October 1964. *Play* was presented on radio on 11 October 1966, with an introduction by Martin Esslin and starring Robert Stephens, Billie Whitelaw and Pauline Jameson. The billing in the *Radio Times* introduced the play with the quotation 'Silence and darkness were all I craved. Well, I get a certain amount of both. They being one. Perhaps it is more wickedness to pray for more'. On Beckett's seventieth birthday, 13 April 1976, Radio 3 broadcast *Rough for Radio* for the first time, produced by Esslin and performed by Michael Deacon, Harold Pinter, Billie Whitelaw and Magee. *A Piece of Monologue* was broadcast on 18 April 1986 on Radio 3, featuring Ronald Pickup, produced by Ronald Mason. The *Radio Times* billing merely offered the suggestive introduction 'Nothing stirring anywhere. Nothing to be seen anywhere. Nothing to be heard.' *Waiting for Godot* was broadcast in an abridged version made for a season of programmes of the cultural highlights of the 1950s on 5 February 1962, with Andrew Sachs and Nigel Stock, produced by Robin Midgley. As late as 3 September 1994, Radio 3 listeners were given the rare chance of hearing the original Théâtre de Babylone production of *En Attendant Godot* recorded on 5 January 1953 with its cast of Jean Martin, Roger Blin, Pierre Latour, Lucien Raimbourg and Serge Leconte. On 4 September 1994, BBC Radio 3 broadcast a new version of *Waiting for Godot*, produced by Peter Wood and featuring Michael Moloney, Stratford Johns, Simon Russell Beale, Alan Howard and Geraldine McEwan. This is a very distinguished record, whose personnel comprised a cadre of Britain's finest stage actors, as well as directors with privileged relationships with Beckett and knowledge of his work.

Given that some commentators on Beckett's television dramas have described them as 'videos' (for example, Russell 1989), it is worth noting that in the context of British broadcasting his work was absolutely not understood as video art but as drama, as the legacy of radio productions suggests. The plays adopted the conventions of dramatic situation, character and narrative to a significant extent, and were made by BBC drama production staff and cast with professional actors. The *Radio Times* (11–17 December 1982) billing for *Quad*, screened on 16 December on BBC2, draws attention to its background in drama, despite the play's concealed actors, lack of dialogue and single camera position: 'A play without words, *Quad* has a musical structure. It is a kind of canon or catch – a mysterious square-dance. Four hooded figures move along the sides of the square. Each has his own particular itinerary. A pattern emerges and collisions are just avoided. From these permutations, Beckett, as writer and director creates an image of life that is both highly charged and strangely funny.' *Quad* was presented as a written play, not as video art or televised dance.

Video art grew slowly in Britain (Marshall 1990), and examples during the period of Beckett's involvement with television show the differences between the two forms. In Britain, against a background of almost total lack of interest in video as medium of art practice, the first major exhibition of British video artists' work was 'The Video Show' at the Serpentine Gallery in 1975. Seduced by the techno-utopianism of Marshall McLuhan's theories, the currency of semiotic critiques of realist representation and a post-1960s commitment to agitprop and dreams of media democratisation, the work was profoundly Modernist in its reflexivity and anti-representationalism. While Modernist painting had reacted against a canonical tradition of fine art, video art reacted against the conventions of broadcast television. Thus many works attempted to discover an 'essence' of video by exploring video feedback. This included pointing the camera at a television monitor to produce infinite regressions of picture-within-picture (in David Hall's 'Progressive Recession'), or time-delayed recording so that spectators saw ghostly images of themselves replaying their recent movements (in Brian Hoey's 'Videvent'). By the 1980s, video artists in Britain had moved away from this quest for a purity of medium and recognised that their work could engage instead with the dominant modes of television representation to critique their conventions and ideologies. In the 1990 exhibition 'Signs of the Times' at MOMA Oxford, for example, the work included David Hall's 'A Situation Envisaged: The Rite II', in which a bank of screens showing broadcast television have been turned to face the wall so that their images are invisible but the colours and patterns of light and shade reflect incoherently back to the spectator, while a central screen shows the moon in a grainy image produced by a scanner like the one invented by John Logie Baird in his 1920s experiments with television. In Susan Hiller's 'Belshazzar's Feast/The Writing on Your Wall', a bank of television screens show flames, alluding to the replacement of the hearth by the television as a focal point in the home and also suggesting the Biblical writing in flames that warned of punishment for social ills. Even from these few examples, it is clear that Beckett's television work might share an interest in television conventions (as Chapter 2 has shown), but its relationship with drama forms is much stronger than its relationship with work designed for gallery exhibition, which has often used multiple screens, engagement with the gallery space and the itinerant spectator, and is primarily non-narrative in form.

When video art has been commissioned specifically for broadcast, it has adopted some of the self-reflexivity of exhibition work, and also the non-narrative, non-dramatic forms of gallery video. For instance, David Hall created ten 'TV Pieces' for Scottish Television in 1971 with the assistance of Anna Ridley, transmitted to coincide with the Edinburgh Festival. They were only a few minutes in duration, were intended to act as interventions in the normal schedule, were unframed by contextual material, and addressed the forms and expectations of the television medium. For example, one film shows a household tap appearing at the top of the television screen and pouring water apparently into the screen itself. The level of the water gradually rises until it engulfs the tap at the top of the screen and the jet of water therefore disappears along with the sound of running water. When the screen is full, the tap is removed and the water drains noisily at a diagonal angle across the screen. The space of the screen, its orientation in space, its relationship to real-world physicality, and expectations of image and sound are all disrupted here. The video references the 'box' in the corner in which images and sounds 'flow' in a 'stream' that is always 'on tap'. By 1976, Anna Ridley worked as a designer at the BBC and persuaded *Arena* to devote a programme to a survey of British and American video art. The programme began with a film by David Hall titled 'This Is a Television Receiver', featuring Richard Baker (a news presenter of the period) in a conventional news studio setting reading a statement about the real and imagined functions of the television set. The image of Baker was then progressively distorted by feeding back the studio monitor's image through the camera. In 1982, Anna Ridley founded Annalogue Limited, an independent production company which produced a series of programmes under the title *Dadarama* for Channel 4 in 1985. Contemporary artists worked with the composer Michael Nyman to produce both conventionally shot videos and animations produced using the Quantel Paintbox system. The programmes were not packaged in a magazine programme format but presented as individual pieces. Later in the 1980s, Channel 4 produced further compilation programmes of video art, and further specially commissioned short films. Channel 4's budget for independent film was £10 million in 1990, later reaching £50 million, and around 1,000 hours of 'art film' were broadcast in its first ten years of operation from 1982 to 1992 (Rees 2007: 147). No work by Beckett was included in this output. The Arts Council has financed artists' films and video since the late 1960s, and in 1981 founded a film and video library to make these works more accessible. Beckett's television pieces do not feature in the Arts Council's video collection because, tellingly, Beckett is regarded as a dramatist. In terms of the aesthetic forms of British video art and its institutional placement, Beckett's television drama is, precisely, drama for television and not video art.

Avant-gardes in the cinema

It is important to distinguish between the historical avant-garde, which encompasses art movements within Modernism such as Dada and Surrealism, the political avant-garde, which denotes those art movements working against bourgeois individualism and capitalist economy such as the art market, and the formal avant-garde which seeks to develop self-consciousness of the artistic media and searches for new forms. The historical avant-garde aimed to destroy the institution of art, in production and distribution, as Peter Bürger (1984) has argued. So as John Caughie (2000) explains, since television is made in and by institutions for institutional distribution, it cannot by definition have an avant-garde. In film, on the other hand, avant-garde films are the products of individual artists or groups working outside the mainstream and without established funding sources. This facilitates the role of the avant-garde film maker as author, along the lines of the Romantic vision of the artist as independent visionary. I have argued earlier in this book that Beckett's collaborations with production personnel and the institutions of television may have been driven by their respect for him as an artist, but nevertheless the work remained within the broad parameters of collective institutional production.

Aesthetically, however, the reflexivity about seeing in Beckett's television work does connect with the self-conscious aesthetic exhibited in much avant-garde film making. For example, there are many shots of eyes in Surrealist and avant-garde film, as William Wees (1992: 13) notes. The opening shots of the protagonist's eye in *Film* could be paralleled with the cutting of a woman's eye in *Un Chien Andalou*, where the parallel is reinforced by Beckett's awareness of Surrealist productions, but also with later work such as Yoko Ono's screenplay *Rape or Chase* in which a camera pursues a young woman, though the film was never made (MacDonald 1993: 21). Scott McDonald refers to the interest in early cinema among American avant-garde film makers, for whom the apparent simplicity of the early single-shot films by the Lumière brothers, using a single tripod camera, suggested alternatives to the dominant narrative tradition of Hollywood and its montage style. Ono's 1968 *Film No. 5 (Smile)* consists of a single shot of John Lennon's face, which looks towards the camera and then smiles twice, accompanied by a dissociated soundtrack (MacDonald 1993: 26–27). The concern with identity and the refusal of its coherence in avant-garde film is evident in Maya Deren's *Meshes of the Afternoon*, which shows what appears to be a woman and her double. These characters' journey across a landscape is incoherent and impossible, resembling a dream. At the end of the film, the dreaming woman awakes. This kind of concern with doubling is evident in *Film* especially, but the interest in visions, dreams and delusions, memories and the summoning of an absent other are also reminiscent of Beckett's television plays.

But despite the connections between the long take avant-garde film and Beckett's screen work, there are also significant differences. Beckett plays do not entirely refuse montage, being composed of a sequence of shots and scenes where temporal and causal relations are plausible even if they are not precisely delineated. Neither do they refuse conventions of performance and casting, though they engage with them paradoxically. David Bradby (2001: 6) notes that Gordon Craig was a figure of considerable interest among the European avant-garde. He aimed to reduce or eliminate the importance of the actor in theatre, using the actor instead as a mechanical body, in parallel to Kleist's theory of the marionette theatre. But paradoxically, Beckett always cast experienced theatre actors in his television work, and cast Buster Keaton in *Film*, suggesting that the reduction of acting technique to minimal forms required actors whose skills were acknowledged and respected rather than ignored.

Film (1964) only partially adopts film narrative conventions because it deprives the spectator of a neutral point of view. In *Film* the spectator is aligned first with E, the pursuing camera point of view that perceives O, the character attempting to escape from it. As E encounters three other characters in the street who express shock and horror at being seen by E, O hurries into an apartment building, secures himself in a dilapidated room but is unable to prevent E from entering the space. Brief point of view shots from O's position identify his look, and at the end of the film, a cut from O to E and back again reveals that E is a double of O, and thus the two points of view become exchangeable. But the film has no unmarked narrative point of view, no neutral point of view that would situate E and O in a space that the unmarked camera position could establish as a real-seeming norm. Thus the spectator cannot fill the role of the transcendent perceiver, as Jean-Louis Baudry (1980: 34), for example, has argued that he or she does in classical Hollywood film narrative: 'the spectator identifies less with what is represented, the spectacle itself, than with what stages the spectacle, makes it seen, obliging him to see what it sees; this is exactly the sort of function taken over by the camera as a sort of relay'. The spectator is obliged to see him or herself as the one who sees in *Film*, a position enforced by the restrictive use of point of view, and this is narratively revealed as a necessary and active terrorisation of the self and others, rather than a pleasurable mastery. This focus on the problematic agency of looking, and the refusal of cinema conventions, aligns the work with the avant-garde's critical investigations of spectatorship at the same time as the film's pursuit motif alludes to the chase films of early Hollywood.

In the 1964 *Film*, the character O is not only observed by a camera, but also owns an envelope full of photographs. It is revealed towards the end of the film that it is the envelope of photographs that O has been hiding under his coat all the way through the film. Photographs have always since their invention had the status of an evidence of the past, a truthful record of being in the world. They entail the mechanical remembering of lived identity for the transcendent individual, and photography therefore becomes a support and guarantee for subjectivity. An early Kodak advertisement proclaimed: 'A collection of these pictures may be made to furnish a pictorial history of life as it is lived by the owner, that will grow more valuable with every day that passes' (Gernsheim 1955: 302, quoted in Neale 1985: 8). Photographic technology claimed to authenticate the being of the individual subject, and to be a pure moment of perception by a transcendent other. The photographs in *Film* are another and different order of image from the rest of the film, promising a truth of the self, a revelation of the past and visual formality and order that are not otherwise represented in it. They are strongly posed and conventionalised representations, in contrast to the moving camera and unconventional cuts and points of view in the rest of the film. The seven photographs apparently of O in *Film* are posed according to the conventions of late Victorian photographic portraiture. They represent significant stages in life, such as the first communion, graduation from university, engagement to be married, the birth of a child, and enlisting in the army. Much later, in ...*but the clouds*..., the image of W is posed like a portrait photograph which memorialises her and has a symbolic value for M as a token of his absent beloved. Yet inasmuch as it is an image made reproducible like a photograph, it also makes W into an exchangeable commodity that can be exhibited for the audience and for M. Although O strokes his photographs as he examines them in *Film*, suggesting precisely the nostalgic construction of a history and identity which Kodak were marketing, the photographs preserve the traces which authenticate his being as visible to an other, or to himself as other, and this seems to be the reason why he tears them up. As Jonathan Kalb (1994: 136) has noted, 'neither a film's characters nor its narrator-surrogate (the camera-eye as subjective "I") really exists until a machine shines incandescent light through celluloid, generating sharp, ephemeral images that fool viewers into believing that the camera-eye is perceiving in the present and that perceivedness is necessarily desirable.' *Film* divides the individual into perceiver and perceived but shows that self as subject and self as object must co-exist. By using photographic technology in this way, being is inescapably split in itself, in a way which recalls the splitting and multiplicity of selves exploited for comic purposes in Keaton's comedy films of the 1920s (see Chapter 4), again uniting popular cinema with a reflexive concern with looking and subjectivity.

On 28 September 1964, Beckett wrote to *Film*'s director, Alan Schneider, about the project: 'I described it to Barney after the first screening as an "interesting failure". This I now see is much too severe. It does I suppose in a sense fail with reference to a purely intellectual schema ... but in doing so has acquired a dimension and validity of its own that are worth far more than any merely efficient translation of intention' (Harmon 1998: 166). The fact that Beckett apparently describes his intentions for *Film* at the beginning of the script has sometimes drawn commentators into simplistic comparisons between the author's intention and the final product. This game of authorial control is explicitly refused, however, by the final line of the screenplay: 'No truth value attaches to the above, regarded as of merely structural and dramatic convenience' (Beckett 1986: 323). The idea of separating perceiver and perceived is an allusion to Bishop Berkeley's philosophy. Berkeley wrote in *The Principles of Human Knowledge* (1949) that the world is divided into ideas, which are perceived, and spirits, who perceive them. Ideas can only exist when they are perceived: *esse est percipi*. Everything exists in God's mind, and God is the ultimate spirit. Thus all objects are eternally known by God and therefore have eternal existence in his mind. This theory does not account for self-knowledge, and Schopenhauer (1966) introduced the idea that perceiving spirits have some notion of themselves as perceivers (Marculescu 1989). E may not simply be the alter ego of O but may also represent aspects of God in Berkeley's system. This idea is supported by the fact that when he confronts O he is standing directly in front of the place where a photograph had hung, a picture described in the screenplay as representing God the Father. Yet since E's perception is itself partial, because of the camera's limited point of view and the few if any connotations that E is an image of God, the parallel is inexact. Beckett substitutes the inescapability of God's perception with the inescapability of self-perception, taking the dynamics of Berkeley's system and reinterpreting the positions laid out by his structure. In a letter to Schneider referring to E's and O's points of view, Beckett requested that Schneider 'make sure that we know that the camera is *subjective* ... in both instances.' (Harmon 1998: 183). This refusal of the conventions of an unmarked camera point of view, and the curious relationships between the behaviour of the persona represented by the camera's point of view versus the person it pursues, are underlined by the performance style adopted in the film. The deliberate bodily movement, stylised and somewhat melodramatic gestures, and dwelling on comic business all serve to distance the audience from any sense that a conventionally realist world is being represented. Issues of perception, artifice and stylisation are immediately apparent. Beckett wrote in a letter to Schneider: 'The problem of the double vision for example is not solved, but the attempt to solve it has given the film a plastic value which it would not have otherwise' (Harmon 1998: 166). The adoption and simultaneous divergence from the conventions of cinema, and the conventions of portraiture in photography, provide *Film* with an ambiguity that is both frustrating and productive.

Critical work has largely connected Beckett's stage drama to Modernism, but as Anne Friedberg (1993) has argued, television has been characterised as postmodern, lacking a historical avant-garde, and only recently in the work of John Caughie (2000) has a modernist tradition in television been identified. According to James Knowlson (1996: 475), Beckett watched avant-garde films when he was a student at the École Normale in Paris, and Knowlson suggests that *Un Chien Andalou* was the possible inspiration for the figure of Winnie in Beckett's *Happy Days*, for example. David Bradby (2001: 4–21) makes the case in his book on *Waiting for Godot* that the play emerges from a European avant-garde theatrical tradition. In relation to television programming, the British public service tradition has created a space for the screening of avant-garde films on television, and for experimentation especially in drama. However, this is not confined to a historical period and is part of the debates around diversity of programming in the public service tradition and questions of quality and taste in the medium. The address to different audience sectors is based on the assumption of recognition and identification by viewers with television forms that connect with their identity and may change it on the basis of that recognition of themselves. But as Thomas Docherty (1993: 16) notes, the avant-garde counters 'the structure of recognition in which the Subject of consciousness finds the comfort of Identity and self-sameness'. For Jean-François Lyotard (1993), the postmodern develops this avant-garde disjuncture with identity, recognition and comprehension. But again, this definition of the postmodern refers not to a historical period but to a formal characteristic that may be shared by some television programmes but does not help in placing Beckett's plays in a tradition or heritage of television forms.

Rather than trying to fit a generalised overview of Beckett's screen work into theoretical definitions of the avant-garde,

Modernism or postmodernism, it is much more helpful to identify specific aspects of structure, tone and mise-en-scène and connect this material evidence to wider conceptual and historical frames. The coherence of space is established to some degree in individual shots and scenes in Beckett's screen work, especially in relation to the indication of rooms as settings. But there is no consistency in how stage productions adapted for the screen adopt spatial conventions deriving from theatre, television or film. The *Beckett on Film* presentation of *Rockaby*, featuring Penelope Wilton, is set in a room which is dressed as a realistic location and which is entered from outside by the camera. After this opening establishing shot representing the whole of the performer's body, the drama settles down to focus on the lighted area of her mouth with the rest of her face and the background in shadow. The domestic setting confined within a room, and the apparently confessional diary form of the woman's monologue has greater affinity with television than with cinema, via for example the BBC's *Video Diaries* series or the confessional speech of television documentary. Long shots of the performer's body alternate with close-ups of hands, also a conventional means in television documentary to signify emotion and also to function as bridges where editing of the soundtrack needs to be matched to a shift of image. On the other hand, the *Beckett on Film* season's *Act Without Words II* was a stage mine that is converted into a pastiche of a silent film short. One after another, two men emerge from sacks when they are prodded by a stick. Like a sequence of vaudeville turns, each in a different performance style, they perform actions such as dressing and tasting a carrot. The film alludes to the early Edison shorts that presented brief sequences of action using one or two performers, often with a comic intention. Leading in the direction of television and film respectively, these two productions confuse any consistent attribution of screen versions of Beckett's plays to the conventions of a specific medium or versions of periodisation.

The relatively verisimilitudinous use of space in the *Beckett on Film* productions can be seen clearly in a comparison between two versions of *What Where*. The German SDR television production of *What Where, Was Wo* (1986), went to elaborate lengths to dehumanise the performers by representing only their lighted faces against a black background, with the rest of their bodies unseen. The performers' heads were conformed to the same shape by the addition of prosthetic masking, their ears were made invisible and their voices were electronically slowed down. In the *Beckett on Film* production (2001), directed by Damien O'Donnell, the same actor appears as the three personae Bem, Bim and Bom. Their costumes are similar but the faces are shot much more naturalistically, though with the paradoxical effect of revealing that each of the 'characters' is identical. Unlike in the SDR production, there is consistent use of close-up, whereas the German production fades the faces in and out of vision as if they were intersecting with a plane of light parallel to the television screen. Anna McMullan (1993: 38) calls the space of the German production a space of memory or fantasy, whereas the *Beckett on Film* production is placed in a three-dimensional set resembling a library. The off-screen Voice is distorted and is relayed through a microphone, and its technological nature is emphasised by the sound of switching circuitry as it is turned on and off. Two of the performers remain static and standing during the play, while the central figure Bem moves freely around the space, connoting his dominance and suggesting the framing of the space as a theatrical environment for performance. Performers in the room are surrounded by books, and the play begins with a shot of the turning pages of a book. This apparent allusion to literary tradition, the dramatic basis of the script being performed, and perhaps to the persona and authorial authority of Beckett himself and his canonical status, have a problematic relationship with the neon lighting in the set and its consequent allusion to science fiction. The play's structure, which is based on the interrogation of the figures and the apparent impossibility of extracting information from them, is left dissociated from the visual style in the SDR production, while the *Beckett on Film* version offers the relatively coherent genre setting of an oppressive future society.

Thus the abstraction towards which avant-garde film moves – and the preoccupation of some avant-garde film makers with the material surface of celluloid – is not as significant in Beckett's screen work as the issues of performance, fragmentary or disturbed narrative and the placing of the performer's body in space that are carried over from theatrical conventions and television forms. In relation to Surrealist film, however, continuities are more evident. As Linda Williams (1981: 81) notes, Surrealist film makers countered dominant forms of realism by manipulating story structure, mise-en-scène, tone and character. They incorporated visual effects (in Carl Dreyer's *Vampyr*, for example) to distort space and time, by using strong light and shadow, stopping and starting the camera, and editing their films in ways that disrupted patterns of cause and effect. By contrast, Expressionist and Dada film makers distorted the photographic image itself. Futurist films shared the interest in geometric shapes, angles and flat planes that was evident in Constructivist art and the interest in mechanical and urban environments. Aspects of this interest in geometry appear in Beckett's television plays and *Film*, but not as a means to dramatise inner psychology or subjective perception, or to comment on the visual forms of modern urban experience. Again, allusions and procedures from the Modernist avant-garde appear in these productions but without consistent patterns of significance.

While not recognisably Futurist, Expressionist or Dada in its formal techniques, the *Beckett on Film* version of *Play* does deliberately fragment visual space, is reflexive about its means of production and its materiality as a text, and alludes much less than some other productions in the series to the domestic settings of rooms, or to stage conventions. In Anthony Minghella's version of *Play*, the camera takes on the role of the light in the stage version to prompt the speech of three actors in urns. The emphasis on characters called into being by being seen picks up the various developments of this theme in each of Beckett's television and film works. Here, however, it is transferred from an original theatre production to film. The opening frames of the film of *Play* show its opening titles in white on black, with a countdown of frames such as would be seen on the leader strip of a film as it is fed into a cinema projector. The space of the production is relatively fluid, with the camera panning and tilting in individual shots, while its position moves significantly across the space of the set by means of cuts which shift it closer to or further from the actors, and to one side of them, above them or behind them. The full range of shots is used, from extreme long shot and overhead shot to extreme close-up, with close-up as the predominant shot type. Reframing takes place within shots where, for example, a whole face is initially shown and then the camera zooms and pans slightly to reveal a facial detail such as a mouth. Occasional images in negative, cuts and joins in the strip of celluloid, and brief moments where the strip of film seems to be broken and reveals the white light of the projector are seen. There is an attention to the material of cinema recording, and its projection in cinema, as well as to the possibilities of camera position and movement, and the relationship of these to montage, editing and narrative structure. Neither image nor speech are offered as means of full revelation of meaning, and instead there is an attention to repetition, deferral and a lack of mastery by the agencies of production over the material that is being enacted and spoken. Across the various television and film versions of Beckett's drama, whether made for the medium or adapted for it, the dramas draw attention to their dependence on a history of formal experiment, and to their allusion to media conventions and sometimes to specific antecedents. But rather than using these as a stable material that can then be transformed, and still less as authoritative 'keys' to the meanings of the material at hand, the work sets them in tension with each other and with the activity of transformation, adaptation or allusion. This raises the question – most forcefully for television plays produced by the BBC and offered to a general and potentially universal audience – why they were made at all if they are so problematic to interpret.

Public Service Broadcasting and the value of Beckett

There were numerous reasons for the BBC to have ambivalent relationships with theatre dramatists and with adaptations of theatre material for television. On one hand, television producers and directors had been concerned that television should find its own form and style of dramatic representation, and Beckett's plays written specifically for television explored televisual forms, as existing critical writing has shown. On the other hand, the use of authors and texts from a theatre background ensured a readily available supply of material during a period of great expansion and potential shortage of scripts. It was assumed that quality programming would result from the use of dramatic material already proven in subsidised theatre, West End theatre, or popular touring repertory theatre, and this rationale underlay the television broadcast of both 'classics' from the British theatre canon and 'middlebrow' plays like murder mysteries. As the actor Timothy West has explained (Bignell *et al.* 2000), the use of theatrical material enabled the BBC to draw on a pool of star performers from the stage, usually accessible to producers based in London. Beckett was a figure who could satisfy demands for both medium-specific experimental television drama and adapted stage successes. But the bald statement that Beckett's stage plays had been 'successes' needs some explanation, since in most cases the plays gained significant public profile through featuring in broadsheet 'quality' newspapers in Britain and in radio and television arts broadcasts. The plays themselves were seen only by a tiny sector of the British population, and the arts programmes that broadcast them or discussed them were predominantly on niche services like the BBC's Third Programme on radio or late-evening discussion programmes on the BBC2 channel. I have already noted that broadcasts of Beckett's plays for television and adaptations for television of his theatre work were somewhat marginal to the schedules and were often presented within arts programme strands. The issue here is the relationship between Beckett and his work and questions of social power and the role of television (and theatre) drama in the specific context of Public Service Broadcasting in Britain.

British television drama has been important to the legitimation of Public Service Broadcasting by connecting the popular medium of television with high-cultural work intended to draw the audience towards 'improved' taste. This was the background to a visit to Paris by Harry Moore from BBC Drama Group in 1964 to investigate television projects with Beckett, Jean Genet, Marguerite Duras and others (BBC WAC T5/2239/7). The European flavour of Beckett's work assisted in its perception as 'quality' programming and confined it to BBC2, the channel that was increasingly tasked with presenting challenging or foreign material as part of the BBC's public service remit. But the making of programmes associated with these great names of European culture also assisted in the export of Britishness internationally through the export of BBC programmes, and although the international sale of programmes and formats is often thought to be a feature of recent decades' globalisation of media forms and institutions, it was a significant factor in British television production as early as the 1960s. For example, the BBC's annual report and accounts for the year 1964–65 (BBC 1965: 28) notes that 7,426 programmes were sold abroad during the year, leading to a 25 per cent increase on the previous year in the gross income from programme sales.

Although the television broadcasting of Beckett's work made a very small contribution to this drive to export British television, for any individual programme about Beckett or featuring his work this export potential was a strong argument that its producers could use when bidding for resources. The television arts programme *Review* did a programme on Beckett on BBC2 in March 1970, for example, in which four repetitions of Beckett's short piece for theatre *Breath* were included. The deal was that the BBC would film the play for a reduced fee in exchange for Beckett's right (through his agent) to make prints from the BBC negative to sell around the world, with the BBC name attached (BBC WAC RCONT20). The BBC's *Lively Arts* strand, like *Arena*, had relatively restricted budgets, and producers sought ways to gain further investment to make their programmes and opportunities to export them to recoup their cost once they were made. Tristram Powell's *Shades* programme in 1977 for *The Lively Arts*, which included *Not I, Ghost Trio* and *...but the clouds...*, cost the unexceptional sum of about £20,000 but was largely covered by a

European co-production agreement. The Munich-based television company Reiner Moritz contributed £17,000, the lion's share of the cost, in exchange for initial rights to the programme in all countries except France and the German-speaking territories of Austria and Switzerland (BBC WAC T51/350). Once the German broadcast had taken place, Reiner Moritz gained control of all broadcasting rights. Reiner Moritz regularly collaborated with the BBC on arts programmes (rather than drama, even though *Shades* featured Beckett's plays). The company co-produced the BBC2 series *Shock of the New* with Time-Life films of New York, presented by Robert Hughes in 1980 for instance, and in the United States financial support was provided by the oil company Exxon to support the series cost of £1.25 million. Reiner Moritz also co-produced the BBC2 arts programme *100 Great Paintings*, a series of 100 ten-minute programmes that began in 1990.

Arrangements like this became increasingly common as the BBC's financing came under pressure from inflation and also from political controversy (especially in the years of Conservative government), and European co-production ran alongside attempts to gain production finance and overseas sales by making agreements with US broadcasters. In the case of the British programmes about Beckett, and the programmes that featured his dramatic work, there was a particularly European dimension to this. For Beckett's work had textual features that linked it to European arts culture, Beckett had biographical connections with France and Germany especially, and his work was admired by a cultural elite which shared interests in a common European legacy of knowledge, taste and experience. In short, Beckett was a totem for a culturally powerful group with links to arts production and television broadcasting, and this made possible the formation of networks of personnel and financial support for television programmes about Beckett and programmes that would broadcast his theatrical and literary work. Beckett had value in cultural terms, and this abstract cultural value could translate into financial value for the producers who were interested in making programmes. Although Beckett's work might admittedly be unappealing in terms of crude audience ratings for television productions featuring him and his work, these productions could be financed by calling on its cultural value. Furthermore, the political and institutional value that the productions could accrue were valuable to the BBC in a time of vigorous questioning about the BBC's role, or even survival, in a climate when commerce, competition and populism seemed to be in the ascendant in British television culture. The assumption of a common European arts culture and audience for Beckett's work had a negative aspect, however. In 1982 the BBC transmitted *Quad* as a play bought from the German television company SDR in Stuttgart, which had made it under the title *Quadrat* in the company's own studios with Beckett's collaboration. The BBC added only a new introduction in English made by BBC itself, presented once again by Martin Esslin who had appeared to explain and discuss Beckett and his work in the 1977 *Shades* production. No original BBC production was made of *Quad*, and by the 1980s the flow of original Beckett productions for television and the money to finance them was from continental Europe to Britain, rather than the other way around as hitherto.

The commissioning of original dramas by Beckett as a writer associated with theatre, and also the presentations of his theatre plays on television, functioned in some ways as advertisements for theatre as quality entertainment and could be justified by broadcasters as a means of supporting theatre as a national cultural institution. This was a particularly significant function for television when the success of the new ITV at drawing and holding considerably larger shares of the popular audience became entrenched. From its inception in 1955 until the middle 1970s (when light entertainment on BBC underwent a renaissance) ITV captured each of the top ten positions in the audience ratings nearly every week. One justification for the BBC's role, and to some extent an excuse for its poor performance in the ratings battle, was that the BBC provided patronage for drama writers, supplied difficult and experimental dramatic work for a small but socially powerful niche audience, and protected the national heritage of theatrical excellence. Nevertheless, as Neil Taylor (1998: 26) has explained, the percentage of television drama on BBC that was adapted from theatre texts and performances drifted downwards from the 1950s to the present day. While in the year 1951–52, 13.4 per cent of programme time was drama, in 1960–61 only 7.4 per cent of BBC programme time was drama. Although the introduction of the new BBC2 television channel in 1964 increased the broadcasting time available for drama, by the end of the decade, in the year 1969–70, still only 8 per cent of broadcast time was drama. By the early 1980s when Beckett was writing *Quad*, the proportion was approximately 4 per cent. These figures apply only to adapted theatre material, and increasingly the expectation was that dramatic writing would be commissioned and written specifically for the medium (often following the technical and aesthetic conventions of cinema).

BBC2's screening of *Quad* on 16 December 1982 shows how the television landscape continued to change. As James Knowlson reports (1996: 667), the BBC had turned down a new production of *Eh Joe* with Rick Cluchey and Billie Whitelaw early in 1980. By contrast, SDR in Germany was making a new production of the play directed by Beckett himself in early 1979. *Quad* was written in English in 1980, directed by Beckett in 1981 and produced by SDR in Stuttgart for transmission on the German RFA channel on 8 October 1981 under the title *Quadrat I & II*. While the assurance of a screening of *Quad* on BBC2 confirms Beckett's continued significance in the context of BBC2's arts output, and the commitment of the BBC to complex and demanding work, this last original television play looked even more distant from the mainstream of British television drama. Against the background of criticism of the BBC for supposedly unpatriotic news coverage of the Falklands War in 1982, the Conservative government were inquiring into the sponsorship of programmes and the introduction of advertising on BBC in the mid-1980s and were selling franchises to operate breakfast television, cable television and satellite channels. Canonised dramas of the period are serials and series, not single dramas, including the literary adaptation *Brideshead Revisited* (1981) and the original series *Boys from the Blackstuff* (1982) for example, representing cinematic 'heritage drama' and contemporary social engagement respectively. The relationship of *Quad* to its television environment, in aesthetic, institutional and generic terms, extends the incongruities of the earlier plays. At the BBC in the 1980s, innovative plays were screened on BBC2, though sometimes later repeated on BBC1 if critically acclaimed. Radical and experimental dramas were likely to be marginalised, if they were made at all (Cooke 2007: 117), and Beckett's work became virtually invisible on television until the production of programmes marking his death in 1989. Access to his television work became confined to the written screenplays and to a specialised academic community, a community that was in any case conversant more with literature and drama than with the broadcast media and audio-visual analysis.

Television, plays and DVDs: *Beckett on Film*

The published screenplays of Beckett's television dramas may be seen as literary texts but are rarely discussed in relation to the technical role and cultural standing of the screenplay form. Studies such as Steven Gale's (2001), for example, discuss films written by famous writers as realisations of a screenwriter's ideas as these ideas are revealed by the written screenplay. But although screenplays are now easier to sell as one among the many commodities associated with films in the contemporary media landscape, they have little literary status unless they are the work of a writer already recognised for productions in another medium (like Beckett or Harold Pinter). The creative work of the screenwriter in the commercial cinema institution is very low in status. The script is a necessary working document that is produced for sale to a cinema institution in order that it may be obliterated by its making into film. Responses to Hollywood by literary writers in the early twentieth century underlie this low status (see, for instance, Latham 1971). The publication of a theatre play provides stability to a performance text, but a film screenplay does not have the same status since the completed film is already a record and no screenplay is required to support its permanence. Nevertheless, there are some interesting features of the screenplay as a medium. Although it is constituted in writing, the screenplay is required to engage with technology by describing the positions of cameras and the occurrences of cuts and changes in lighting or framing. This relation with technology is often removed in publications of screenplays of popular films, such as those published by Faber or the British Film Institute, where camera directions and other technical information are edited out. In Beckett's screenplays, also published by Faber among a collection of his shorter dramas, this information remains in the published form, making the verbal and literary aspects of the screenplay one component in a text that is also directed towards system, mechanism, craft and collaboration, contrasting with the conventional individualism and assumption of artistry in literary publication. Beckett's screenplays are not like the texts of his theatre plays in this respect, although Faber publishes them alongside his short theatrical works in one volume (Beckett 1984). Whereas film scripts are always typed in courier 12, the editions of Beckett's screenplays have been printed in Faber's conventional font. The letter-forms that are used are in themselves signifiers of literary artistry, though often what these letters are used to denote is technical instructions for the realisation of the plays in the specialist environment of the television studio. The reason for the choice of letter-form is the context of publication in a volume of stage works, and the canonical name of Beckett attaching to them. Publications of screenplays that derive from the film industry look quite different because they are close to the site of their industrial production as partial commodities attached to the films they originated.

A desire for permanence lay behind the production of the *Beckett on Film* series. Michael Colgan, Artistic Director of the Gate Theatre, Dublin, was the animating force behind the 1991 production in Dublin, as part of an international Beckett festival, of all 19 of Beckett's stage plays in the period 1–20 October. The festival had financial backing from the Irish public service broadcaster RTE (Radio Telefis Eireann) and Trinity College, Dublin, where Beckett studied for his degree. The 1991 Gate productions were periodically revived and toured, staged in 1996 at the Lincoln

Center, New York, in 1997 in an abbreviated form in Melbourne, Australia, and in full at the Barbican Centre, London, in 1999. The co-producer of *Beckett on Film*, Alan Moloney, explained that the initial intention was to record the 1991 Dublin stage versions, and as the international tours of the productions continued, this aim to create a permanent recording of them appeared increasingly desirable. But as the project developed, Moloney began to seek a form that would give the recordings 'a cinematic feel, rather than just filmed plays' (Sierz, undated). Furthermore, the Gate is an 'alternative' National Theatre of Ireland, and since the stage productions had originated there Colgan and the production team wanted to present Beckett as an Irish writer but also to involve international performers and directors, befitting their understanding of Beckett as an Irish writer whose themes and appeal were 'universal' (Saunders 2007). So, for example, international directors behind the camera were often working with explicitly Irish characters portrayed with Irish accents (in *Waiting for Godot*, *Endgame* and *Happy Days*). As Graham Saunders (2007: 80–1) has suggested, this links the plays with the BBC Television Shakespeare series (1978–85) where all of the author's works were presented as 'universal' and simultaneously Southern English. The country where production originates (Ireland for *Beckett on Film*, England for the BBC Shakespeare) adopts its 'national' and 'universal' writer by assimilating accentual neutrality, despite other circumstances of production (like the BBC Shakespeare's co-production with US finance, and *Beckett on Film*'s production with the British Channel 4). But the aim of keeping Beckett's Irishness to the fore in the *Beckett on Film* productions was a strike not only against his possible Englishness but also his Frenchness. Writing many of his texts in French and only later translating them into English, with few markers of setting that would firmly place them in England, Ireland or France, and residing in France for much of his adult life, Beckett's Irishness was far from obviously his dominant cultural locus. More than 20 years before the Gate's festival of Beckett theatre, a similar event took place at the Théâtre Récamier, Paris, in 1970. In Paris in 1981, the Festival d'Automne marked Beckett's birthday with a theatre season, academic conference and a retrospective of Beckett's film and television work (Saunders, 2007: 86).

Some of the funding for *Beckett on Film* came from the Irish Film Board, a public body subsidising productions, especially those that are perceived to have an overseas appeal, and also from the Irish broadcaster RTE. *Beckett on Film* was screened on PBS in the USA and also on German and Dutch television, without subtitles, but despite this overseas distribution which assisted with the production's costs, there was no take-up of cinema distribution rights for the project as the producers had initially hoped. RTE has public service aims that are similar to the BBC's, and it is funded by a public licence fee but also by advertising. The broadcaster supports what are perceived as the cultural traditions and national identity of its audience, broadcasting traditional seasonal festivals, folk music and programming about writers and the arts (as well as a conventional mixed programme schedule). RTE programming thus not only reflects this perceived Irishness but also constitutes it, especially in the case of traditions re-invented to satisfy a national hunger for identity, such as Irish dancing. The other co-producers of *Beckett on Film* were a partnership of the Irish companies Blue Angel Productions and Tyrone Productions, the latter having produced the stage dance spectacular *Riverdance* in 1994 and thus expert at exploiting Irishness internationally. The *Beckett on Film* project was launched at Dublin Castle, where the invited guests matched the simultaneous Irishisation and internationalisation of the product, numbering among them the pop group The Corrs and the lead guitarist from U2, as well as the pop singers Marianne Faithfull and Lisa Stansfield, who both lived in Ireland despite their English origins (Saunders 2007: 88).

The *Beckett on Film* recordings made use of many (though not all) of the actors from the Gate Theatre's season (Saunders 2007), with the Irish actors Johnny Murphy and Barry McGovern as Vladimir and Estragon in *Waiting for Godot* for example, supported by the Irish resident Alan Stanford as Pozzo. The Irish actress Rosaleen Linehan played Winnie in *Happy Days*, and the Irishman David Kelly (known in Britain for his roles as stereotypical sitcom Irishmen, in the restaurant comedy *Robin's Nest* for example) played A in *Rough for Theatre I*, having taken the role of Krapp in the 1991 Dublin stage version of *Krapp's Last Tape*. *Endgame*'s director was the Irish playwright Conor McPherson (writer of the international Irish-set success *The Weir*), and Irish film director Neil Jordan directed *Not I*. Many of the productions signalled Irishness through accent, such as in McPherson's *Endgame* where British actors Michael Gambon and David Thewlis imitated Dublin accents. While implemented unevenly, the *Beckett on Film* adaptations had a significant aim to mark their belonging to a notion of Ireland fit for export (rather than to specifically Irish locations in their setting, for example), such as is seen in the *Riverdance* show, the franchised Irish pubs around the world, or the phenomena of St Patrick's Day parades. The branding of *Beckett on Film* as this kind of high-cultural export is more significant to its production, reception and impact on interpretations of the drama than its status as a thoroughgoing contemporary reworking of Beckett's oeuvre.

RTE screened *Beckett on Film* from 19 March to 2 April 2001, but the plays could be seen in Northern Ireland only on satellite and cable services, since terrestrial broadcasting was limited to Eire itself. This vitiated some of the series' ambitions for national status and national cultural unification around Beckett as a totem of Irish achievement. Four of the *Beckett on Film* plays were presented as separate programmes by RTE: Michael Lindsay-Hogg's *Waiting for Godot*, Conor McPherson's *Endgame*, Atom Egoyan's *Krapp's Last Tape*, and Patricia Rozema's *Happy Days*. Five programmes consisted of three short films each: first was David Mamet's *Catastrophe*, Katie Mitchell's *Rough for Theatre II* and Damien Hirst's *Breath*. Second, Richard Eyre's *Rockaby*, Karel Reisz's *Act Without Words I* and Charles Garrad's *That Time*. Third was Charles Sturridge's *Ohio Impromptu*, Kieron Walsh's *Rough for Theatre I* and Neil Jordan's *Not I*. The fourth compilation was Enda Hughes' *Act Without Words II*, Robin Lefevre's *A Piece of Monologue* and Anthony Minghella's *Play*. The last programme comprised Damien O'Donnell's *What Where*, Walter Asmus's *Footfalls* and John Crowley's *Come and*

Go. But the timing of the broadcasts was outside conventional prime-time, and their audience ratings were comparatively low (see Chapter 5). *Krapp's Last Tape* and *Act Without Words II* were presented in the earliest slot of any of the plays, at 9.30 pm, and the rest were shown after 10.00 pm.

Historically, in Britain there has been a long-standing assumption that television in itself is not valuable, but it becomes so when it transmits something valuable in a democratic and socially useful way (Brunsdon 1990). As we have seen in this chapter, Beckett's work benefited from this ideology inasmuch as it was conjoined with aims to bring high culture, such as literature, theatre or music, to a wider audience. But Beckett's plays could not be assimilated into the other means for television to acquire value by making use of its supposed privileged relationship to reality, exemplified by broadcasting public events, or connecting with public sphere concerns around news or current affairs. Television broadcasts of Beckett's work are not 'popular' or 'commercial' television, but inasmuch as television is regarded as a bad object, it functions as the other against which valuable forms of culture or cultural viewing practice are constructed. Since the viewing practices of television have been understood as variable, distracted, domestic and private, the identification of aesthetic value in programmes by assuming an attentive, concentrated, public and socially extended viewing of them, such as is given to art cinema, serious theatre or painting, poses problems for television producers and television analysis. The mode of viewing required for sensitive aesthetic judgement seems alien to the medium. It is in this context that criticism has addressed Beckett's television work as valuable because of its difference from the programmes surrounding it, and its requirement of a different mode of viewing engagement from that which is assumed for those other surrounding programmes. It is telling in this respect that the life of the plays in the *Beckett on Film* series is now as a DVD commodity for solitary home viewing, primarily in the educational market, rather than as television broadcast for collective audiences or in cinema exhibition.

3

Institutions and authorship

Introduction

In television and film it is very common for institutional constraints and working practices to remove control over production decisions from the author and for directorial decisions to be influenced by the demands of the broadcasting institution and, in particular, its perception of the desires and competencies of the audience. But on the other hand, the cultural authority of the mass media of radio and then television as cultural forms were bolstered by employing established literary figures as writers, directors or producers, making programmes featuring interviews with and features on literary figures, or presenting adaptations of their work. As Ros Coward summarises in relation to radio in Britain, 'The history of BBC radio is marked not only by an extreme reverence to the great authors of the literary establishment, but also by "episodes" where significant literary figures were courted by the new mass medium' (Coward, 1987: 81–2). This chapter discusses the strategies used by the BBC to secure good relationships with Beckett so that programmes could be made about him and both original work and adaptations of his theatre plays could be broadcast.

This story began with BBC radio, and especially in relation to its explicitly high-cultural channel the Third Programme, and continued in BBC television production throughout the 1960s until at least the mid-1980s. The process of legitimating broadcast media by connecting them with Beckett and other writers relied not so much on those writers' provision of original work for broadcast as on their established reputation in literary culture. Coward argues persuasively that: 'The only hope which television offers itself for claiming an intrinsic cultural quality is through the notion of the playwright. And this notion of the playwright owes nothing to specific skills within the medium of television, and everything to the institution of literature. The playwright is the lure held up to television. If the playwright is good enough, television too might become an art' (Coward, 1987: 83).

In parallel with this process, the commissioning of original work by figures who already had reputations beyond radio in literature, or later, beyond television in either radio or literature since radio inherited cultural cachet as television overtook it as the most popular medium, brought with it the desire to establish authorship as a marker of value. For Coward (1987: 79), 'the higher the evaluation of the medium *as an art*, the more likely you are to find the quest to establish an author for a work.' So once authorship attains cultural value and significance for a broadcasting institution, legitimating a medium's claims, it becomes one of the forces contesting the means of realisation of a programme. The desire to include authorship as a legitimator of a programme brings with it a requirement for the broadcasting institution to give up some of its power to the author. In Beckett's case, this posed some difficulties for the BBC because of Beckett's refusal to appear on screen, or in radio or television interviews discussing his work, and because of his comparatively rigid views about how his work should be realised on screen. He had a reputation (as does his estate after his death) for being a controlling and precise director of his own work and a highly prescriptive author, in whose writing stage-direction, set design, lighting cues and costumes are all very carefully described. This authorial control exercised via the scripts and subsequently the published texts of the plays is supplemented in Beckett's case by his own involvement in productions or even his direction of them.

Staging authorship

The fact that many of the performers in Beckett's television plays are voice-over narrators produces a direct connection to the audience they address, and this provides them with an authorial role mediating between the television audience and a represented environment. This separation between the audience and the representation of the environment reinforces the possibility that the represented environment is in some sense a creation or an illusion. Much greater distance and separation between the image and the audience is achieved in Beckett's plays than is conventional for television drama. The question of abstraction and illusion is connected to the role of the author and narrator. It has been argued that Beckett's television plays take place within a human consciousness and are therefore divorced from the concrete particularity of the real. The voice in *Ghost Trio* is able to predict the movements of the male Figure, so that the action of the drama seems to be brought into existence in an unreal space. The voice in *Eh Joe* may be the product of Joe's consciousness, or Joe may be the product of the consciousness of the voice. W and M1 in ...*but the clouds*... are summoned into existence by M. The dreamt self B in *Nacht und Träume* is represented in a way that allows him to seem to be the projection of the dreamer A's mind, though the repetition of A's actions by the identical figure of B, which take up the whole of the screen space, suggest a *mise-en-abyme* in which either, both or neither the A and B sequences might be dreams, and this begins to displace the activity of witnessing to the 'dreaming' of their creator or even the television viewer (Herren 2000, 2001). Issues of authorship and authorial control are alluded to in Beckett's television plays and *Film*, and this relates to questions of agency that affect writers, characters, the camera and the audience.

Since the late 19th century, photography has been used for collecting criminal evidence and to record scenes of crime. In *Eh Joe*, the camera and voice take on an investigative look, and a surveillance role, but the event that they seek to bring into presence has already happened in the past and has not been recorded, and Joe makes no confession and reveals nothing. The effect for the audience is to produce expectation but also to be suspended in an aesthetic of waiting. It is sometimes assumed that Voice belongs to Joe's unconscious (Gontarski 1983: 426, Miller 2000: 266, Lamont 1990: 230). But the phrase 'Behind the eyes' (Beckett 1986: 362-3) shows that although Joe may believe this, Voice is more accurately to be understood as being behind the eye of the camera. In the original manuscript of *Eh Joe*, there are occasional references to eyes and looking that do not appear in the eventual television production. For example, Voice says 'Why don't you put out the light? ... In case there's an eye you've forgotten' (Beckett undated a). The machine of the camera becomes less evidently dependent on the human body of its operator and appears to become an independent technology of reproduction (Weiss 2002). Furthermore, despite their theatricality, Beckett's television plays were not filmed before a studio audience, which further emphasises their technological production and reproduction and their distance from the bodily and material qualities of performance and reception. Toby Zinman (1995) and Clas Zilliacus (1976: 191) contrast the camera's roles as an apparent informational device and as a voyeur: 'The surest sign that the camera is a peeping Tom, not an illustrating device, is – for the viewer unfamiliar with the author's written directions – its firm refusal to translate any of the voice's rich verbal stimuli into pictures'. It is worth noticing of course that in the BBC's adaptation of *Krapp's Last Tape*, the decision was taken to turn some of Krapp's reminiscences into pictures, a decision that has been universally condemned in Beckett scholarship because of its reductive attribution of the reminiscences to a camera agency standing in for Krapp's imagination or memory, and thus attaching the camera's visualisation to the character.

The issue here is the agency of the camera and its relationship with the viewer and the fictional world. The camera could appear to have a subjective identity (especially if it is connected directly with a voice-over) or it could function as an external and mechanical narrating agency. In *Film*, the camera's focus is on the eyelid not on the iris of the eye in the opening shot. This seems to underline a theme of refusal or inability to see, but it could also be a marker of technical failure. In terms of the conventions of film making, the film seems to be badly made with imprecise cuts and lack of narrative flow. The eye is reminiscent of a camera, but a camera does not blink, and by contrast the camera exhibits a forensic and interested look which can gain access to a great deal of information but only at the cost of excluding everything that is outside the frame. The medium of film introduces the notion of a restriction of vision as well as a privileged vision. There is a strange unmotivated cut in *Film* as O goes along the wall in the opening scene, and the camera demonstrates its power to follow him even though he runs away, since the camera can simply cut and leap ahead to a position alongside him again. But the camera never leaps in front of him, demonstrating that it is not omniscient. The camera is an agent and not a character, so it is unclear how the camera can take on O's point of view. The editing of the film is not part of the agency of the camera: editing happens later, in post-production, so there is also a cinematic agency outside of the operation of the camera itself. The camera can cut in the sense that it can stop recording, but the joining and assembly of the narrative is a cinematic process not a camera process. The editing agency above and beyond the camera can select and emphasise particular shots, such as the close-ups of the eyes of the cat and dog in O's room. These shots are from O's point of view but are not at the logically correct distance from his body to be optical point-of-view shots. So these shots of the dog and the cat have the status of a third level of agency that is distinct from the point of view of a character and also from the point of view of the observing camera as an independent agent. These uncertainties of the attribution of vision can certainly be explained away as faults during *Film*'s production, but their effect is to destabilise the viewer's ability to establish a system for understanding whose point of view is offered and what the agency of the camera represents. Its control over vision is not consistently presented, and further directing agencies (such as editing) intervene to question who or what has authority over the expressive means of the piece.

Many of these problems of agency in *Film* stem from the different aims, expectations and experience among the production team. *Film* was edited by Sidney Myers, who had made the film *The Savage Eye* a few years before working on *Film*. Alan Schneider (1972: 88–90) recalled: 'Sidney always gently trying to break the mold we had set in the shooting, and Sam and I in our different ways always gently holding him to it.' Beckett (1972: 58) realised that the aim in the third part of *Film* to turn the camera on itself so that it could perceive itself was hard to realise visually in a way that would make the two points of view of E and O comprehensible: 'I feel that any attempt to express them in simultaneity (composite images, double frame, superimposition, etc.) must prove unsatisfactory.' At the time of writing this outline, Beckett was envisaging a single-sequence film where point-of-view shots were to be used in an unspecified way, and where the difference between E's and O's points of view in Part Three would be marked by visual style rather than by postproduction processes such as double frame or superimposition: 'a succession of images of different *quality*, corresponding on the one hand to E's perception of O and on the other hand to O's perception of the room'. He suggested that this might require establishing early in the film that the two points of view were visually different: 'it might be desirable to establish, by means of brief sequences, the O quality in parts one and two' (1972: 58–9). This method would mean abandoning the idea of shooting Parts One and Two as single long takes (or at least making them appear to be single takes) and also threatening the aim to make the audience identify with E since the audience would also be positioned with E. The cinematographer on *Film* was Boris Kaufman, who had experience of using long takes through his work on *Twelve Angry Men*, where a six minute-long take at the beginning of the film is cut only when the main character is introduced. In the finished *Film*, the opening shot has the camera E in a static position, using pan and tilt to look around the space. Once O enters the visual field E follows O, and camera movement within the space begins, in a similar long-take format apparently driven by the main character's arrival.

While Beckett's outline for *Film* suggests that Part One should be a single sequence of pursuit, because of limitations of time and equipment the production team decided to introduce cuts into Part One and thus break down the tension that a long take from E's point of view would have created. There is a cut between the first shot from E's point of view during which O appears, and the following shot, also from E's point of view, when E is simply looking at the wall. Another cut returns E to a shot looking at O. The enforcement of E's point of view as a long take is segmented, without any apparent narrative reason, and confuses the idea that E is a character rather than a 'neutral' camera master-shot. Similarly, brief cuts connect whip-pans across the wall to the shots of O being pursued, giving the impression of pursuit but breaking up the sequence into further segments and thus fracturing the consistency of E's point of view. And again, after E has been diverted by the encounter with two people and momentarily loses O, the camera does not dolly forwards to catch up with O and enter the stairwell of his building, but instead there is a zoom that brings the shot closer onto O, and then a cut leads to E's arrival in the stairwell. E's point of view is fractured once again by cutting within the sequence and the impression of a temporal ellipsis is introduced since E (if a character) could not have got there so quickly. As O enters his room the cuts are motivated by shifts between E's and O's point of view as O fumbles with his key and enters the room with E following. Here the reasons for cutting are comprehensible, but the use of unmotivated cuts previously has diminished the audience's chance to understand E and O as characters with specific and different points of view that are presented in long takes individual to them. Again the question of who or what is in charge of *Film*'s realization is raised by specific moments within the mise-en-scène.

Graley Herren (1998) argues that *Ghost Trio* establishes a pattern which seems to constrict the possibilities of the text, but that in fact it presents a power struggle between the forces that seek to dominate, and that there are moments in which the framework of agency in the drama is deconstructed from within. Voice could be addressed to the director of the play, telling them what to shoot. Voice seeks to author the play, but Figure undermines her authority (Knowlson 1986). Figure rebels against the system of repetitions established by Voice in Part Two, when Voice orders Figure 'Now to door' and he instead goes to the stool, sits down and resumes his pose as in the opening of the play. Voice describes Figure as the 'Sole sign of life', whereas of course the television viewer is a sign of life that she occasionally acknowledges, and she is unable to enforce her command to the viewer to 'Keep that sound down'. Figure behaves mechanically when he thinks he hears her, raising his hand with a jerky motion. The repetition of his assumption that he hears her is in itself mechanical, and of course it is prompted by music produced from a mechanical source. Knowlson argues that the style of movement in *Ghost Trio* may be influenced by Beckett's reading of an essay on marionette theatre by Kleist. Kleist argued that since puppets defy gravity, they have greater mobility and harmony of movement than human performers. It is also significant that puppets do not have a will of their own, they lack subjectivity, and they are thus more open to manipulation and directorial control by the figure of the author.

This would reinforce a reading of *Ghost Trio*, and Beckett's drama in general, as determined almost entirely by Beckett's authorial signature and the details of his own work as director in the realisation of his drama. It is this view that underlies Linda Ben-Zvi's (1985: 207) case that Beckett regarded television as a voyeuristic medium that gave entry to experiences normally prohibited or restricted from view. When the characters in the dramas are interpreted as puppets manipulated by an unseen controller, the implication is that Beckett neglected the humanity of his characters and performers and regarded the realisation of television drama as a purely technical and formal matter. This issue is reflexively raised by Voice's incomplete territorial control of Figure's movements; there are momentary recognitions that the authority of Voice may not be complete. Yet the dominant motif of the play is to consider everything in the represented space as an object. The space of the room is itself divided up and separated as if it were a series of objects under investigation, and this same dissection and control applies to Figure. As Knowlson (1986: 196) has pointed out, he is immobile, like an object, and seems to be under the instruction of Voice in the same way as the objects in the room when the initial shot of Figure, black and white against a grey background and sitting still, parallels him with the fragments of setting which Voice introduces to the viewer.

Ghost Trio has different relationships to power and spectatorship in each of its three parts, and some early scholarship on *Ghost Trio* (for example, Esslin 1983) gives priority to the image, and foregrounds Voice as an introductory device whose significance diminishes. Figure is introduced as the object of the look by Voice in Part One. In Part Two, Figure explores his own space but there are no camera shots from his point of view until his point of view is introduced in Part Three. His face is seen in the mirror, the rain is seen outside the window, and the boy is seen in the corridor from Figure's optical point of view. Each of these shots opens onto another space (in the case of the mirror it is a virtual space). The use of the character of the Boy to introduce a notion of otherness and other space is parallel to the function of the Boy in *Waiting for Godot*, to prove the existence of an outside to the performance space, and the possible existence of an other, such as the woman in *Ghost Trio* or the eponymous Godot, who the plays need to concretise the characters' object of desire. The conventional gender distribution of subjective authority and passive object are reversed in *Ghost Trio*, since Voice is female and Figure is male. The play also alludes in this respect to the cinematic convention of a masculine point of view, made concrete in the look, and on the other hand the relatively passive and feminine glance attributed to the viewer's relationship to television in theories of television spectatorship. Peter Freund (1998: 42) argues that 'by melding his or her attention with the perspective of the camera, the flattered viewer penetrates and masters a scene from any and every possible angle'. There is a holograph copy of *Ghost Trio* at the Beckett International Foundation, at Reading University Library (Beckett undated f). This notes, for example, that the camera 'stops and stares' at Figure and at the contents of the room. It also contains some physical business in which Figure has to unlock the door and window before he can open them. This would have reinforced the notions of imprisonment and spatial containment, as well as drawing further attention to the room as a domestic and interior space. Having removed this physical business, the space becomes more abstract and the agency of the camera appears less like a subjective point of view. The camera position in a static and externalised relationship to the action, and the grainy black and white image, draw attention to the television medium as a voyeuristic and intrusive gaze of surveillance that objectifies its objects. Graley Herren (1998: 77) argues that initially Voice acknowledges the viewer's power over *Ghost Trio* as an author figure by suggesting that the viewer will determine the volume of the sound. Later, however, Voice gains authority by determining the editing of the camera's look from one part of the space to the other, moving from door to floor and so on. The predictive quality of the line 'He will now think he hears her' emphasises Voice's authority.

This apparent subjection of the visual field and the personae within it conduces to the argument that the plays concern authorial control and the potential destabilization of that control. In *...but the clouds...*, M is also mechanical, repeating his attempts to describe how 'she' appeared to him, and when this is unsuccessful he retreats into a routine of mathematical calculation of cube roots. In the same way that Voice describes Figure in *Ghost Trio*, M says at the beginning that in his little sanctum no one could see him. But of course, the camera and the spectator can see him. Interestingly, in the untitled holograph draft of *...but the clouds...* (Beckett undated g) Beckett has a reference to God as the one being able to see him, as in *Film*. The line (with Beckett's deletions as marked) is: 'Right. (pause). Now sitting there, where ~~only none but~~ God ~~alone~~ can see me...'. Stan Gontarski's (1983) analysis of *Eh Joe* makes significant use of archived drafts, and connects the play to theatre works including *Krapp's Last Tape* and *Footfalls*, as well as to prose works and Beckett's interest in philosophical and psychological models of subjectivity. Gontarski is aware of the medium-specific features of the work but concentrates on its relationship with Beckett's continuing creative concerns and the development of the written drafts of the play. Existing critical work has assumed Beckett's centrality as the authorial agent and attributed any confusions of agency in the plays to a deliberate strategy of deconstructing agency on the part of their author.

The performers in *Quad* are called 'Players', like the pieces in a chess game. The Players are indistinguishable, so they are open to interpretation as parts of one identity, as individual characters, or as allegorical representations. The Players' movement in space, and the space in which they move, can be interpreted metaphorically in many ways, and this parallels the openness to multiple interpretation that has often been discerned when Beckett's language has been analysed. Faced with the difficulty of interpreting this play by psychologising its personae or connecting it developmentally to thematic concerns in Beckett's dramatic or literary work, academic criticism has tended to emphasise the play's geometric abstraction and to revel in its ambiguity. For example, Martha Fehsenfeld (1982: 361) refers to the painterly qualities of the image, in the process mistakenly assuming that the play was shot on film rather than electronic cameras: 'He [Beckett] has painted a picture, deliberately choosing color for the first time in using film.' Phyllis Carey (1988: 147) and Mary Bryden (1995: 112) stress the religious connotations suggested by the cross-shaped diagonals of the set. Enoch Brater (1987: 107) comments that 'The work in this instance is more like the scheme for some avant-garde modern dance than anything even vaguely recognizable as traditional dramatic form.' Stan Gontarski (1986: 404) says that *Quad* parallels 'postmodern literary theory and literal decentering'. This range of interpretations is remarked by Christina Adamou (2003) who also notes that Bryden (1995), Fehsenfeld (1982), Brater (1987) and Gontarski (1986) all relate the Players to Dante's damned in the *Inferno*. However, a persistent motif in the writing about the play is the reliance on what authorial information there is in Beckett's written outline for *Quad* and in reminiscences about the circumstances of its production. In other words, agency shifts from the cameras and the personae to Beckett and his directorial collaborators. Fehsenfeld (1982: 360) explains that the posture of the Players recalls the bent position of the woman in *Footfalls*, and the geometric pattern resembles Beckett's outline for *J.M. Mime* created in 1963. In looking for a 'centre' of meaning critics attempt to find one by displacing their gaze to resonances between *Quad* and earlier plays and by metaphorising the central node represented on the floor of the set. There is much written about why the central point is called E. The written text describes E: 'E supposed a danger zone. Hence deviation.' But Carey (1988: 146) notes it is 'the "supposing" of "E" as a danger zone that creates and sustains it'. A new question then emerges about who the agent is who supposes. Perhaps the Players 'suppose', or the actors who are playing the Players, or the audience, or Beckett the author. After Beckett watched a tape of *Quad I* in the studio gallery in black and white to check its image definition for viewers with monochrome receivers, he said that *Quad II* looked like ten thousand years later than the time of *Quad I*. This remark has functioned to close down debate about temporality in the play, for there is little evidence in the transmission to substantiate Beckett's remark. Black and white could represent an earlier time than colour in a television context since that matches the history of the medium, and this would produce an interesting reversal of the assumptions about causal linearity that have governed interpretation so far. What has been interpreted as a vision of a distant future might also be understood as a recapitulation of television drama's past, thus rendering volatile the notions of temporal progression and teleological development within the drama, and its relationships with histories of its medium.

Beckett and conventions of television authorship

Historically, authored television drama had a legitimating function for the relatively new television medium. Both the adaptation of recognised high-cultural work and the promotion of the television 'author' were significant in attempts to shore up the cultural worth of the medium, which was widely regarded as irredeemably shallow. Beckett's fame (or notoriety) as a stage dramatist, and later as a Nobel Prize winner, made the broadcast of his work for television significant for these reasons. Critical writing about Beckett's television plays has tended to follow the trajectory of this mid-twentieth-century discourse. Academic analysis of television drama in Britain takes its bearings from work on the 'Golden Age' of the 1960s and 1970s, which focused on a canon of television playwrights and on questions of realism (Bignell *et al.*, 2000: 81–92). The politics of television drama, in relation to its mobilisation of the mass audience, were especially significant. The role of the BBC as a Public Service Broadcaster was both supported – as a space for work which is alternative in its content and its form – and critiqued, as a stale and elitist institution distant from the popular audience. The effect of these concerns on critical approaches to television drama was to establish a canon of original dramas, to lionise the new figure of the 'television writer', and to focus on his (there were few women) relationship to political arguments over form and audience address. Policy makers and executives within television institutions discussed television drama on an analogy with literary and dramatic authorship, rather than cinema. In the 1976 Richard Dimbleby lecture, at the time that the BBC's prestigious strand of one-off original dramas for television *Play for Today* was coming to an end and the year before *The Lively Arts: Shades* broadcast of Beckett's plays, the senior television executive and former producer and presenter of the BBC's arts programme *Monitor*, Huw Wheldon (1976: 266), stated:

> If the business of movies is pleasure, the business of literature and drama, in the final analysis, is truth … The truth of a news bulletin is the degree to which it accurately describes an event that has taken place. The truth of a play is not so different. It is the degree to which it accurately embodies a world conceived inwardly. It is the degree to which that world, inwardly conceived, has been accurately embodied. The degree to which it is not meretricious. The degree to which it hangs together as a single object, cutting no corners, cheating no-one, including the author.

Wheldon sets news in parallel and in opposition to drama, pointing out their shared origin in the description and mimesis fundamental to realism, and assuming a consensual and hegemonic discourse about both these forms of broadcasting. The playwright is the key figure, since it is the author's imagination (on the model of the literary author) which is the origin of creativity. Wheldon's conception of drama is that, like news, it is about the contemporary world. This assumption paralleled debates in theatre in the same period, where the tradition of the well-made play had been countered by works in the Royal Court style motivated by contemporaneity, class issues and a realism of political engagement.

Beckett's work was understood in relation to the ambivalent dynamics moving between the pop art culture of the 1960s and Modernism. Links can be seen between, for example, David Oxtoby's painting of Mick Jagger's mouth and *Not I*, the late 1950s and 1960s Parisian left bank style in café culture and Beckett's characteristic sartorial style of black polo necks. His work was taken up by young avant-garde artists (like the video artist Bruce Nauman) as well as by an intellectual elite that included figures such as Martin Esslin with whom Beckett had a close relationship. Beckett's interest in experimental theatre suited well the programmes of the Royal Court Theatre, with their exploration of Gordon Craig's, Antonin Artaud's and Bertolt Brecht's ideas, and the exploration in the West of the formal possibilities of Noh theatre. Productions of Beckett's plays sometimes featured iconic figures of stage and screen in the 1960s, such as Nicol Williamson and Billie Whitelaw. In the reverse direction, from Beckett's work to popular culture, the television playwright Jack Rosenthal cast Jack MacGowran, who had appeared in a widely seen stage version of *Endgame* in 1964 and in *Eh Joe*, as a rubbish collector in his successful ITV situation comedy *The Dustbinmen* in 1969 whose iconography alluded to the bins seen on *Endgame*'s stage set. This relationship between Beckett as a representative both of high culture and of popularised versions of that intellectual fashion is also evident in the *Beckett on Film* project at the turn of the millennium, where fashionable artists and directors like

Damien Hirst and Atom Egoyan were brought into the project. As Eckart Voigts-Virchow (2000–1) suggests, Beckett still retains this cultural meaning, as shown by the use of his image in advertising for the design-led and expensive Apple computer, with its connotations of creativity, fashion and good taste.

But this sense of modernity as contemporaneity, authenticity and relevance, related to post-1956 theatre among other cultural currents, was paradoxically supported in television by the use of film versus 'theatrical' studio recording. The BBC producer Tony Garnett, who worked at the BBC in the 'Golden Age' of the 1960s and whose plays shot on film are central to the realist canon, saw his work as in opposition to the West End theatrical tradition that was carried on in television by his colleagues at the BBC Drama Department. In a 1972 interview (Hudson 1972: 18) Garnett said of his BBC colleagues, who had been trained in a more conventional and theatrical tradition, 'if somebody had pointed out that what they were doing was not remotely like the real world or anybody's real experience, they would say "We're doing art".' But referring to his own very different assumptions about television drama, shared by his then collaborator the director Ken Loach, Garnett distanced their approach from that of their colleagues: 'We were very firmly not doing art, right? We were just trying to make sense of the world.' With film productions like those of Garnett and Loach, authorship itself was displaced as the director became the authorial centre of power when using film in exterior locations. The use of film was reserved for an elite of drama producer–director–writer teams, where film was not used as it would be in the Hollywood cinematic tradition of fictional melodrama and classical narrative but was instead the medium for fictional work that borrowed the conventions of the documentary mode. But in terms of the relationship of this work to academic (and other) criticism, filmed plays produced a paradoxical return to auteurism since Garnett and Loach become canonised as much as the writers whose scripts they shot. Nevertheless, historically, the end result of this complex set of negotiations around the role of scripts, theatre, film, and aesthetic choices in television drama was to displace the writer as the central creative figure. Such displacement, however, did not extend to Beckett and interestingly replicates the prominence of authorial agency that is evident in academic discussion of his work.

BBC documents (BBC WAC T48/74/1) reveal that as early as 1960 negotiations were opened for the rights to produce a television version of *Godot*. Beckett was able to impose strictures, such as wanting Donald McWhinnie to direct and refusing to have the play cut to 60 minutes. Beckett had exceptional control over the production of his work and contributed to decisions about design, costume, direction, editing and acting. BBC staff valued this and were keen to establish good relations with him in order to secure continued broadcasting rights. A 'culture of authorship' was created from the working relationships between Beckett and the directors and production staff. For *Eh Joe* in 1966 Beckett came to Britain and consulted with Michael Bakewell, Head of Plays at BBC television, about details of the camera direction that Bakewell could not interpret in conventional technical terms. The phrase in the script 'constant remove', in particular, was puzzling to Bakewell, and on 21st January 1966 he wrote to Beckett asking for clarification (BBC WAC T5/1296/1). Bakewell, in common with most of Beckett's collaborators, regarded himself as subject to Beckett's written instructions, no matter how far their language was from the technical vocabulary of television production. Normally, either authors wrote using correct technical vocabulary or their scripts were altered by story editors and script editors to fit the requirements of standardised production practices. Beckett was consulted by the designer Peter Seddon about the set for *Eh Joe* (BBC WAC T5/1296/1) partly because Beckett so much disliked the set for the television production of *Godot*, and the BBC was very careful not to alienate him. So when the discussion programme *Late Night Line-up* on 18 May 1971 included extracts from *Film* and *Eh Joe*, and a reading from *Watt*, the BBC Copyright Department sent an angry memo to the producer saying that Beckett was very sensitive about the use of cut versions of his work and they must not do this again (BBC WAC RCONT20).

In the 1960s and 1970s, British television producers and heads of departments were keen to find original or adapted television plays to fill longer daily schedules. Sydney Newman, head of BBC Drama in the 1960s, separated the roles of producer and director, and also divided the production of single television plays into two strands. *Festival* was produced by Peter Luke and largely presented adapted theatre or literary works, while *First Night*, produced by John Elliot, commissioned new writers. It was in the *Festival* anthology that Beckett's *Krapp's Last Tape* was screened in November 1963, in a run which also included adaptations of James Joyce's *Ulysses* and plays by Jean Cocteau and T. S. Eliot. *First Night* was shifted from Thursday to Wednesday night in 1964 and was renamed *The Wednesday Play*, while *Festival* ceased to exist, signalling a shift of emphasis away from the literary, the theatrical and the 'high-brow'. A team of producers worked on *The Wednesday Play*: Peter Luke, James McTaggart, Lionel Harris, and Tony Garnett, and the strand reflected individual producers' interests, from the literary and theatrical to politically engaged, contemporary drama with a realist aesthetic. Throughout the 1960s, and especially after the advent of BBC2 in 1964, considerably more broadcast hours meant that more and more drama was required. Shaun Sutton, as the BBC's head of Drama in the early 1970s, presided over the broadcast of over one hundred single plays annually, in anthologies like *Play for Today*, *Theatre 625* (on BBC2), *Play of the Month*, and *Thirty Minute Theatre*. The growth of drama as an output category made reliable and well-known creative staff valuable to producers, and made producers keen to develop a stable of newer writers and directors. The forces at work in the BBC in the years when Beckett's television plays were made conduced to bringing him into the fold of established cultural figures whose work would be screened, but it also distanced him from developments in television drama forms and changes in the culture of authorship. Similarly, Beckett's persona and oeuvre were both fashionable and obscure, contemporary and anachronistic.

Collaboration and networking

The authority accorded to Beckett after the theatrical success of *Waiting for Godot*, and the numerous BBC radio productions of his work that Martin Esslin oversaw as head of Radio Drama at the BBC from 1963 to 1977, meant that he was perceived by television producers as part of a cultural elite. Esslin himself was both a prime mover in commissioning Beckett's media work and also the author of academic publications that emphasised its aesthetic significance (Esslin1975, 1982, 1987, 1991). Esslin made his first broadcast on 20 September 1959 and worked on programmes until 2002. His numerous entries in the BBC's programme database include mention of Beckett's television plays *Eh Joe*, *Happy Days*, the three dramas in *The Lively Arts*: *Shades*, *Rockaby* and *Quad*, but also television contributions to programmes on morality and religion such as *Doubts and Certainties* (1968) and *Religion in the Sixties* (1970), and cultural commentary including *Workshop: Brecht on Music* (1964) and *Writers' World* (1965). On radio, his production of Beckett's radio plays ran alongside a profile of the director Peter Hall (1960), the actress Glenda Jackson (1970) and the documentaries *Our Changing Theatre* (1970) and *An Actor from San Quentin* (1978). Similarly, Donald McWhinnie made his first broadcast in October 1949, and his numerous directing credits on television, in addition to Beckett's plays, include episodes of the period dramas *Elizabeth R* (1971), *Fall of Eagles* (1974) *Moll Flanders* (1976) and the World War I series *Wings* (1977). On radio, he worked on *Headlong Hall* (1950), *An Inspector Calls* (1950), *Peer Gynt* (1959) and *Darkness at Pemberley* (1973), and the radio feature *These Our Actors* (1980). This partial selection from Esslin's and McWhinnie's distinguished records demonstrates not only their lengthy and active broadcasting careers but more particularly the literary, high-cultural and theatrical associations and skills they acquired, alongside expertise in the more mainstream fare of middle-brow drama and personality profile programmes that made up the bulk of arts broadcasting. Beckett's links with them added to their kudos and also gave Beckett access to a powerful professional culture at the BBC in which they were important players.

Beckett's first television play, *Eh Joe*, was sent to the BBC on his agent's suggestion, rather than being commissioned. Beckett sent it to Michael Bakewell, then head of Plays at the BBC, who had been the director of his 1961 radio play *Words and Music*, and by 1966 Bakewell was producing television plays that included the award-winning quartet of studio-shot dramas, *Talking to a Stranger* by John Hopkins. In 1966, Beckett's later collaborator on *Ghost Trio* and *...but the clouds...*, Donald McWhinnie, was working on *Theatre 625*, having also directed for ATV on its *Studio 64* slot and on BBC's *Play of the Month*. Each of these anthology slots presented a variety of kinds of play and attracted sizeable national audiences, with *Play of the Month* in particular focusing on popular naturalistic drama. McWhinnie's involvement provides a bridge between Beckett's television plays and the mainstream drama of the period, but Beckett's plays themselves, as author-led, studio-based, experimental television drama, have nevertheless been sidelined by developments in technology, institutional politics and academic television criticism.

There was a significant context for the production of the BBC2 programme *Shades*, containing three Beckett pieces, broadcast at 9 pm on Sunday 17 April 1977, because of the involvement of Martin Esslin, Donald McWhinnie and Tristram Powell. Esslin, who had published early and significant critical work on Beckett's theatre, wanted to celebrate Beckett's seventieth birthday in April 1976 by presenting his work on radio, using existing recordings of *Embers*, *All that Fall*, Jack MacGowran's readings of Beckett's poems, and the newly translated *Rough for Radio II*, and also to present Beckett's work on television. The 1966 *Eh Joe*, written for television, and the 1972 television adaptation of Beckett's stage play *Krapp's Last Tape* were available since recordings of each had been preserved, so it seemed at first that no new drama from Beckett would be required. The efforts to bind Beckett to the BBC meant that not only Beckett himself but also his collaborators acquired institutional power. The first contract to make a film of

Beckett's stage play *Not I* for later television broadcast on the arts programme *Second House* was drawn up in May 1973, but the play's performer Billie Whitelaw did not approve the form of the television version proposed, and since Beckett respected her judgement he would not agree to the recording (BBC WAC RCONT20). It was only later in the year that these problems were smoothed over and the film was made. Tristram Powell produced the film in February 1975, using a film camera with an unusually large reel to avoid cuts at points when one reel of film would be used up and another one would need to be loaded. The slot for the three pieces was to be the *Second House* arts series, whose title significantly indicated its connection with theatre rather than presenting items concerning television drama. But Billie Whitelaw featured in *Not I, Eh Joe* and *Krapp's Last Tape*, and the editor of *Second House* wanted to avoid a sequence of plays based on one performer. He was in contact by letter with Beckett, and a further obstacle to this selection of material was that Beckett thought the television adaptation of *Krapp* had become too well-known. In response to these problems, the director Donald McWhinnie was asked to make a selection of Beckett's prose that could be spoken over images and that would take the place of one or more of the proposed dramas.

By this time the *Second House* series had been supplanted by its successor *The Lively Arts*, made by substantially the same production team. But when Tristram Powell, now the producer of *The Lively Arts*, was planning the *Shades* programme for this series in 1975, Beckett's agent Warren Brown wrote to Powell on 22 December 1975, saying that Beckett could not agree to the programme until he knew what it would contain and that a discussion with the proposed director, Donald McWhinnie, would be essential before he would consent to the project (BBC WAC T51/350). Beckett did not like the filmed adaptation for television of his theatre play *Play*, which the BBC had made and which could have accompanied the *Not I* film in Powell's programme. Beckett proposed instead (Knowlson, 1996: 620) that he 'try to write a new piece for TV to be directed by Donald'. This was agreed and Beckett delivered *Tryst* (later titled *Ghost Trio*), having already consulted Donald McWhinnie about how McWhinnie should direct it. To accompany *Not I* and *Ghost Trio*, Beckett wrote *...but the clouds...* in 1976, and both new plays were produced and directed by Powell and McWhinnie respectively, with Beckett's close involvement. McWhinnie had already worked as producer–director (in British radio these roles were combined) on Beckett's 1957 radio play *All That Fall*, commissioned the previous year for the BBC's Third Programme, and Beckett was regarded sufficiently highly by the Third Programme to meet personally with its Controller, John Morris, in 1956. But it was very unusual (as it still is today) for there to be an interaction between television and radio commissioning, and this meeting and the link between Beckett and the radio and television personnel is further evidence of the networks of professionals and creative figures who valued Beckett's work.

Shades was commissioned, scheduled, organised and presented in a quite different way from the majority of BBC drama output in the period. That Esslin had promoted Beckett's work on radio, was in contact with him personally, and could appear in *Shades* as an expert interviewee, were ways of facilitating the television programme and were a rare instance of planning across the two media. Esslin appeared in *Shades*, commenting on Beckett's life and work, and the programme was an unusual contribution to *The Lively Arts* since it departed from the usual format and content of programmes in the series. The notable, even defining, feature of *The Lively Arts* was that it was an arts feature programme which each week presented interviews with, and documentary features about, contemporary cultural figures. On the following Sunday, for instance, *The Lively Arts* consisted of a documentary on, and an interview with, the aristocratic cultural commentator Jessica Mitford. There was an expectation that Beckett would talk about his work in the programme as a living (*Lively*) writer, and Esslin's presentation between the plays substituted for this. Beckett was asked whether he would consent to be interviewed, but he promptly turned down the request, as he always did in such circumstances. This could potentially have scuppered Powell's plans for the programme since it could not contain the expected discussion with the living writer who would be its subject. But the production team's respect for, and interest in, Beckett's work meant that even though he did not appear as a participant in the programme, new plans were made to get around the difficulty. It seems also that Beckett himself was enticed by the prospect of having two new plays broadcast by BBC.

Clearly, one significant point about the BBC institution's attitude to the production of programmes about Beckett and programmes featuring his dramatic work is that the author was given paramount importance, transcending the usual format and production methods that would be employed. But furthermore, some of this authority extended to the collaborators both within and outside the institution with whom Beckett had worked before in television and theatre contexts. People such as the actress Billie Whitelaw and the director Donald McWhinnie acquired leverage over the producers because of Beckett's relationship with them, and this could mean that performers and directors, as well as Beckett himself, could scupper programmes if they failed to meet expectations. On 26 July 1976 Warren Brown wrote to Powell, referring to Beckett's suggestions to McWhinnie about the use of the camera in the version of *Play* that was to be screened in *Shades* (BBC WAC T51/350). Although Beckett replied in his letter back to Powell that he regarded his own suggestions about direction as merely recommendations, and wanted to allow McWhinnie the customary freedom to direct as he wished, Beckett later refused permission for the broadcast of *Play* because he did not approve of the lighting. Although the BBC had the legal right to use the programme, having secured Beckett's permission to make the adaptation, they acceded to his wishes.

Stephany Marks, the production assistant on Powell's *Lively Arts* programme sent the actor Ronald Pickup a copy of *...but the clouds...* on 23 November 1976 (BBC WAC T51/350). In the covering letter that she included with the script she wrote: 'Sam has asked particularly that the parts should be played by you and Billie ... Donald will be directing and we have asked Sam to come over and supervise again ... We have written to Sam asking for more specific instructions and information regarding costumes & makeup.' The outcome of Marks's letter to Beckett was a very detailed response, dated 27 November 1976 (BBC WAC T51/350), which included instructions such as:

> Greatcoat: 'the old green greatcoat my father left me' of *That time* [sic] and the novels. 1900 motoring coat ... Greatcoat should stand out darker, rober [sic] lighter, from ground of shadow. Such difference between the two, one dark, stiff, heavy, hard, the other all the contraries that scarcely recognisable as the same ... Woman's face: CU not so tight as for *Not I*, but not whole face. Identity with figure of G.T. not to be stressed. Stool and narrow table out of shot. This shot probably a little from above ... Essential for this shot to be as strange, unreal, intriguing as possible.

This degree of involvement by an author in a television production is and was exceptional. Normally, even in prestigious authored drama, the control is in the hands of the producer, who commissions writers and directors, casts performers, and works with story and script editors to mould a screenplay into the required form for a predetermined length, expected audience and production schedule. Much of the published academic writing about Beckett's television plays has made a point of attributing to Beckett an exceptional interest and competence in the techniques and conventions of the medium. Scholars have also praised Beckett for his patient and meticulous instructions to the producers and directors of his work about matters of staging and interpretation. These points are certainly valid, but they neglect to point out how unusual this level of authorial involvement is and was, and what its consequences might be in relation to the collective and industrial production of television programmes. Beckett's (and some of his collaborators') authority over the realisation of his work could be a double-edged sword for the institutions of television production and their staff. It gave exceptional cultural status and legitimacy to the television productions that were made, and it ensured a close relationship between the 'intentions' of Beckett as a dramatist and the finished programmes. But it also caused significant problems in the process of production of programmes and prevented production staff from carrying out their roles in the ways to which they were accustomed.

Authenticity, identity and performance

Leslie Hill (1996: 25) suggests that 'Increasingly, Beckett's later plays, when they experiment with theatrical and other forms, are seeking to redefine performance in non-anthropomorphic terms (and this, at bottom, is probably the main reason for Beckett's sustained interest in the use of technology on stage and in the development of radio and television drama).' It is certainly the case that the use of close-up, high key lighting to create contrast, and the separation of the body from the set or a sense of surroundings, tends to reduce the anthropomorphic and realist aspects of Beckett's later television work. The body can be fragmented, separated from its visual background, and manipulated as an image in relation to other non-figurative images within the television frame. As Katherine Weiss (2002) shows, both Beckett and Walter Benjamin were writing about Marcel Proust and were interested in photography as a means of both composing and decomposing identities. For Proust, Benjamin and Beckett, the mechanisation implied in habitual behaviour enables subjectivity across temporal extension by creating the persistence of subjectivity, but it also dulls and routinises subjectivity. Furthermore, Weiss argues that the inevitable running-down of a mechanism, or the breaking-down of a technology, are parallel to the representation of the human body in Beckett's work, and also parallel to the fading and minimisation of language. Beckett, like Benjamin, wrote in *Proust* about the act of narrative as a fragmenting process that is similar to the decomposition of the object by photography. The continual and complementary processes of decomposition and recomposition produce the perpetual potential for new narratives and narrations at the same time as they prohibit their proper resolution.

Sound has similar functions in Beckett's work. This mechanical production of memory and identity as imperfect and repeating narrations is demonstrated in *Krapp*'s use of the tape recorder. The reproduction of sound, and its supposed indexical relation to the real and its role as the vehicle of memory, are explored in Beckett's radio plays *All That Fall* and *The Old Tune*. The title of *Eh Joe* is a conventional punctuating phrase which offers the possibility of replying to a statement by the first speaker in a conversation, and this injunction to speak is reflected more strongly in the French title of the play, *Dis Joe*. In place of such speech, the play moves towards the close-up on his face. While it might be more expected for the movement towards Joe's face to end in a close-up of an eye or both his eyes (Ziliacus 1976: 190), especially in the 1960s when extreme close-up was used more than it is now, the ending on the face draws attention to bodily expression and its ambiguity. Furthermore, with Beckett's interest in Modernist art and film, Tim Armstrong (1998: 230) makes an apposite comment when he notes that the Surrealists disapproved of sound film because the fluid unreality of the cinematic image would be normalised and grounded by speech. While *...but the clouds...* is a production that makes use of sound, it uses repetition, ambiguity and the absence of dialogue, and the ventriloquism by M of W's recitation of the Yeats poem, to retain a ghostly and fluid quality in the image, at the same time as drawing attention to the mechanical reproduction and apparent fixity provided by the television technology. Both M and W are said to 'appear' or 'reappear' as if they were ghosts. Ghostliness seems to have been aimed for very deliberately in the SDR production of *Was Wo*, as Garforth (1992: 442–57) shows. So the point made by Richard Bruce Kirkley (1992: 609, see also Katz 1995) that 'language controls the image' in *...but the clouds...* is wrong, especially because of the dominance of the image and the reflexive attention given to its production. In relation to television, drama requires the performance of the actors and the assumption of roles. Furthermore, the broadcasting of a programme is a further kind of performance, similar to the use of this term to describe a cinema showing or a theatrical performance where a text is exhibited to its audience. The patent lack of realism in the settings, costumes and actions of Beckett's television plays draw attention to them as performances in a double sense. They are fictional works performed by actors, and they are also opportunities for the exhibition of a constructed text for an audience. Such features as the introductory discussions in *Shades*, and the fact that the plays are almost exclusively broadcast in black-and-white, give particular prominence to their performative features (see Austin 1971, Butler 1990, Parker and Sedgwick 1995), in distinction to the illusory realisms of many television programmes.

It is important to separate the representation of absence that is so central to Beckett's plays from the negative theology which attributes a Romantic and transcendental presence to this absence. It is certainly the case that there is an absent beloved in *Ghost Trio*, and another absent beloved and an ungraspable past for M in *...but the clouds...*, an illusory representation of grace in *Nacht und Träume*, a dead and absent beloved in *Eh Joe*, and an empty centre in *Quad*. The personae of the plays constitute themselves in relation to these absences, but this does not posit the absences as the origins or centres of meaning. Instead, however, the personae are constituted as subjects in relation to these absent objects of desire, and both subject and object are constitutive of each other. The plays are the drama of this mutually interdependent relationship, and the plays end once the recognition of this relationship has been established for the persona and thus, ideally, for the audience. Many of these absent others are gendered feminine, in distinction to a masculine persona, and as Judith Butler (1990) has argued, gender identity is produced through actions rather than essences, in which the repetition of conventional gender behaviours produce a temporarily stable gender identity. In the television plays, there is a repeated structure in which an apparently masculine subject ambivalently and questionably constitutes itself by imagining a feminine other from which it is separated and which it desires. Yet the feminine that the masculine subject imagines is not represented as a fictional fantasy. The feminine is not simply a production of the masculine, and therefore subservient or subsequent to it, for the feminine and masculine are established in relation to each other. There has been a significant difference of approach in the criticism addressing close-ups of the face of Joe, for example, and critical work on the function of the close-up on women in cinema. The close-up on Joe is assumed to invite a reading of psychological depth, interiority and character. By contrast, close-ups on faces and other parts of the female body have been described in terms of the fetishisation of vision of a surface, of an appearance behind which there is no depth. Critical production in cinema and television, such as avant-garde film, draws attention to the presence on the screen of an absent object, and the television plays have a similar critical function. The aesthetic of the productions is thus anti-realistic in this specific sense that reflects on their realisation as virtual and mediated representations, and as performative in Butler's sense. Within the plays, the present figure draws attention to its performance status and the possibility of conjuring up an image of the absent other (presented, for example, in the image of the woman desired in *...but the clouds...* as a superimposed television image). Drawing attention to absence becomes equivalent to drawing attention to presence, in the context of the simultaneous presence and absence of the signified in television. The temptation for interpreters of Beckett's screen work has been to subsume this flickering between absence and presence under Beckett's intentionality and authorship, whereas that authorship too is unstable and reflexively debated by means of the work itself.

Beckettian 'signatures' in *Film*

Beckett's work critiques the notion of subjective plenitude and intentional agency by exploring how the subject is both determined by psychic histories, discourses and circumstantial forces beyond his or her control and, yet, struggles to attain agency. So it would be contradictory to attribute the meanings of Beckett's work to his own subjective intentions as author, yet his agency nevertheless enables his name to be cited as the source of the plays. Beckett's authority depends in part on the authority of the author as producing agent (*auctor*) behind the work, and also on the authority (*auctoritas*) of the traditions from which the plays' aesthetic forms derive. The effect of composing a work from these diverse materials and placing emphasis on their diversity rather than their possible unification into a narrative or a set of themes is, of course, to distance the author or the authorial voice from the text much more radically than is normally the case. Nevertheless, paradoxically, because this technique is so unusual in television and so significant as an example of a formal device, it is almost always the case that the particularity and significance of work like this are attributed specifically to the name of Beckett. In other words, the author himself as the unconventional and significant creator of the work is picked out from the group of writers and creators involved in the production of a work which in terms of its textual meanings specifically does not privilege the role of the author.

This complex set of paradoxes around authorship had been evident before Beckett wrote any of the plays commissioned for television, when he wrote the outline for *Film* in 1964 having thought of it first as a possible television piece. Beckett's name seems to authenticate *Film* as a cinematic work, in the manner of a signature. The author's name is superimposed over a close-up of Buster Keaton's eye in the film's closing shot, in a caption which reads 'Film by Samuel Beckett'. This caption's citation of Beckett's name refers the spectator to the eye and 'I' of Beckett as the originator of the film, by posing the shot of the eye as potentially the eye of its author (since the close-up disallows the spectator from identifying whose eye this is). The eye might also signify metaphorically the notion of unique authorship, simply by connoting the privileged point of view that creativity is conventionally held to require. So the first function of the name is to act as a sign of the film's creative origin. Secondarily, the presence of Beckett's name marks the film as Beckett's property and guarantees its authenticity and authorship. This is a conventional function of signatures and identifying marks, with its origin in contractual and legal contexts associated with property and copyright. The same function remains common in feature films, where the director's name connotes creative authority and ownership. This placing of the director's name was a common distinguishing mark of French New Wave cinema in the 1960s, where it would be unsurprising to see the caption 'Un film de' preceding the director's name at the opening of an auteur film, and Hollywood directors took up the same convention subsequently as a way of claiming authorial creativity.

But the proper name is actually invoking Beckett's authority as the writer of the screenplay, and not as the director, the usual 'author' of a film. This might be somewhat disorienting for a cinema audience who are not familiar with the genesis of the *Film* project, but in theoretical terms its effect is certainly to signal the literary conventions of authorship rather than cinematic ones, and to distance the film from commercial cinema practices. A further function of the caption showing Beckett's proper name and the film's title is to mark the physical limits of the film and thus construct the textual frame within which the narrative proper is delivered. The closing shot is a boundary device, which offers to ground what has come before it for the spectator. The film frames that the audience sees on the screen as *Film* ends are at once part of the film and also tell the audience that these frames are not part of the main body of the film. This function of the name is to enforce a border between the inside and outside of the film, separating the text as an object from the subject who authored it. This reinforces the reading of the title *Film* as designating a surface separating one thing from another, and this interest in surfaces can also be seen in the camera's attention to textures, including Buster Keaton's skin, especially his eyelid, the decaying wall in the opening scene, and the badly plastered walls of the room to which Keaton goes. But since the closing frame reflexively reads 'Film by Samuel Beckett', it suggests that the separation announced in the idea of surface and film is itself under the authority of the author. Some of the same paradoxes appear because of the title's reference to the film medium. *Film* is a unique work, but its very name refers the spectator to what is generically filmic about it, what is not unique. Here the contextual frames offered by other films are significant, and I develop this issue below. The title frame, as a bordering device, has a double status. It separates the work from Beckett and from other films, especially films made by and starring Buster Keaton, and paradoxically denies this separation.

Film was produced at an auspicious time as far as authorship is concerned, for in the 1950s and 1960s the film journal *Cahiers du Cinéma* argued for a 'politique des auteurs', inaccurately translated as 'auteur theory', which sought to take film seriously as an art-form and to elevate selected film makers to cultural prestige by undertaking sustained and detailed analyses of their work. This approach focused not only on contemporary French directors' films but also on Hollywood productions and films made in earlier decades. The aim was to approach popular cinema seriously through study of authorship, and to avoid film criticism that focused only on socially relevant content and analysis of themes without attention to the aesthetic processes by which films produce meanings. A selection of film directors whose work was identifiable as the creation of a distinct author's vision became established, including John Ford, Howard Hawks and Alfred Hitchcock. The director's work on the script and the assemblage of the meaning creating procedures of film making, such as the arrangement of setting, movement of the camera, performance style and editing system, were studied in detail to establish the distinctive vision of the director as author. The journal's valuation of directors as auteurs adopted the ideology of expressive individualism which underlay discussion of literary works, and in the context of this 'literary cinema', in 1965 and 1966 *Film* began to receive awards at European film festivals. It won the New York Film Festival award and the Diploma di Merito at the Venice Film Festival, and was selected as the film of the year at the London Film Festival. When Keaton made a personal appearance in 1965 at the Venice Film Festival, for the first European showing of *Film*, he received a standing ovation from the audience. However, this reaction was not primarily because of his work in *Film*. It was result of European intellectuals' recent revaluation of his silent comedy films of the 1920s, a revaluation carried out in part in the pages of *Cahiers du Cinéma*, and because of his status as an elder statesman of the cinema. But the 'seriousness' of *Film* as an art movie, and the critical acclaim of Keaton by European intellectual culture were becoming linked together. The following year *Film* won awards at the Oberhausen, Tours, Sydney and Krakow film festivals.

But despite the emerging critical framework which valued directors as authors, the director of *Film* considered himself a translator and not an author, because he thought of Beckett as its author. Alan Schneider suppressed his role as an auteur director in order to give greater prominence to Beckett's role as the author of the written outline that *Film* had been made from. Schneider's view was that he had simply been translating the written outline into the film medium. Schneider worked as a theatre director, had little ambition to gain a reputation as a film director and had never directed a film before he embarked on the *Film* project. He saw *Film* as an investigation of the medium by an author who was properly a playwright. Schneider (1972: 63) portrayed himself as the facilitator of Beckett's vision, consciously reversing the auteurist slippage from literary author to film director: 'With every new wavelet of contemporary cinema turning directors, in effect, into authors, it took the surprising author of *Film*, playwright Samuel Beckett, to become, not too surprisingly, its real director.' As produced, the film is different from the written outline, but even this was seen by Schneider as a result of Beckett's influence over the project. Schneider attempted modestly to deny the film's independence of its author by invoking the author's 'vision' as an anterior authority for the written outline, and he saw the outline as an intermediate partial object, a transparent film through which the author's creativity had to be made visible. Schneider wrote a commentary on *Film* when it was published by Grove Press, the publisher of Beckett's prose work and theatre plays. In describing his and his crew's intentions, he included a quotation of an approving remark made by Beckett to him: 'it was the special vision and tone set by Sam which all of us were dedicated to putting on film ... acquiring "a dimension and validity of its own that are worth far more than any merely efficient translation of intention". But, in the process, it was exactly that faithful translation of intention we were all after.' (Schneider 1972: 63) Schneider claimed to be using the film medium and film production techniques purely as translation machines through which Beckett's authorship would pass. He included Beckett's approving words only to deny the compliment that was paid to him, and gave back to Beckett the authority of the signature.

Posthumous reverence

The iconic role of photographs of Beckett has already been discussed (Voigts-Virchow, 2000–1) and has been a persistent feature of television broadcasts of Beckett's work and in documentary features about him, as in the photographic montages in the introductory commentary by Melvyn Bragg and Martin Esslin in *The Lively Arts: Shades*, and in the BBC's tribute documentaries *Beckett at 80* (1986) and *A Wake for Sam* (1990). Most recently, the presentation box and booklet supplied with the *Beckett on Film* productions on DVD are notable for their many images of Beckett. The iconic status of Beckett, signified in part by these pictures, raises interesting paradoxes in relation to the *Beckett on Film* productions as regards the relative significance of author, directors and production institutions.

Channel 4's investment in the Beckett season is to some extent consistent with the channel's original remit yet marks an interesting difference from the terms of its foundation in the early 1980s (Greenhalgh, 1998). Channel 4 was devised with a large and guaranteed income provided by the advertising revenues of ITV companies, yet with an injunction from government not to pursue the large audiences that gained ITV that money but, in contrast, to be distinctively different from mainstream television, to be innovative, to provide programmes for minorities and to articulate the concerns of those whose interests were rarely represented on television. This set-up was clearly based on the post-war consensus that had established Public Service Broadcasting throughout the twentieth century, and it represented an enterprising yet troubled yoking together of commercial funding and the values of subsidised public service. There are several ways to regard the position of Channel 4 in the broadcasting landscape. First, it can be regarded as a strategy of repressive tolerance, in which marginal and potentially radical broadcasting can be contained yet expressed without posing a threat to the established duopoly of BBC and ITV. Second, it can be regarded as a safe haven for television producers and creators whose work is amenable neither to the broad middlebrow audiences sought increasingly by a BBC anxious to defend its licence fee by drawing audiences of substantial size, nor to an ITV increasingly threatened in its address to downmarket mass audiences. These threats consist of audience fragmentation created by a multi-channel environment, advertisers' increasing interest in valuable niche markets and decreasing interest in masses, and an audience profile of increasing age and diminishing income. Third, the fact that Channel 4 is a publisher broadcaster rather than a programme maker means that it is able to respond quickly to the rapidly changing fortunes of the television industry, as an enterprise business driven by market forces. These three very different ways of understanding the cultural role of Channel 4 fit in different ways into the seemingly hesitant and unplanned attitude of the channel to the Beckett season.

Michael Kustow, the first Commissioning Editor for the Arts on Channel 4, came to the channel from the National Theatre, and before that from a post as Director of the Institute of Contemporary Arts. It was intended that drama on Channel 4 would refuse the comfortable forms of costume heritage drama and the adaptation of classics. Instead, contemporary, unfamiliar, immediate, innovative and consciously televisual work would be created. The results of this aim can be seen in, for example, *Nicholas Nickleby* (adapted by David Edgar, 1982) which mixed the 'live' relay of theatre performance with a classic story told through ensemble performance based on alternative theatre practice, *The Mysteries* (adapted by the poet Tony Harrison, 1985), in which the conventions of the multi-camera outside broadcast used for sports events or rock concerts were used to present the epic promenade performance, and *A TV Dante* (painter Tom

Phillips in collaboration with film maker Peter Greenaway, 1989), where state-of-the-art post-production methods were used to present Dante's text using montage, overlays, animations, voice-over commentary and picture-within-picture. By 2001, however, Channel 4 was competing much more directly with BBC2 on a range of programmes designed for attractive niche audiences, in particular the 18–25 audience captivated by such programmes as *Friends* and *Big Brother*, and its significant Film on Four production arm had failed to move from low-budget but successful films to Hollywood-scale productions and was scaled down radically in 2002. The ambitions of Channel 4 had become much more conservative, and much more conscious of audience value, because the channel had been empowered to sell its own advertising and make its own money, and this was directly reflected in the fate of the co-productions of Beckett plays and their scheduling and transmission (and non-transmission).

The first British screenings of *Beckett on Film* in 2001 were on Channel 4 in an irregular collection of schedule positions in either the early or late evening. While the plays were sometimes given trailers before broadcast, in which they were presented as a special arts event, it was difficult for viewers to know more than a few days in advance when they would be shown, and they bore no obvious relation to the channel's normal scheduling policy. They were neither part of a regular series of drama programming nor connected to arts magazine programmes (like BBC's *Arena* or *Lively Arts* series) or dramas by other writers. Individual plays were broadcast singly, with whole longer plays and shorter plays in different slots of unequal length rather than as a package occupying a consistent period of broadcast time. The uncertain relationship between the plays and the rest of the channel's output, and the unconventional pattern of scheduling, must have contributed to the season's low ratings and confusion about which viewers the plays were aimed at. This first showing of the *Beckett on Film* season harks back to some extent to British broadcasters' policy to mix programmes together in the schedule so that audiences might come across them by chance and be stimulated by relatively demanding fare that they might not consciously choose to view. This kind of scheduling is now rare in British television and belongs to a pre-1980 conception of Public Service Broadcasting in which the audience is conceived as a citizenry whose cultural knowledge and involvement could be gently raised by insinuating 'quality' material amongst popular entertainment.

However, the second period in which the *Beckett on Film* adaptations were shown was quite different in character. By 2004, the plays were being scheduled as if they were educational broadcasts for schools, thus adopting an explicit pedagogic address to the audience (see Chapter 4). In the week of Saturday 28 February to Friday 5 March 2004, for example, Channel 4 showed the *Beckett on Film* productions in their schools programme slot in the middle of weekday mornings. The plays were repositioned as educational programmes for secondary school viewers who may be studying the plays in their English or Drama syllabus. Listings magazines such as the *Radio Times* grouped all of the day's Channel 4 programmes for schools together in one block of text giving information such as programme titles and starting times, but also noting the age group for which each programme was intended (as an aid to teachers or parents). For instance, on Thursday 4 March, the *4Learning* educational slot from 9.30 am to 12.00 pm included four plays from the *Beckett on Film* season. They were preceded (at 10.40 am) by the programme for English literature students aged 7–11, *What's So Good About J.K. Rowling*, which discussed the well-known author of the Harry Potter novels. At 10.55 am, *What Where* appeared, targeted at a suggested 14–19 year-old age group. These are secondary school students who may be taking GCSE examinations (at age 16) or the final school examinations that can prepare them for Further or Higher Education. Following *What Where*, and filling the rest of the educational programmes slot, came *Footfalls, Come and Go*, and *Act Without Words II*, with the same suggested age of audience. Clearly, the plays were not being offered to a general audience but were a contribution to British television's statutory support for the school curriculum, as resources for study.

Beckett's plays for television need to be understood in relation to British television culture, and the institutional culture of the BBC in particular. The linkage between Beckett's television dramas and the Modernist aesthetic that Beckett was perceived to represent functioned through the value of Beckett's name and associations, which played an important role in legitimating the educative and conservational values underlying Public Service Broadcasting. The formal experiment, theatrical background and admitted complexity of Beckett's television plays supported the claims of the BBC and later Channel 4 to present the best of contemporary arts practice despite, or even because of, the distance between such practice and the mainstream forms of television dramatic entertainment. The culture of authorship connecting Beckett with the producers and performers of his television plays worked as a supporting structure that facilitated their realisation according to the instructions and wishes of their author, in contrast to the more usual subsidiary status of the writer for television. Beckett's authorship was at once granted exceptional primacy and yet was also dependent on a network of professional relationships and networks within British television that could easily be disrupted or damaged, and which underwent change over time.

Furthermore, these contextual and cultural issues can be directly connected to the paradoxes and reflexive foregrounding of agency, authorship, narrational control and textual framing that occur in Beckett's television work itself. In the wider context of critical writing on Beckett's work, Daniela Caselli's (2005) study of authority in his prose writing offers a theoretical approach to authorship that situates and illuminates these issues. Her work posits Beckett as 'not the origin of these texts but a figure of power emerging from them, which inevitably remains powerful even when professing his own powerlessness' (Caselli 2005: 3). For the network of collaborators working on the realisation of Beckett's screen dramas, assumptions about his cultural authority and the value of his work led to their granting of extraordinary power to his own authorial direction over the work. This led to the subsuming of their own power under the rubric of carrying out his instructions or what they perceived to be his intentions. But it also gave them institutional power themselves through their association with Beckett and his work, thus refracting Beckett's authority beyond his own person and stated ideas. Within the dramas themselves, questions of power are an important part of their textual structure and their thematic patterns, whether through ambivalent relationships between past and present selves, voice and image, or present and absent characters. In proposing interpretations of the work, critical discourses have attempted to stabilise the texts by invoking biographical information about Beckett and the processes of writing the dramas, and locating patterns of similarity or development across a series of texts that also ultimately legitimate their claims by grouping them together under their author's name. In all of these ways, a figure of authority who is not the 'real' Samuel Beckett emerges, but one who is a figure representing a desire for the stabilisation of meaning and of a textual corpus. The institutions of television and film, and of academic criticism, have in their different ways consistently invested in authorship as a strategy of control.

4

Intertexts

Introduction

This chapter addresses the relationships between uses of visual space in Beckett's television works and *Film* and his theatrical works. It also uses reference to Beckett's novels and prose essays on painting and other topics to discuss visual space, framing, and spectator positioning, and relates these to interpretations of the television works. This involves discussion of formal and compositional issues, and aesthetic and philosophical theories of vision in Beckett's oeuvre, considered in relation to theories of visual meaning in Television Studies discourses. It also requires a discussion of the prevalent motif identified by Beckett critics of increasing formal simplicity or minimalism in his theatre, prose and media works. It has been argued that Beckett's persistence with the unfamiliar and problematic television and film media was a way of moving towards a 'language' of pure visual form, through the spatial and abstract qualities of the television image, and its manipulability by technological means (for instance superimposition, exaggeration or paring down of colour, exact repetition, and separation of image and sound). My work on Beckett's television dramas is connected to theoretical traditions which have explored problems in the conceptualisation of television's visual space and the relationships of television and film with other media. Paradoxically, a distinguishing feature of Beckett's television plays and *Film* is their inclusion of a combination of forms deriving from different genres and modes of television, theatre, painting and film. In other words, the distinguishing feature of the work is that it is not homogenous but is itself dialogical and internally differentiated. The implication that a concentrated form of spectatorship is required by Beckett's television plays connects them with the gaze of cinema rather than the glance of television. The reduction of the visual field to self-consciously two-dimensional surfaces and geometric arrangements recalls twentieth-century abstraction and Modernist painting. But the prominence of interiors and the domestic space of the room, together with the centrality to image compositions of windows and doors, connect the plays' visual aesthetic with Dutch 'Golden Age' painting. Some of the effects of depth produced by light, figures and darkness are similar to Renaissance religious art such as the paintings of Caravaggio. The different implications of these traditions, in relation to their interest in subjectivity, psychology, family dynamics and romances, or mythological and religious commentary, load the plays with potentially elusive and ambivalent meanings.

The problem with most studies of intertextuality where such borrowings and ambivalences are discussed is that they identify sources and origins for components of the work they are addressing, leaving those sources stable as explanatory keys to the work that has adopted them. This chapter, on the other hand, shares with Daniela Caselli's (2005) study of intertextuality in Beckett's work a desire to show how Beckett's allusions and borrowings rework that material and lead the television plays and *Film* in different directions. The unity and coherence of the dramas is thereby fractured by the ways they point outwards and backwards to what they have transformed, to the extent that the competing 'keys' to their meaning do not coalesce with each other or create a stable hierarchy of levels of interpretation. Furthermore, there are evident similarities and repetitions between the dramas that might suggest that they have a teleological and developmental relationship with each other as a body of work. But this chapter argues that, in Caselli's (2005: 2) words in relation Beckett's prose writing, these correspondences are 'part of a larger internal (intratextual) strategy of reduplications, mirrorings, echoes and *mises en abyme* which shape the

Beckett corpus'. By reflecting back and forth to each other, the dramas invite a reading based around their author's consistent exploration of related concerns, but also render such consistency impossible because the materials from which they are constituted are drawn from somewhere else, from other texts, media, artistic traditions and conventions of production. While Beckett's work is infused with cultural knowledge and reference and has been presented in arts contexts in television and as art film in the cinema, it persistently deconstructs the pedagogical function that this implies.

The association (especially in Western Europe) of the television medium's social embeddedness as the primary mass media apparatus, with a social project to enlighten its audiences, offers the possibility for television to collapse neither into commodification, commerce and populism nor into elitism and special pleading for work that is identified with high culture. In Britain especially, television has a close relationship with the arts. The principles of Public Service Broadcasting underwrite the presence on mainstream channels of programmes about the arts and programmes that adapt painting, music, theatre or dance for the screen. One of the fundamental assumptions governing the regulation and the culture of British television is that a requirement for diversity of programme content includes programming designed to inform and educate the audience about the arts and, in the first four decades of British television history at least, a desire on the part of broadcasters to contribute to the enhancement of the population's aesthetic faculties and interests. Since television began as a live broadcast medium, and still remains so to an important extent, it also has a close relationship with the representation of the present and the modern. Furthermore, the presence on television of a range of modes and genres of representation, some of them drawn from antecedent representational forms such theatre or journalism, conduces to possibilities of formal experiment, mixing of genres and modes of address, and self-conscious experimentation with representational techniques. The fact that television has drawn its programming ideas and modes of representation from other media, from both elite and popular culture, and from sources associated with the past as well as from the immediate present, complicates the relationship between Beckett's allusive television and film work and the media for which it was produced. Modernism as a cultural phenomenon looked back to antecedent traditions as part of a desire to break from them, and incorporated technologies and representational forms from elite and popular culture. Framing Beckett's television plays and *Film* in the contexts of artistic histories and movements illuminates how they are both innovative and anachronistic, and both revisionist and deeply dependent on the artistic and theoretical currents of previous times.

Beckett among the Modernists

A Modernist aesthetic can be traced in Beckett's plays written for television, where the reduction of verbal and spatial textures, and concentration on geometrical forms and music, represent experiments in medium-specificity. It is this reflexivity that has been noted already by scholars that include, for example, Linda Ben-Zvi, Enoch Brater, Stan Gontarski, Anna McMullan and Catherine Russell. Although television drama is necessarily part of popular culture because of its integration into this most popular medium, television drama in Britain is linked with the aesthetic, institutional and political debates around realism and Modernism which have informed British and European culture since the late nineteenth century (Caughie 2000). For television, Modernism means several things: a set of reflexive formal techniques, work produced in a culture of mechanical reproduction that nevertheless seeks to avoid commodification, and work which responds aesthetically to the specific conditions of the present. Television drama is important to these Modernist concerns because it is necessarily at an intersection of art and the popular. Television is embedded in social life and popular culture to a degree that matches the significance of radio in the earlier twentieth century, and because the television set occupies a place in the home it is arguably more embedded in the routines of daily life than cinema, even compared to the years in the mid-twentieth century when cinema attracted diverse audiences in enormous numbers. It is not only in high art that Modernism is evident; for example, some films in the popular form of Hollywood cinema also show evidence of the kind of aesthetic exploration, drive for change and relationship to the contemporary (urban) situation that characterises Modernism in high art. Some of Hitchcock's films (*Rear Window* or *Psycho*, for example), have the reflexive interest in perception, knowledge and identity that is found in Modernist literature and drama. Beckett's television plays play with the aesthetic possibilities of the popular medium of television in a similar way. The conventional form of the studio television drama, the room, the still-present narrative and the narrational linearity of the plays show their connection with the generally naturalistic form of television fiction, but they clearly also have a serious, experimental and reflexive interest in their own form and the ways in which looking, knowledge and action can be represented.

For television producers, production staff and reviewers, Beckett's work for television was understood in relation to current conceptions of Modernism in literature and theatre. A television version of *Waiting for Godot* was commissioned by the BBC in 1960 among a group of plays by newer playwrights: the BBC planned to produce Pinter's *The Dumbwaiter*, Doris Lessing's *The Truth about Billy Newton*, M.F. Simpson's *One Way Pendulum*, and Arnold Wesker's *The Kitchen*. Beckett's status continued to be high thereafter, and throughout the 1970s the fees paid to him by the BBC were one-sixth higher than the standard contractual amount for playwrights. Given Beckett's standing in theatrical drama, and his recognition as a Nobel Prize-winning author, it is not surprising that he was positioned among a Pantheon of significant contemporary writers. There are of course significant differences between, for example, Wesker's exploration of kinds of realism and the documentation of work and working-class characters, and Beckett's formalist investigation of language, space and performance. But in their different ways, the writers courted in the early 1960s by the BBC with a view to commissioning works specifically for television were all exploring questions of form and signification in ways that connect with the reflexivity and self-consciousness of medium pioneered by the artists of the early twentieth century who had, by the early 1960s, been labelled as 'Modernists'. A television version of Beckett's *Krapp's Last Tape* was screened by BBC in November 1963 in the *Festival* anthology of one-off plays, in a run which also included an adaptation of Joyce's *Ulysses* and plays by Jean Cocteau and T.S. Eliot. It was in this company of British and continental European writers that Beckett was placed.

This contextualisation of Beckett among Modernist practitioners continued into the 1970s. As the production files relating to *The Lively Arts* programme *Shades* of 1977 show (BBC WAC T51/350), in 1976 BBC producer Tristram Powell was planning a television tribute for Beckett's birthday, to include *Not I*, *Play*, and a specially written television play. The links between Beckett and a tradition of high-cultural literature, theatre and art were to be signalled by contributions from Harold Pinter, Roger Blin, Donald McWhinnie, and some of the distinguished actors who had appeared in Beckett's theatre plays. Powell commissioned a translation of Beckett's preface to a catalogue that Beckett sent to him of paintings by Henri Hayden for the National Museum of Modern Art in Paris in 1968. As well as three Hayden paintings, the eventual programme, *The Lively Arts: Shades* showed 'The Scream' by Edvard Munch, Francis Bacon's 'Pope II', and Alberto Giacometti's 'Woman of Venice VIII', as still images against which voice-over discussion by Melvyn Bragg and Martin Esslin of Beckett's drama was heard. Beckett was positioned among twentieth-century European Modernists, not only from the literary scene but also from a broader arts culture that included painting and sculpture as well as theatre. For the BBC, Beckett existed in a transnational cultural and economic context that enfolded his work in a set of assumptions about contemporaneity, formal experiment and aesthetic and historic value, and was an exception from increasingly dominant norms of production, scheduling and competition for popular audiences. By framing the plays in this way, Beckett s work was given a pedagogic relation to its audience, seeking to provoke unconventional ways of seeing, hearing and experiencing represented space and time. Mise-en-scène, point of view, and relationships between image and sound or music in the plays were implicitly paralleled with formal devices from the visual, theatrical and plastic arts that could be assimilated into television arts programme discourse.

The unconventional cinematography in Beckett's first cinema work in the 1960s, *Film* (1964) can be partially explained by its author's interest in Modernist cinema (Bair, 1980: 177–8). In 1935 Beckett was reading books by and about Eisenstein, Pudovkin and Arnheim, and the journal *Close-Up*. He would therefore have known about Eisenstein's montage experiments, for example, in which he used images of the same face backed by different music and found that test audiences understood these image–music conjunctions in different ways. Beckett wrote to Eisenstein in 1936, offering to go to Moscow and work unpaid as his assistant. Eisenstein did not reply, but Beckett also wrote to Pudovkin about his interest in silent cinema, which had by then been eclipsed by developments in sound and colour. These attempts show that Beckett was aware of and interested in modes of film making which were different from the commercial cinema of the time. The production context of *Film* illuminates this interest further, as Enoch Brater (1975) has described. Barney Rosset, Beckett's American publisher, commissioned *Film* as part of a composite of three works called 'Project 1, Three Original Motion Picture Scripts by Samuel Beckett, Eugene Ionesco, Harold Pinter', suggesting a desire to make films by significant playwrights of the time, whose work was regarded as intellectually challenging and serious. Of the other two films, Ionesco's *Hard-Boiled Egg* was never made, and Pinter's *The Compartment* became *The Basement*, broadcast by BBC television in 1967. Following up this context in the European avant-garde, Brater (1975) points out that *Film*'s short running-time and its juxtaposition of odd perspectives recall Dada Surrealist films of the late 1920s, and that the close-up of Keaton s eye in the first frame might refer to the slit eye in Buñuel s *Un Chien Andalou* of 1928. Avant-garde cinema has drawn attention to the link between the cinematic gaze and ordinary vision (Wees 1992:

13–14), and close-ups of eyes are common for this reason. Both Beckett and Buñuel contributed to a special number of the periodical *This Quarter* of September 1932 in which the filmscript of *Un Chien* was published, along with Beckett's translations of works by René Crevel, Paul Eluard and André Breton.

Small details of production technique and mise-en-scène reinforce these Modernist connections, as well as biographical and historical contexts. There is a typescript with production notes for *Nacht und Träume* at the Beckett International Foundation's Reading archive (Beckett undated h). This records that a blue cloth was used to conceal the body of the person whose arm is seen in the play. The same technique was used in Cocteau's *La Belle et La Bête* (1946), and in Cocteau's 1950 film *Orphée*. Surrealist notions of the autonomised body were also explored using reverse motion. Roger Blin, director of the first French production of *Godot* and thus a contributor to the system of bodily movement that set the tone for later productions of Beckett's theatre, acted in *Orphée*. The notion of the blurred boundaries between fantasy and reality is the subject of both Cocteau's films and *Nacht und Träume*. *Nacht und Träume* establishes a difference between a waking world and a dreamt world, only to blur the distinction between them by using fade and zoom to replace one by another. The use of the technical device of a wipe produces blurred borders around the inserted dream image and literally breaks down the distinction between them ontologically and epistemologically by the way they share lighting and compositional forms. Beckett's self-consciousness of medium and consciousness of the materiality of the work of art and its means of production is a Modern characteristic, as opposed to the interest in institutions that characterises the avant-garde, and the volatile relationships explored in post-modernism. Eckart Voigts-Virchow (2000–1: 121) argues by contrast that Beckett's work is avant-garde, in the sense that it refuses the popularising conventions of television aesthetics: 'The real alternative that Beckett's minimalist abstract TV vision has to offer to contemporary media culture is its definition of space as a void and an absence – the denial of vision and spectacle.' But the objective of the avant-garde was to destroy the institutions of art, yet television is by its nature institutional, and Beckett's work was enabled significantly by his institutional and personal relationships in television and also by his interest and experience in film and theatre alongside collaborators who also drew on experience from several media.

Film and silent cinema

As earlier chapters have shown, Beckett's television Modernism relies on a conscious engagement with the current conventions understood by the audience, and their manipulation rather than their rejection. The mixing of forms in contravention of apparent conventions relies on the existence and familiarity of those conventions as the ground against which the works are measured. In parallel with intertextual relationships with European art cinema, *Film* can also be understood in relation to Hollywood's silent film tradition. Miriam Hansen (1991: 23) begins her study of spectatorship in American silent cinema with a passing reference to Buster Keaton. Her concern in the book is the gradual establishment of the regime of spectatorship which we now refer to as 'classical Hollywood cinema', and she mentions Keaton's *Sherlock Junior* (1924) in this context as a film which dramatises the new spectatorial relation which is being constructed:

> With the elaboration of a type of narration that seems to anticipate – or strategically frustrate – the viewer's desire with every shot, the spectator became part of the film as product, rather than a particular exhibition or show. As reception was thus increasingly standardised, the moviegoer was effectively invited to assume the position of this ideal spectator created by the film, leaving behind, like Keaton in *Sherlock Jr.*, an awareness of his or her physical self in the theater space, of an everyday existence troubled by social, sexual, and economic dependencies.

For Hansen, *Sherlock Junior* is poised between the film as show and the film as narrative product, and there is a possible history here in which Keaton's earlier shorts and his subsequent narrative features could be placed in relation to the shifts in American cinema. As Chapter 6 will show, forty years after *Sherlock Junior*, audiences who saw Keaton in *Film*, based on a screenplay by Samuel Beckett, were unsure whether they were spectators of a Keaton 'show', or a narrative product in which he starred, or an avant-garde movie organised around Beckett's authorial reputation. After a discussion of Keaton's comic mode of performance and the reflexivity around identity in the examples of two of his silent films, *Sherlock Junior* and *The Playhouse* (1921), I shall outline the emergent re-evaluations of Keaton's significance in the mid-1960s. It was in this mid-1960s context that Keaton appeared in *Film* (1964), directed by Alan Schneider, produced by Evergreen Theatre Inc. As the correspondence between Beckett and Schneider (Harmon 1998: 146) reveals, first choices for the character of O were Zero Mostell, then Jack MacGowran. Keaton was only suggested in late May 1964, but the use of the comic actor in this 'art' film was consonant with the new respect being given to Keaton at that time. Yet *Film* is now regarded primarily as part of the canon of Beckett's work, and by 1964 Beckett was already becoming well known after media controversies around productions of his plays *Waiting for Godot* and *Endgame*. Beckett's role as auteur and centre of meaning for *Film* bypasses the role of its director, the usual candidate for authorial status, and underestimates the significance of Keaton's presence in the film (Bignell, 1999).

In *Sherlock Junior*, Keaton plays a film projectionist. While sleeping at his post he splits into two people and becomes an actor in the film he is projecting. Initially he cannot control the world of the film, and is partly in the cinema auditorium and partly beyond the screen's surface in the film itself. By a shift in point of view, Keaton's vision becomes entirely that of the film 'reality' and he is inside the film, in the costume of Sherlock Holmes. He projects his desires onto the film world, becoming a successful detective, saving the girl he loves from the villain, with all the fictional characters being 'played' by the 'real' people Keaton had been rejected by in 'reality'. Back in the real world, he takes on the heroic characteristics of his film self, clears his name, unmasks the villain and regains the woman he loves. In

Film, Keaton also plays a character split into two, an observing self and a pursued observed self. But the doubling of the Keaton character is not a comic device, or a means of empowering the anterior 'real' individual behind the dream double, but instead a means to dramatise notions of subjectivity as a matter of perception and self-perception. The elements of the Keaton star image are multiple, and as Richard Dyer (1998: 127) remarks, a 'film may, through its deployment of the other signs of character and the rhetoric of the film, bring out certain features of the star's image and ignore others. In other words, from the structured polysemy of the star's image certain meanings are selected in accord with the overriding conception of the character in the film'. Splitting and doubling of the central character, a 1920s setting, the use of black-and-white film and the narrative form of the chase are alluded to in *Film* and support a mode of viewing oriented around Keaton's star image, while other features of his performance and the narration of *Film* counteract this mode of spectatorship.

Splitting of identity and metafictionality also appears in *The Playhouse*, a short in which Keaton plays all the parts on stage and all the theatre staff in a minstrel show by the use of multiple exposure techniques. The number of doubles escalates from Keaton as audience member and conductor of the pit orchestra, until all the orchestra players, stagehands, minstrel players and audience members are his doubles. As in *Sherlock Junior*, the implication is that this is a dream, and the next sequence shows him being awakened, and his bedroom being disassembled, since it is a stage set. Keaton is in 'reality' a stagehand, pursuing twin young women, who then takes the role first of a performing monkey and then an acrobat, and then rescues a woman from an underwater act. Like *Sherlock Junior* and its use of cinema, *The Playhouse* uses theatricality and dreaming as a means to reflect on identity as performance, and as arenas into which identity can be displaced in fantasy, then reconnected to an anterior 'real' world. This splitting and reconnection works differently in *Film*. Rather than opening a space of fantasy in which the double's activities play out the desires or potentials of the 'real' conscious subject, *Film* shows how, as Keaton himself remarked (in Dardis, 1979: 270) about the role he played in it, 'a man can get away from everybody, but he can't get away from himself'.

The casting of Keaton in *Film* corresponded to a critical view, which was being developed at the time, of his work as reflexive and intellectually significant. I refer here mainly to the European, and especially the French, re-evaluation of Keaton in the late 1950s and 1960s, though Keaton s status as a great comic had been signalled in the United States at around the same time (Bishop 1958a and b). Writing in 1964 about his comedies, inspired by a season of Keaton shorts and silent features at the French Cinématèque in Paris in 1962 and articles and interviews in *Cahiers du Cinéma* and *Cinéma* in the late 1950s and early 1960s, Jean-Patrick Lebel (1967: 15) dismissed the critics who had regarded Keaton's face as a comic trick: 'They felt obliged to reduce his opaque mask to something they themselves could understand, and not accept it for the disquieting thing it was: a face turned in upon itself, concentrating upon itself with a prolonged and unbearable determination.' This notion of the comic mask as a surface which points to a concealed depth is remarkably similar to the questions which *Film* poses. The transparency or concealment of identity entailed in the media of film and photography are part of its narrative content and are marked by the title *Film* itself. Further, the 'disquiet' Lebel refers to is parallel to the questions of interpretation which *Film* poses for its audience, and parallel to the disquiet which audiences felt when in the film's final moments the expected passivity of Keaton's face turns suddenly to a horrified expression. And finally of course, the double point of view of Keaton's mask, appearing to look out but also looking in at itself, is the structural logic of perception which *Film* attempts to render in its construction via the two points of view of Keaton and his double. Lebel's (1967: 16) reassessment of Keaton goes on to the problem of reading and interpretation, the same problem which *Film* generated the year after Lebel's book was first published; 'whether one makes of Keaton's mask a trick and the mark of comic superficiality or one makes of it the image of tragic human destiny; whether one sees in him mere dead indifference or one sees the ridiculous symbol of human pathos, there is no getting around the expressive fixity of his face. His impassivity is sanctioned by being reduced to the concentrated expression of a single emotion turned upon itself.' Lebel offers a series of interpretive frameworks for the reading of Keaton's face. There is a wide range of possibilities of reading, from the dismissive to the metaphysically emblematic. Reduction, concentration and self-reflexiveness are the features which he regards as essential to Keaton.

The casting of Keaton in *Film* links it to vaudeville and slapstick, and its theme of pursuit also recalls the chases in urban settings which occur in Keaton's and others' silent comedies. However, these silent comedies would make considerable use of wide shots through which the action moved, and a static camera in front of which the actor exhibited his routines. The moving camera in *Film*, and the lack of wide shots to establish space, make this kind of comedy very difficult to achieve. It is not possible to call *Film* a 'silent film' in the sense of an imitation, throwback or pastiche of films made before synchronous sound was common. 'Silent films' was a phrase rarely used before the coming of sound in 1926, since films were not silent. Apart from the noise of the projection machines and the audience itself, there could be spoken commentary, phonograph music, mechanically or manually produced sound effects, pit orchestras and singers, and piano or organ accompaniment. In the 1920s Keaton's films would have been accompanied by orchestra or piano. Keaton himself preferred the use of the orchestra to a single instrument and also expressed a dislike for sound effects matching narrative events (McCaffrey, 1968: 136). But the modern cinema audience is geared to expect the conventions of presence offered by synchronous image and sound, the conventions of narrative point of view, the modulation of one scene to another in a gradual unfolding of narrative significance, and the complexity of character interaction within scenes. Most of this unification and audience positioning is absent from *Film*, but so is the viewing experience of silent cinema, because of the lack of music, intertitles, or gestural acting style of the period. Although *Film* alludes to silent films by its own silence, and the reflexive 'Ssh' which is its only sound, it does not repeat the experience of viewing silent films in the pre-1926 period. The silence of *Film* has the effect of reminding its audience of silent cinema and depriving them of the narrative continuity provided by dialogue and music. The silence enforces a concentration on visual perception and reminds the audience that they are experiencing the film as a silent collectivity in the cinema itself. This kind of concentration works against the comedy which Keaton's performance and expectations deriving from previous silent movies might arouse, and is part of a general strategy to allude to previous kinds of cinema while repudiating important aspects of their history and form.

Picture planes and performance spaces

There are both obvious and less obvious relationships between Beckett's television plays and painting. The emphasis on framed static images in the plays and the immobility of the figures is one clear example. The face of the woman in *...but the clouds...* is static and composed, perhaps alluding to the slightly inclined and composed faces of Madonnas and angels in Renaissance painting. The evocation of phantom-like figures summoned up by memory is especially significant in *...but the clouds...* and in *Ghost Trio*, where their simultaneous presence but ambiguous status as present or past is enforced by the use of superimposition or their presentation in central lighted areas of the composition surrounded by indefinite dark shadows. As Jonathan Kalb (1989: 100) has pointed out, the use of powerful contrasts between light and shadow and arrangements of composition in the work of Caravaggio are similar to those of Beckett, though the painter's evocation of the tints of human skin against darkness, and especially his placement of foreground objects to generate spatial extension into the viewer's space, are significantly different from the planar compositions of the settings in Beckett's television plays. As Chapter 3 has argued, invocations of authority for Beckett's television work raise distinctions and problems of attributing origins, as well as useful correspondences. Furthermore, fundamental geometric forms become principles of image composition, where for instance Beckett moves from the grey squares representing the setting in *Ghost Trio* to the lighted circles that comprise the acting area in *...but the clouds...* The representation of the room as a series of rectangles in Part One of *Ghost Trio* changes the representation of the space from that of a room defined by its potential uses and dramatic possibilities to a two-dimensional and pictorial series of forms rendered in geometrical and abstract ways. Since the television screen is in itself rectangular, providing a frame around what is seen, the various rectangles presented by Voice to the viewer can be interpreted as intertextual allusions to the framed rectangular spaces of gallery painting. In *Ghost Trio*, Voice focuses attention on these geometric surfaces. The effect of subdividing the rectangular space within the frame is to energise parts of the space and to suggest relationships between the frame and the spaces demarcated within it. As Martha Fehsenfeld (1982: 357–8) suggests, 'In the 1977 television plays *Ghost Trio* and *...but the clouds...*, limited movement within strictly prescribed boundaries produces an intensely concentrated focus'.

Movement is across the plane of the set in left-to-right directions, entering and leaving the spotlight, in *...but the clouds...*, whereas the movement in *Ghost Trio* is into and out of the set, from the front to the back. In *...but the clouds...* there is an almost immobile male figure and a static female figure in the closing moments, returning to a static framing on the television screen, and in *Ghost Trio* also, the Figure returns to a position that recapitulates its opening. The circles of *...but the clouds...* are ellipses because of the perspectivally viewed space of the floor of the set, drawing attention to the three-dimensionality of the space and not simply to the plane of the television screen. The two plays use similar ideas of the picture plane and the flatness on the television screen of three-dimensional objects and spaces, but they use different means to achieve these. Even *Quad*, where the figures in Part One move rapidly, has a static camera framing a rectangular shape. The wipe effect that creates the shift in the image from 'real' space to apparently dreamed space in *Nacht und Träume* is also parallel to the panning of a camera across the surface of a planar picture. The most striking television-specific effect in the play is when the window-like area on the top right of the screen expands to fill the screen with the 'dream image'. This achieved by the technique of overlay where the output of one camera is superimposed over the output of another in part or all of the visible frame. This inlaid picture can be electronically expanded (or contracted) by means of a wipe effect to take up more or less of the screen.

In *Nacht und Träume*, the title suggests that what the television viewer witnesses is the young man's dream images. But the religious connotations of many of the objects featured in the dream, and the fact that the image of the dream enlarges to occupy the whole of the television screen in the repeated version, problematises this. There are three lighted areas in the play: the area containing dream imagery, a small window of light on the wall facing the camera, and the larger lighted area like a window on the wall behind the dreamer's body. As soon as the dream image appears, the other two lighted areas disappear. The square of light on the wall produces a parallel between A and his dreamt self, B. But the similarity highlights the difference between the two scenes, since A is enveloped in darkness while B is surrounded by light. It is also significant that the visual space of the dream is in some respects parallel to the space of the television screen itself. Although the boundaries of the dream image are not defined in the same way as the solid framing of the television screen, the differentiation of the dream space from the rest of the represented visual field produces a window-like effect, along with the other window-like areas of light in the image, and when the dream occupies the whole of the television screen it matches the dimensions of that space. The overall result is to question the television screen as a revelatory 'window' and to suggest that its function is to purvey dreams, or at least non-naturalistic narratives, times and spaces. As is necessary in television, the camera is the route of access for the viewer to the visible, and therefore the freedom to look across represented space and to choose which details to focus on is restricted. Television images in Beckett's plays are like and unlike painting, for the duration of camera shots and the common use of long shots giving access to the completeness and depth of the space militates against the camera's restriction of choice about where to look, so that the camera's agency as an instrument of selective perception is diminished.

The result of these emphases on static compositions and geometric figures carved out by light and contrast is that the television viewer is presented with an image on screen which invites the movement of the eye across its dynamics, offering both restriction and freedom of vision, like someone contemplating a painting in a gallery or sitting in the auditorium of a theatre and contemplating the set. However, as in television programmes about paintings, a voice-over appears to guide the viewer's gaze at and understanding of what can be seen. There are restrictions on the display of works of art on television, including the flattening of the picture surface, the distortion of colour values and the presence of an outer frame created by the frame of the television screen. Factors such as smell and sound environment are also eliminated. For these reasons, television representations of paintings generally introduce spatial movement created either by camera movement or by zooms into or away from details in the picture. This has the effect of emphasising particular details and generating a sense of dynamism in the image. It is very unusual for the television camera to linger on a shot of a whole canvas. It is also unusual for television to present paintings without either music suggestive of the tone of the work or the voice-over of a presenter or expert. As Benjamin (1968) argued, mechanical reproduction of works of art, including television representations of them, contribute to the loss of the aura of uniqueness that characterises the status of the artwork in contemporary culture, separating Beckett's picture-like compositions from the experience of looking at paintings. Television representations of paintings attempt to enfold the relatively poor reproduction of the image with audio-visual elements that seek to contextualise, explain and energise the work. The presence of narrators and expert contributors is often designed to supply a sense of intellectual depth and sensory engagement that the camera itself is unable to provide. The invitation to look at the surface of the screen as a composition and a surface rather than a window through which action and movement are perceived counteract the assumption in studies of television spectatorship that the viewer is a passive being characterised by his or her glance (Ellis 1982: 137). Beckett's plays encourage attention to the tones, textures and forms within the image in a way that is close to the conventions of representing painting, as well as to art cinema or quality television as forms where the high production values of what can be seen, the lavish detail of settings or costumes, or the nuances and details of performance are offered for the viewer's visual pleasure. But neither are Beckett's television images the same as looking at art, because of their parallels with television re-presentations of art and their consistent adoption of drama conventions.

Whereas Benjamin's lament for the loss of art's 'aura' of authenticity and cultural value was countered by the entertainment media's potential for the democratisation of pleasure, Beckett's aestheticisation of the television image and his allusions to high culture are the opposite of what Benjamin called 'the liquidation of the traditional value of the cultural heritage' (1968: 221). As Herren (2007: 49) argues, Beckett 'returns over and again to meditate upon' that heritage by using the media that might seem to disempower it. Benjamin argued that mechanical reproduction, in photography or cinema, for example, did not do away with the fascination of seeing an original work of art such as a painting, where that fascination was understood as a property of the work itself that he described as its 'aura'. Rather, the original's aura becomes unstable and open to doubt when perfect reproductions of the work can be produced, so that the stamp of authenticity that legitimates the work's cultural and economic value leads to the development of a culture where that authenticity is not a determining criterion. Art, inasmuch as it is defined by its aura of authenticity and uniqueness as a material object, loses its privileged status. In parallel with this change, new kinds of cultural production emerge that do not depend on uniqueness and authenticity, and here Benjamin's example was the recently emergent cinema in the form of films as entertainment commodities for widespread consumption. The necessity for geographically extended and simultaneous distribution of films to cinemas requires the production of numerous identical copies of the film, and the very reproducibility of the film is essential to its social being since audiences expect to see the same film at whichever exhibition venue they attend. Benjamin concludes that 'the work of art reproduced becomes the work of art designed for reproducibility' (1968: 224). Benjamin regarded this development positively, whereas in a discussion of this in relation to Beckett, Herren (2007: 49) has lamented the 'deracination eventually caused by the inundation of mechanically reproduced simulacra into every facet of contemporary reality. Beckett had the historical (dis)advantage of seeing the larger trajectory of this authenticity crisis', which Herren advances as an argument for Beckett's resuscitation of art in the popular medium of television. Herren's (2007: 135) forceful declaration of his own 'allegiance to Beckett's work as art' and his 'commitment to construct, deconstruct, and reconstruct Beckett in that category', however, is in my view insufficiently cognisant of the situation of television as a domestic apparatus, and the disjuncture between television 'art' and the material conditions of its viewing. Beckett's television plays problematise the meaning of domestic space, and the ways that 'art' reflects on the homeliness and potential unhomeliness of television in it, in a way that would work differently for cinema and other audio-visual media that are exhibited in the public sphere. Again, Beckett's work alludes to art, television representations of art, and television as art, but always in a way that reminds its viewer that television is rarely and problematically assimilable in these terms.

The heritage of domestic stories and settings in television derives from a literary and theatrical history which is crucially bound up with individuality, family, home and social class, and which represents these concerns spatially in three dimensions rather than as a planar surface. Raymond Williams (1990: 56) described television drama as 'the ultimate realisation of the original naturalist convention: the drama of the small enclosed room, in which a few characters lived out their private experience of an unseen public world.' Critical writing on Beckett's prose has often drawn attention to the relationships between the room and the womb. This supports the idea of the room or home as the place of privacy, family and the reproduction of social relations that are associated with women and bourgeois naturalism, finding a theatrical staging in the work of Ibsen and Chekhov. Rooms in Beckett's television plays might seem to be refuges but they are also lonely and empty environments into which the camera and voices can enter. The exteriors beyond the windows and doors are never given concrete or representational features. The interiors in the television plays are quite clearly constructed sets rather than locations, drawing attention to the composition of space by means of the dividing flats of a set or the selective lighting of the television studio, and to the disposition of objects, entrances and exits within this set and the manipulation of proportion and perspective. This is especially evident in the strangely sized windows and doors of *Eh Joe*, or the studio non-space of *…but the clouds…* in which the absence of walls and doors marks the space as one created by and for drama, and existing within its conventions. Beckett's television dramas both allude to the spectatorial conventions of seeing paintings in a gallery, but also create a dialogue between the planar surface of a picture and the spatial and temporal extension of television. In addition, the requirement of attention that accompanies the social and public contemplation of art is reconfigured for the domestic and private experience of television viewing. Beckett's dramas negotiate a position between art for television, art on television, and television as art.

Beckett's interest in painting began while he was at college (Knowlson 1996: 71–2), and in discussing his drama Martin Esslin (1987: 67) noted that throughout his life he was 'more at home in the company of painters than that of writers'. As Graley Herren (2007: 163) has explained, 'Beckett knew London's National Gallery well enough to apply for a job as assistant curator in 1933 … and his intimate familiarity with Dublin's National

Gallery is evident from his ongoing correspondence with Thomas MacGreevy, who served as longtime Director. He devoted much of his seminal trip to Germany in 1936–37 to viewing dozens of art collections, and he spent the rest of his life frequenting museums and galleries throughout Europe and collecting their catalogues.' Beckett was interested in the tradition of classical painting as well as contemporary art. In the paintings of the Dutch masters that Beckett admired, such as Jan Vermeer, the setting of relatively still figures within rooms is connected to the rise of the bourgeois home and the intimacy of domestic private life. These political and social developments were the preconditions for the novel and for naturalism in theatre. The relationships between the domestic and the public were emphasised in Dutch painting by the frequency and significance of doorways and windows, marking the boundaries between the inner and the outer and associating these uncertain boundaries with the inner dramas of the paintings' subjects. These dramas were expressed externally by relationships with objects, other people and the intrusion of the outside into an inner world, such as through a map, a letter, or the arrival of a guest. *Nacht und Träume* begins with a rectangular lighted shape that resembles a window, and windows also figure in *Eh Joe*, *Ghost Trio* and *Film* as the figures protect themselves from the outside by drawing curtains and closing doors, before something or someone arrives to question the boundaries and significance of the interior space.

The moulding of space by internal framing in the work of Nicolas Poussin, another of Beckett s favourite painters, also establishes interior or exterior space as a stage or enclosure. The development of paintings of rooms, from Renaissance art to the Modernism of Paul Cézanne, Vincent van Gogh or the American painting of Edward Hopper, can be seen as the development of ideas about private space, property and possessions, and the home as a refuge. Since the television set is likely to be placed in a room, among the domestic objects of the household, the plays' focus on domestic interiors, most striking in Voice's attention to the layout and space of the room in *Ghost Trio*, both makes a link with the viewer's own environment and also establishes the difference and distance between the represented room and the viewer's own space. It is particularly striking that the Voice not only describes the set, the colours and shapes of the items in it, and the disposition of the Figure, but also remarks on the technical and material means of the viewer's perception of this information. Voice's command that the viewer should not raise the volume on the television set, for example, is a recognition not simply that the drama is conveyed by means of the camera and sound recording equipment but also that it is being received on domestic television apparatus in the home of the viewing audience. Again, this not only draws attention to the means of representation in a self-conscious and Modernist way but also affects the inclusion and exclusion of the audience from the drama. As a conduit for images and sounds, the television apparatus provides access to those images and sounds, and mirrors the represented room with the viewer's, but it also announces the viewer's separation from the moment of their recording and excludes the viewer from the room supposedly matching the one in which the viewer is watching this.

Jonathan Kalb (1989: 105) suggests that Voice in *Eh Joe* could be painting Joe's portrait, and this remark opens up a specific series of questions about the relationship of figures to the spatial ground against which they appear, and the stakes of psychological insight achieved by television's ability to use the close-up. Portraiture, especially, is a mode of painting practice that seems relevant to understandings of Beckett's television plays. As John Adams (1998: 154) has noted, the close-up is a particularly significant type of shot in television drama, in comparison and contrast to theatre:

> the body is decisively fragmented; the character is detached from setting; the character is privileged, emerging from the encounter and/or the group. Above all, the looks and personality of the actor are imposed on the narrative persona: the physiognomy of the player provides a map of the landscape of individual thought and feeling, to be read in terms of the narrative context. In dramatic terms, the close shot is primarily a signifier of significant thought or feeling. Such readings are then further structured by the

sequential context and the camera position – the extent to which a CS is aligned with a camera position associated with the viewpoint of another character in the scene, for example, or whether it sits within a sequence of active/reaction shots. In other words, camera placement and choice of lens position the viewer to share and respond to the inner process of the character (that is, a subject of the drama) or as an object of the look, where judgments have to be made about the process of thought.

In the television version of *Not I*, the separation of the mouth from the rest of the body diminishes the significance of bodiliness, yet at the same time the use of extreme close-up on the detail of the mouth's movement, and the mechanics and visceral qualities of that movement, make the materiality of speaking all the more evident. The BBC version of *Not I* shows only the mouth on the screen, which, although it is a part of the body, is the whole of the speaking agent. By contrast, in the *Beckett on Film* version of *Not I*, the body of the actress is shown approaching the camera and the chair in which she will sit, and her speaking mouth therefore appears as a fragment of a known larger whole. The relationship between the agency of the voice and its body is different in the two versions. The body as the site of perception, and the bodily process of perception through the senses, are particularly evident in Beckett's dramas. This continuing concern is a means to explore on the one hand the paradox between the abstraction and metaphor that the plays seem calculated to suggest, and on the other hand the embedded quality of representation in the physical and situated bodies of performers and the television audience.

The images of the sets and the performers remain iconic signs referencing objects and people present in front of a camera, as television images almost always do. But the recognition of facial expressions, bodily poses or familiar objects rarely leads to the possibility of decoding a definite meaning for them, as the naturalistic and psychological heritage of television drama might imply. As television theorists have argued in the past, close-up may be the most natural shot in television, because it offers the resources for psychological interpretation on a small screen in dramas about people. But in Beckett's plays, the reading of these surfaces on the surface of the screen does not seem calculated to work as psychological revelation. Jonathan Kalb's (1989: 106) comment on portraiture finally leads to the interpetation that *Eh Joe* 'evokes the genre of portraiture only to turn directly around and question its very principle of sublime wholeness'. The movement of the camera towards Joe's face leads Kalb to argue that Beckett is questioning the notion of framing, and this is reinforced by the use of lighting in Beckett's plays to frame lighted areas within surroundings of darkness. Kalb (1989: 99) argues that like the work of Caravaggio, the television plays are like 'windows looking inward on particular souls' and represent 'Man existing on his own in a kind of nothingness'. He presents a variation on this argument (1989: 97) when he parallels the dreamer in *Nacht und Träume* both to Christ and to the adoring figures of classical religious painting.

A similar interpretation is offered by Graley Herren (2007:166), who suggests Jan Grossaert's painting 'Agony in the Garden' as a source for *Nacht und Träume*. The painting depicts a redemptive moment when Christ prays for the avoidance of his forthcoming crucifixion, and 'Beckett replicates the painterly traditions for depicting the scene by incorporating conventional iconography and arranging his graphic elements on screen after the fashion of the old masters. These graphic affinities are subverted, however, by his deft manipulation of the temporal dimension, a televisual tool at his disposal unavailable in the exclusively spatial medium of painting.' By presenting the dreamer's comforting by a sympathising figure, then fading the dream out in the next sequence of the play, Beckett radically reverses the religious hopefulness of the classical painting's meaning by introducing temporal extension into the motif. Beckett's biography also suggests that the iconography of *Not I* was inspired by Caravaggio's painting 'The Beheading of St John the Baptist' (Knowlson 1996: 520) and Herren (2007: 70) approves the suggestion that Don Silvestro dei Gherarducci's 'The Assumption of St Mary Magdalene' was a visual precedent for Beckett's theatre play *Footfalls*. However, this raises the question of the particularity of the figures in the plays, because of their specific realisation on television in temporal, spatial and performance forms that allude to, but do not repeat, a specific source or iconographic motif. Along with Sidney Feshbach (1999: 343) in a discussion of *Film*, I would argue that the plays insist on the specificity of the actor's face and body, the detail of the set, and the precise shapes established by effects of lighting, for example. This contradicts the assumption that the figures, and their stories and settings, represent an essence of human nature or the instantiation of a transcendental or abstract idea and so removes them from that artistic tradition at the same time as they reference it.

Parallels between the body and a machine in Modernist art, in both Futurist and Cubist ways of representing the body as a series of planes, volumes and lines, were used to question the body's articulation and relationship with its environment. In Beckett's plays too, figures move slowly, unnaturally and deliberately, suggesting an analytical and deconstructive way of representing the body. This has made it possible for critics to argue that Beckett's work explores the notion of the divided self, or the subject under erasure as proclaimed by post-structural criticism. As Stan Gontarski (1986: 404) remarks of *Quad*, the play could be seen as 'Beckett's most vivid image of postmodern literary theory and literal decentering'. Working from an earlier critical tradition concerned with negation and existentialism, Beckett (1983: 152) himself expressed an interest in artists whose work seemed to seek representations that excluded the conventional notion of the self, commenting on the work of his artist friend Avigdor Arikha that it was 'Eye and hand feverish after the unself'. But although the bodies in Beckett's plays conform to what is for Beckett an almost stereotypical male figure dressed in an overcoat or a nightshirt, for a television audience they will appear highly specific. They look like figures from the past, with outlandish hair and clothing, perhaps suggesting old people living alone in city apartments, as in a drama of social or political critique.

This kind of concreteness of bodily representation needs to be distinguished from gallery video work in which short pieces explore the body as an object in relation to a containing space. These works, exemplified by the experimental videos made by the American artist Bruce Nauman in the late 1960s, meditate on movement and repetition, but not in the form of dramatic or narrative forms, and are not made for broadcast. Nauman is a privileged example of this kind of visual art because he explicitly acknowledged the debt his work owed to reading Beckett's prose and theatre texts. In six one-hour videos, Modernist concerns with the body as a mechanical assemblage enacting repeated movements combine with a similarly Modernist interest in the possibilities of the recently invented domestic video camera to frame and record bodily movement. In *Slow Angle Walk* (1968) the static camera is placed on its side, producing a canted frame that destabilises the relationship of Nauman's body with conventional representations of interior space. In his studio, Nauman has his hands clasped behind his back, kicks up one leg at right angles to his body, bends forward and shifts his weight onto the extended leg as it reaches the floor. Extending the other leg behind him, he drops onto it and repeats the sequence many times, producing an eccentric walk across the floor that results in him sometimes disappearing from the frame. *Bouncing in the Corner* (1968) also uses a canted camera that frames Nauman's torso and legs (but not his head) crammed into a corner of the wall. He falls backwards into the corner, stopping his movement with his hands and pushing out again into the room, but since the camera image is presented on its side, he seems to be rising from and falling back to a lying position. *Stamping in the Studio* (1968) uses an upside-down camera shooting Nauman pacing diagonally and spirally across the floor in increasingly complex syncopated footstep rhythms. *Wall-Floor Positions* (1968) shows Nauman standing against a wall, leaning outwards, bending forward, squatting, sitting then lying down, in a repeated sequence that begins each time from a different position in relation to the wall (facing it, facing left, facing right, etc.). In *Walk with Contrapposto* (1968), Nauman walks with his hands clasped behind his head in a hip-swinging movement back and forth along a narrow, specially-built corridor along which the camera is looking and which frames his body in an exaggerated telescopic space, bringing his body from small and distant to large and close to the lens. Finally, *Revolving Upside Down* (1969) has a camera positioned upside-down recording pirouettes, goose-steps and angular arabesques similar to *Slow Angle Walk* that appear to be conducted across the ceiling of the studio. In each of these videotapes, Nauman draws on the movements suggested by Beckett's characters in his novel trilogy, and to a lesser extent his theatre plays, to defamiliarise the body and its component limbs, articulatory possibilities and relationships with the interior spatial dimensions of a room. But their lack of narrative and dialogue places much greater emphasis on compositional form, the sounds resulting from body movement and the orientation of the visual frame than Beckett's television work. As non-broadcast visual art they are distinct from the engagement with television conventions that I have emphasised in this book, but their significance for my argument here is their relationship with Modernist concerns with technology and representation, and how they explore the stakes of audio-visual representation in dialogue with conventions of seeing.

Learning to see

Modernism involves a questioning of perception that is the ground on which formal experiment and reflexivity of communicative means in language and visual arts can be built, as in the film work of Sergei Eisenstein or Dziga Vertov for example. By reproducing the perceptual processes of the eye through the use of the camera, the fundamentals of perception could be explored. Furthermore, the recognition of differences between perceptual machines such as film cameras and human perceptual organs both de-naturalised human perception and offered possibilities for thinking otherwise (Crary, 1992). The art historian Ernst Gombrich (1960, 250), for instance, quoted John Ruskin's nineteenth-century invocation of the 'natural' innocence of perception only to refuse it: 'The whole technical power of painting depends on our recovery of what might be called the *innocence of the eye*; that is to say, a sort of childish perception of these flat stains of colour, merely as such, without consciousness of what they signify'. For Gombrich, modern art thematises and reflects on perception and representation in a way which debunks the Ruskinian myth of childlike, innocent perception. From this perspective, Beckett's return to the apparent building-blocks of perceptual sense-making can be understood as a critical project to repeat the process of 'learning to see' in order to defer and differentiate it: to suggest precisely the non-necessity of its conventional forms. In this regard, the notions of the child's perceptual capacities and of childlikeness function as terrains for critical experiment in television aesthetics and audience address, as long as television allows a space for that kind of pedagogical research. This notion of teaching the audience by conducting a series of experiments in and with vision provides a historical and cultural context in which the assumptions in existing critical writing on Beckett's television plays can be grounded historically and culturally.

The Voice in *Ghost Trio* forms a mediating function between the drama and the viewer. This has the effect both of including the viewer in the unfolding of the drama, offering a passage for the audience into the space of the action, and of separating the audience from the drama by assuming the necessity of a figure that can conduct the audience from his or her viewing space into the space of the action. Rather than beginning the performance as a self-contained and naturalistically rendered world, by contrast in *Ghost Trio*, Voice invites the audience to consider the means of staging itself, and the construction of the fictional space in which the drama will unfold. Rather than focusing attention on the performers and the beginning of the narrative, attention is focused on the apparatus of television representation and its rendering on the two-dimensional space of the screen. Walls, floor, pallet and door are mentioned first, while the figure is the last focus of attention for Voice and the camera. The Figure is also immobile and at some distance from the camera when first observed. All these factors reduce the affective involvement of the viewer in the drama, and instead promote distance and abstract contemplation of the form of the programme. As Linda Ben-Zvi (1985: 35) has noted, Voice has a pedagogic educative role in outlining the means of representation and the disposition of the apparatus of the drama. Voice's authorial and interpretive control is also evident in the directions given by Voice to the camera and to the Figure. Similarly, in ...*but the clouds*... (1977) and *Quad* (1982), the frame of the screen is accentuated by the framing of the characters by lighting, producing an unlit off-screen space which is neither identifiable with the studio set nor a fictive location. This continues the emphasis on framing produced in *Ghost Trio* by the rectangles of the floor, wall and F's pallet, which each mirror the square television screen. The audio-visual forms in Beckett's television plays have legitimated approaches that emphasise their reflexivity and their critical work on the television audience.

The presentation of the spaces of the room in the manner of projected slides or stills in a gallery presentation or a television documentary on the visual arts may also be regarded as part of the pedagogic and educative function of the play, and the address to the viewer as someone who must learn a visual language of abstraction in order to understand and appreciate the work. The connections between the visual form of *Ghost Trio* in Part One and visual art clearly affect the status of the play itself. If it borrows the conventions of contemporary Modernist abstraction in painting, and Voice's address to the viewer suggests that a specific means of understanding beyond everyday perception is required, then the play positions itself as an artistic work itself. Considerations of value, experimentation, the authorial signature and the social distribution of specialist knowledge about the arts become relevant to the play. This risks the alienation of the audience and connects the play to television and other media representations of elite culture. The fact that the play was broadcast in the *Lively Arts* strand, and framed by interpretive discussion by Martin Esslin and Melvyn Bragg, further confirms this class specificity. In various ways, the play risks categorisation as a forbidding and elite work, in which special knowledge and cultural authority are required in order to understand it.

The presence of Schubert's music further connects the play to this stratum of specialist knowledge. But there are powerful discourses which would support the function of television as a pedagogic device for illuminating and teaching about vision.

Recent defences against the scapegoating of media draw on the concept of media literacy, which concerns children's knowledge of media codes and conventions, genre, narrative and production processes (Hodge and Tripp, 1986). The revealing of television conventions and apparatus valued by Beckett critics as self-reflexive and critical uses of the medium, is in effect a pedagogic strategy to teach media literacy to adults in the way that programme makers aim to teach it to children. In a similar way, the screening of introductory material in which television presenters set parameters for the viewer's interpretation of Beckett's television plays establishes these plays as 'difficult' material that requires explanation and guidance. However, the emphasis in Beckett criticism on the viewer's acquisition of skills, and the drive for rational control by the child or adult viewer over media interactions, risks repeating the binary oppositions between rational child and irrational child, active and passive, agent and victim, which have underlain much of the debate on both childhood and popular culture for more than a century. David Buckingham (1993a and b, 1996) draws on a Cultural Studies approach to address this, adducing children's and parents' talk about television to focus on the 'positive' and 'negative' emotional responses to television. Buckingham discovers that both watching television and talking about television are important means for children to understand themselves and others, and also to perform their own identities to themselves and others. This dynamic interaction involves gaining and deploying knowledge of television codes and conventions, such as distinctions between genres, narrative forms, and contextualisation of the programme text through knowledge about the production processes which gave rise to it. Buckingham's research has shown that children sometimes seek out disturbing programmes in order to test their own maturity at coping with troubling emotions. It is not simply pleasure that drives viewing preferences (paedocratic impulses), but also a desire to self-educate and confront challenging material (a pedagogic viewing position). These notions of child development that Buckingham's work relies on, however, have been critiqued for accepting the unequal power relationships between the sexes, between children and adults and between less developed and the more developed nations that are sustained through the institutions of developmental psychology themselves (Burman 2007). Mapping a model of development onto children implicitly supports the existing hierarchies between the less developed and the more developed in these discourses.

In a similar way, critics have valued Beckett's plays as ways for viewers to understand and explore problems of identity, death, love and meaning in general, as a counter-strategy to some of these critics' assumptions about television's role in cultural dumbing-down. Jonathan Kalb (1994, 137), for example, claims that 'television has been dominated by the narrowly circumscribed formats of commercial programming since its birth, and those formats have contributed to egregious, worldwide psychological changes: shrinking attention spans, discouraging reading and encouraging passive, narcotized habits of viewing art of all kinds'. These are exactly the effects that television has been claimed to have on children. Kalb (1994: 138) argues that Beckett can 'augment human perception and, by implication, dignify it', thus leading adults away from television's pernicious influence and constructing a developmental teleology that positions Beckett's kind of television drama as the destination towards which a television viewer ought to aspire. This rhetoric can be reversed in other discursive models, however, as discussed below, and thus each mobilisation of the concept of childhood is revealed as contingent and rhetorical rather than necessary.

The adoption of textual strategies such as the explicit address to the audience by V in *Ghost Trio*, 'Keep that sound down', and the lengthy shots showing the rectangular shapes of the set are pedagogic inasmuch as they discipline their audience and explicitly prescribe ways of viewing and comprehension. If Beckett's television plays 'teach' the audience how to watch television, as in *Ghost Trio*, they can be compared to the programmes with pedagogic aims made by producers for child audiences. Linda Ben-Zvi (1985: 24) has argued that Beckett's plays for television and radio educate the audience about their means of production: 'Beckett foregrounds the devices – radio sound effects, film and video camera positions – and forces the audience to acknowledge the presence of these usually hidden shapers of texts'. Thus the plays are argued to empower the audience by requiring attention to the conventions of signification in the medium. This matches educationalists' arguments for children to study the media at school, learning 'media literacy', which comprises knowledge of genre, narrative codes and production processes. Critical discourse on Beckett's television plays values their pedagogic strategies for teaching media literary to adults, paralleling the adult audience with children and paralleling Beckett's plays with children's programming. Parents, educators and regulators have argued that programmes for children should have greater regard for the functions of television in education and child development. These responsibilities on the part of programme makers and broadcasters have underlain much of the discourse of British television production in the public service tradition.

An insight into this discourse can be gained from the work of Roger Singleton-Turner, a BBC producer whose book *Television and Children* (1994) is not only a guide for programme makers but also addressed to the wider audience of educators, parents and officials concerned with children and television. He argues that the competencies and knowledge held by children and the adults who make children's television are different. The explanatory discourses which legitimate Singleton-Turner's sense of quality and appropriateness derive from developmental psychology and from the professional discourse of television production. A discourse on media literacy draws on developmental psychology to promote the notion that television is a language, and Singleton-Turner (1994: 23) claims that: 'The whole grammar of television needs to be learnt by each viewer. There is evidence that the language of film and television is learnt in a similar way to spoken language and that children of increasing maturity accept with understanding an increasing vocabulary of filmic conventions.' Therefore, narrative forms should be relatively linear and clear, to avoid the child creating 'extraordinary constructions in his [sic] mind to explain what he has seen'. A discursive model of child development is constructed as an evolutionary learning process which moves teleologically towards the normative adult viewer. The specific results of this developmental schema are to proscribe the audio-visual form of programmes, according to the 'stage' in development which the child is assumed to be at, with the simplest forms for the youngest audience. Relations between long shots and close-ups should be signposted (to avoid confusion over the sizes of objects and people), time ellipses between shots should be rare in programmes for young children, and cutting rates should be slower than for an adult audience. In essence, the form of children's programmes comes to resemble early cinema, and children's programmes repeat the 'evolution' of film from the static camera shooting theatrical boxed sets, with little cutting or change of frame size, to a contemporary style of rapid montage, fast cutting and 'unmotivated' use of pan or close-up in programmes for older children.

This institutional discourse from within the BBC suggests striking similarities between the professional codes adopted for the making of programmes for children and the structural principles and audience address of Beckett's television plays. In each, there are simple relations between shots, long takes, clear establishing shots, guiding narration, and use of compositional and editing conventions deriving from early cinema and television. *Eh Joe* (1966) and *Ghost Trio* both begin with static establishing shots that present the whole of the acting area, and only then proceed to segment that space by cutting and camera movement, while *Quad* uses only one camera position that has a similarly complete view of the space where action takes place. Eckart Voigts-Virchow (1998, 235) asks: 'How does this formal examination of Beckett's camera plays, then, position their reductive, repetitive, static, monochrome, interior closeness in the TV environment?' He answers that it sidelines them as outdated and rarefied (both rarely-seen and aimed at an elite audience). But the learning curve of child viewers in watching programmes made for them is parallel to the notion of 'learning to see' that Beckett's plays use as their mode of address to their viewers. It could be argued therefore that, like programmes for children, Beckett's television plays become a condensed version of the normative and teleological history of audio-visual communication, thus producing a reductive view of both media history and audio-visual 'language acquisition'.

The pedagogic relation to the audience has an institutional and cultural authority that reaches back to the foundation of broadcasting in Britain. But over the years in which Beckett's plays for television were being produced by the BBC, the power of the pedagogic discourse waned substantially and has now in many respects been overtaken by a paedocratic relation to the audience. Existing academic work on Beckett's television plays inhabits this dialectical tension between paedocracy and pedagogy and is a component of a wider issue of the legacy of Modernism that structures debates about the function of both 'high' and 'popular' culture. The institution of Beckett criticism derives its notions of the politics of textuality and spectatorship from the Modernist culture in which Beckett was a leading figure. As I have argued earlier in this book, Beckett's television plays represent a television tradition that connects to Modernism in television, film, radio, theatre, literature and the visual arts. In the 1960s, a liberal discourse on contemporary media gained currency by linking Modernist pedagogical aims to expand audiences' intellectual horizons with a paedocratic discourse that claimed childlike openness to experiment, and the valuation of childhood as a mode of experiencing that liberated perception from the dry conventionality of 'adult' relationships with contemporary media. Marshall McLuhan (1987, first published 1964), for example, argued that media users, especially television viewers, interacted with media in a parallel way to children's supposed creative and involved relation to the world around them. McLuhan's work proposed that electronic media like television surpassed the linear, rationalistic and literary heritage of Western civilisation by returning to an iconic, tribal and bardic mode which he associated both with 'primitive' tribal societies and with Modernist art. Young people, for McLuhan, were equipped with valuable interests and competencies in responding to television and other recent media forms, as well as with the energy to embrace social change which he also valued and saw around him in the 1960s. Like some of the popular movements of the time which drew on Romantic conceptions of nature, childhood and organic social utopianism, McLuhan's use of the figure of the child represents a call for the reinvigoration of technological culture by a paradoxical return to a pre-existing Nature. Both broadly positive and negative theories of media draw on childhood in ways which largely reinforce conventional understandings of the child as different from adults, and socially and culturally in process. For both pessimists and optimists, the figure of the child was a key component in understanding a Western metropolitan society perceived to be dominated in new and significant ways by mass media culture. While I am not suggesting that Beckett was consciously a disciple of McLuhan, the cultural visibility of McLuhanism as a means of validating popular media technologies such as television forms a bridge between intellectuals' attitudes to pedagogical Modernist concerns with experimental art-forms and the paedocratic discourse in which television audiences can be valued because of their childlike predilections rather than in spite of them. The upshot of this debate is that Beckett's work is both pedagogical and paedocratic, for it both 'teaches' its audience how to look and sets up modes of address that discipline how the dramas can be understood, and also critiques notions of authority by questioning the hierarchies of voice and image and the ability of figures in the plays to control their perception, memory and emotions. Despite their apparent seriousness, sobriety and elite cultural positioning, the dramas are self-consciously playful about their use of dramatic conventions and their reflexive invocation of television forms as well as textual elements drawn from other media.

Viewer and viewed

As this chapter has shown, there is a long tradition of discussing Beckett's television (and other work) in relation to painting, and remarks abound such as Martha Fehsenfeld's (1982: 361) suggestion in relation to *Quad* that 'He has painted a picture'. The approach has often been useful, but historically the recourse to reference to painting has often been made out of frustration with a dominant literary and theoretical tradition. For example, Lois Oppenheim (2000) produced her study of Beckett's relationships with painting in order to shift the critical focus on his work away from his disputed status as Modernist or post-modernist, by discussing earlier traditions of figuration and Cubism, Dada, German Expressionism, Mark Rothko, Surrealism, Bram van Velde and Andy Warhol. There is very little in Oppenheim's book that discusses the painterly qualities of Beckett's theatre work, and almost nothing about his television plays. Arguments about the status of the television screen's image as a two-dimensional plane and the figuration of television images draw attention to the abstract composition of the television image as a moving pattern of dots and lines rather than the photographic assumption of a finished and concrete object. Making Beckett's plays in black-and-white draws attention to the material base of the image, by contrast with the colour programmes surrounding them. Moreover the problems of interpreting the non-naturalistic action and space of the plays draw attention to the role of the viewer as interpreter, working with the audio-visual materials presented to him or her. This kind of awareness of interpretation as a relational structure was what Marshall McLuhan (1964: 313) was keen to emphasise: 'The TV image is not a still shot. It is not a photo in any sense, but a ceaselessly forming contour of things limned by the scanning-finger. The resulting plastic contour appears by light through, not light on, and the image so formed has the quality of sculpture and icon, rather than of picture ... the viewer of the TV mosaic, with technical control of the image, unconsciously reconfigures the dots into an abstract work of art on the pattern of a Seurat or a Roualt.' The viewer is then a sort of artist, with a deep involvement in the process of representation, and is no longer the alienated consumer of a fragmentary commodity object. In dialogue with Georges Duthuit about the works of Bram van Velde, an abstract painter whose work he particularly admired, Beckett (1965: 19–20) described him as 'the first to submit wholly to the incoercible absence of relation', and described the art as other to the conventional tradition of representing its subject but having rather a performative status, actively mediating the relation between making, object and perception, 'an expressive act, even if only of itself, of its impossibility, of its obligation'. Reference to painting as an explanatory discourse for Beckett's screen work opens up the simultaneous connection and separation of that work from pictorial art, as discussed above. Each of the component terms in the comparison between television and art becomes unstable, as each threatens to adopt the characteristics of the other.

At least since his essay on Proust, Beckett had been interested in the relationships between perception and vision, the relations between people, and the desire to know. In *Proust*, he writes, 'the observer infects the observed with his own mobility' (1957: 6). Since both the perceiving subject and the object of perception are mobile and in process, Beckett concludes that 'whatever the object, our thirst for possession is, by definition, insatiable' (1957: 7). In the novel *Murphy*, looking and consuming the object of the look is also associated with 'the type-tragedy of the human relationship whose failure is preordained' (1957: 7). In *Murphy* the title character scrutinises Mr Endon's eyes, and later, at the end of *The Lost Ones*, the last remaining figure inspects the unseeing eyes of a vanquished woman. What the television plays and *Film* do is to turn this questing and failing relationship between the subject who looks and the object looked at into a quest for perception of the self (and this is also pursued in *Krapp's Last Tape* by means of aural records of past selves reviewed in the play's present). The eye searches for its object, an object that is perpetually ungraspable. The failure of this visual relationship means that both the subject of seeing and the object of sight cannot constitute themselves through an achieved relationship. Each of them remains mobile and unfixed, incomplete and unable to establish the boundaries between self and other. The television plays are structured as observation, whether solely by the camera or also including an observing voice or figure. But since the perceiving subject and the object perceived remain ungrasped and lacking, these audio-visual texts deconstruct the stability of observation on which they appear to be based.

Beckett's work for television and film engages directly with the issues of illusion, the elusive and evanescent properties of the television and film image, and the allusion to other works in the same and in different media, that are signalled by the titles of the dramas. *Ghost Trio*, *...but the clouds...*, and *Nacht und Träume* are titled respectively in direct reference to Beethoven's *Geister Trio*, Yeats's poem 'The Tower' and a Schubert *Lied*, and each of them incorporates direct aural quotations from those sources. The invocation of voice present in the title of *Eh Joe* is also significant, and the title of *Quad* can be regarded as an allusion to the space of the television screen. This use of allusion is closely connected with questions of illusory presence, fantasy, evanescence and illusion, in which absent others and acts of memory and repetition form the structural conceit of each work (Herren 2007). However, by contrast, the cultural situation of television has conventionally privileged the opposite pole of television and film representation: the ability of the media to reflect and reproduce the real. The naturalistic form of the majority of television and film drama, the iconic quality of visual and aural signifiers in both media, and the assumption that the image is an analogue of what it represents, have placed television and film in the tradition of mimetic arts.

This tension between the mimetic and the abstractly formal is crucial to Beckett's television and film work. On one hand, sets, action and narrative are progressively reduced to a set of elements that are combined and juxtaposed with a systematic and almost mathematical quality that signifies the unimportance of conventional realism. Yet on the other hand, the specificity and concreteness of visual and aural signifiers are insisted upon. The particular connotations of the greatcoat in *Ghost Trio*, the bowler hat in *...but the clouds...*, the goblet in *Nacht und Träume*, and the costumes in *Quad*, are strikingly significant in contrast to this formal abstraction. The abstraction of the visual form of the plays, especially perhaps *Ghost Trio*, seems to call for a Cartesian concept of matter and space, in which the universal forms of geometry and algebra are applicable. Despite the command by the voice in *Ghost Trio* to pay attention to the specificity of the floor, the wall, the pallet, etc, it is the geometric regularity of these forms and their potential exchangeability with each other that is most evident. The plays require the viewer to engage with objects inasmuch as they correspond to concepts, rather than objects in their particularity, yet at the same time insist on the particularity and concreteness of objects. The position of the observer or observing agency, and the material conditions in which visibility can occur, are offered in problematic forms. Thus the dramas simultaneously invoke the relationship between vision and knowledge and also introduce the incompleteness of desire and the failure to apprehend self and other that undercuts vision and knowledge. The same structure underpins the intertextual allusions to works of art and cultural traditions in the dramas, where Beckett 'approaches his traditional sources from a critical modern perspective; and, where he finds their examples inadequate for his purposes, he freely refutes his predecessors and revises their forms' (Herren 2007: 22). But where Herren positions these related works of art as 'sources' adopted for an authorial 'purpose', they should more accurately be understood as part of an intertextual network that includes Beckett's own reiterations of an encounter with television and motifs adopted elsewhere in his oeuvre. The position of the 'source' and its reconfiguration, the medium and its allusions to other media, and the author and his role as one node among a paradigmatic and syntagmatic complex of textual sites, are all rendered volatile in the relationships that this chapter has collected under the term 'intertextuality'.

5

Evaluations

Introduction

As earlier chapters have shown, critical response to the canon of British television drama from the 1960s to the present focuses on oppositions between critical realism and aesthetic modernism. Critics' responses to Beckett's work reflected the changing emphases of this critical debate over naturalistic political drama versus avant-garde form. The movement of British television drama from the 1960s to today has been away from theatricality and Modernist experiment with the medium, in favour of elaborations of filmic naturalism, seen as relevant, contemporary and politically progressive. Thus Beckett's television plays are situated within a complex dialectic of critical discourses around the aesthetics and politics of television drama, which are important to studies of television history. Part of this debate is over the address to the television audience, and the chapter will connect critical work on Beckett's television plays with discursive models of how television audiences have been discussed by authors, critics and television institutions, since assumptions about audiences for drama and arts programming affected the presentation and scheduling of the plays. The chapter also presents archival research on data collected by BBC Audience Research, which reveals how the plays were received by actual viewers, and thus the chapter complements existing studies of audience response to television which have focused on popular television drama and its viewers in both theoretical and empirical terms.

Broadcasting and conceptions of audience

In the context of a tradition of critical discussion that characterises Beckett's plays for television (and his other work) as attempts to engage with nothingness, absence and death, this chapter argues that the television plays are critical explorations of the problematics of presence and absence inherent in the conceptions and histories of broadcasting. Broadcasting has been understood for over a century by means of two different metaphorical and ideological frameworks. In the first, broadcasting is speaking into a void. Until the advent of interactive television at the end of the twentieth century, its apparatus (more appropriately named by the French term *dispositif*) consisted of centrally generated broadcast signals received by a mass audience which is nevertheless atomised by its separation into single viewers or small groups of viewers watching their television sets. This entailed the necessary non-response of the audience to whom a broadcast is addressed. The viewer/listener is posited as a destination or receiver, but cannot be present as an interlocutor and is instead solicited or delegated within broadcast texts. These viewer delegates include representations of internal auditors or addressees (like Joe in *Eh Joe*, or Figure in *Ghost Trio*), and visible or audible audiences within programmes. In television programmes other than Beckett's drama, such as chat shows or situation comedy, audience groups are seen and heard in programmes with a similar function of standing in for the television audience, but in drama these forms of represented delegation are rare. The opening words of *Ghost Trio* are 'Good evening'. This is the conventional means to welcome the viewer to the start of a television programme, particularly in programmes belonging to the genres of news, magazine programmes and light entertainment such as game shows. The common factor in these different television genres is their setting in a television studio, their use of a presenter who speaks directly to the audience, and an assumption of immediacy or liveness such that the television programme appears either to be broadcast live or before a studio audience that is present at the recording. The effect of the phrase 'Good evening' is obviously to acknowledge the presence of the viewer, and to include him or her in the broadcast. By contrast, television drama almost never uses this address to the viewer, since the positioning of the audience for the programme is different and is closer to the notion of spectatorship deployed in theories of cinema.

The psychoanalytic theory of spectatorship is used much less in the discussion of television than in the analysis of film. One of the reasons for this is the different kind of attention presupposed on the part of the viewer in each medium. Whereas the film spectator is encouraged to give full attention to the screen because of the darkness of the cinema, the surrounding sound and the commitment to the film produced by payment for a ticket, the television viewer has been regarded as a glancing and often inattentive spectator. For these reasons, notions of the spectator's identification with the projection apparatus as a source of vision, identification with the camera as perceiving subjectivity, and identification with on-screen characters as fantasised and desired subject-positions for the spectator have been gradually abandoned in television analysis. Furthermore, television is experienced as a flow, in which the boundaries between texts are not always clear, and where interruptions by advertisements and trailers are common. However, Beckett's plays are structured to demand attentive viewing because of their relative lack of camera movement, long takes and lack of visual spectacle, and this brings them closer to cinema. Writing from a US perspective, Graley Herren (2007: 49) characterises the television medium's conventional mode of spectatorship as determined by its political economy, which in the USA depends on advertising to support programme production: 'The medium traditionally demands no more activity from its audience than that they buy its advertised products. Conversely, Beckett's teleplays attempt to reinforce a strict modernist sensibility upon a medium generally oriented toward mass appeal.' As earlier chapters have shown, the actual historical conditions of the production of Beckett's dramas by BBC (and by SDR in Germany) were not influenced at all by this consideration, because these productions were firmly within a non-commercial tradition of Public Service Broadcasting. However, Herren's reference to Modernism accurately points to the mode of address to the viewer in Beckett's drama that involves the intense engagement of the addressee with the programme as a text, largely detached from the extended social reality of the viewing experience and dependent on the viewer's absorption and concentration on the programme.

In the rare instances when Beckett's dramas have been screened in Britain on a channel funded by advertising, this mode of address and requirement of spectatorship was carried across into that different context in a very unusual way. When Channel 4 broadcast its *Beckett on Film* adaptations of Beckett's theatre plays, they were not interrupted by advertisements unless the original text contained an internal break where a theatre interval could occur. In *Happy Days* and in *Waiting for Godot*, there were interruptions for commercials between the first and second acts, but all the other plays were broadcast uninterrupted. On channels without advertising breaks, like the BBC or Germany's SDR, Beckett's plays were shown uninterrupted, like any other programme. In television drama performance, following the conventions of theatrical and cinematic representation, the audience is coded as an unacknowledged observer of the action, which takes place in a space that is removed from the space of the audience and is not open to the response or reaction of the viewing audience or an audience represented within the programme. Clearly, Beckett's television plays work within a tradition of hollowing out the place of the viewer/listener, akin to the spectator position established in film, but they also engage with the different situation of the viewer in television watching. Beckett's plays do this occasionally by directing an address to him or her, or including figures within the text who may stand in for the television viewer as destination for a communication. In terms of the disposition of the viewer, Beckett's plays are hybrids between conventionally cinematic and televisual forms of spectatorship.

In a second understanding of television broadcasting as communication, broadcasting has been understood (especially in Western Europe) as the casting of seed that may fruitfully grow in the soil of the audience community. This is evident in the British concept of Public Service Broadcasting, for instance, where the universally available broadcast of material considered socially valuable, like Beckett's work, bets on its future productivity for some (at least) of its audience. This quasi-religious and hopeful vision of broadcasting as communication is evident in Beckett's television work too, not only in the historical circumstances of its production in Britain and Germany, discussed in earlier chapters, but also in the risk or hope of, or the belief in, communicative effectivity that the plays' dialogic scenarios depend on. The pedagogic functions of Voice in *Ghost Trio* and her relation to the viewer, the authority of Voice's tone and her instructions as to how to view, could be interpreted in relation to the mythology of BBC programmes including drama in the BBC's public service functions. 'Auntie BBC', with a Reithian heritage of education and improvement, could be connoted by the play's address to its viewer. However, although Part One of the play introduces the audience to the space, and Part Two to the movement of the figure, Part Three has no voice-over. The dynamics of the audience's relationship to the play therefore change, with a consequent implication that the viewer has learned how to find his or her place as the audience imagined by the play's discourse. This chapter analyses the television plays, and the conceptions of medium and audience they suggest, in terms of these dual understandings of broadcasting as dissemination.

Beckett and television criticism

Television theorists are part of the audience for television, obviously, but this fact has not always been recognised, since the discursive forms of theoretical writing set up the analyst as an other, both to the programmes he or she discusses and to the empirical 'ordinary' audience. The issue of why academic television criticism does not refer to Beckett's work requires an evaluation of the ways that television drama is cited in academic writing, and on how a particular identity for 'Beckett' would be produced by Television Studies if it were to cite him as an example. If Beckett's work is separated by television theory from the context of its production as an example, and from an awareness of the subject-position of the theorist discussing it, this runs the risk of fetishising the work as an apparently unitary and undetermined object. A reflexive approach to the significance of Beckett's work restores it to the conditions which govern its citation and non-citation and therefore generates a dialogue between the plays and the dynamic politics of theory. I briefly explore the reasons why it is not cited, and thus recognise that the citation of Beckett is part of a struggle around the politics of theory as well as of television drama. Such a reflexive approach also responds to the dialogic and situated form of his work itself, since his dramatic work for television features dialogic structure and is in dialogue with television forms and reception contexts, as earlier chapters have demonstrated.

When academic studies of British television drama began to emerge after the late 1950s and 1960s, they largely focused on the one-off television play and on the authorship of these texts. The studies of television which emerged in book form were focused on the single play and on the authorship of play texts (Thomas 1959, Shubik 1975, Brandt 1981, Bull 1984), or interviews with writers (Pike 1982). Despite the emphases of Raymond Williams (1990, first published 1974) and Horace Newcomb (1974), for example, who wrote about popular series and serial drama too, critical conceptions of television drama centred on single plays in prestigious anthology series. Newspaper reviewing of television, largely confined to upmarket broadsheet papers, also focused on these dramas. Beckett's television plays were not screened in drama anthology series on BBC1 or ITV, but in arts programming slots on BBC2, and this militated against considering them in relation to work by such writers for television as David Mercer, Trevor Griffiths, or Dennis Potter, whose plays were seen in that more mainstream context. BBC arts programming screened plays both by writers whose work was known in other media (like Beckett), and also by writers who produced work for anthology drama as well (like David Mercer). But the academic canonisation of television drama did not extend to works in this arts programme context. While Beckett's television plays lend themselves to being considered in the dominant critical discourses around authored drama, the fact that they were not screened in drama anthology slots separates them from the canon being developed by academics of the time. But a significant critical tradition in the field neglected single television plays entirely. Theorists of television including Williams or John Ellis (1982) had an interest in the 'flow' of television – in other words, temporal sequences which are not bounded by the beginning and end of programmes. It is a Cultural Studies agenda, rather than a theatrical or literary one, which underlies this attention to dynamic audience response rather than textual meanings. Television Studies shifted its focus away from the one-off television drama, and within broadcasting too, powerful institutional and economic forces have been working against Beckett's kind of television drama, as later work in this chapter explains.

A significant aspect of the agenda of television criticism has been the unevenly successful dialogue between academics and television professionals (Millington and Nelson 1986, Tulloch and Alvarado 1983, Tulloch 1990, and Bignell *et al.* 2000a). Unlike those socialist writers whose topics and dramatic forms often concern power-relations, dominant histories and hegemonic institutions, and the agency of 'the people' in political struggles, Beckett's work is not closely aligned with the agendas of the cultural formation in which many British academics and dramatists work. That cultural formation could be broadly defined as one in which, as Raymond Williams (1981) powerfully argued, culture is seen not only as the expression of social forces but also as an agent of social change. British Television Studies academics and creative workers have shared a commitment to this progressive leftist ideology of culture. This left-wing agenda conceived of the television play as a communicative statement, in which questions of form were in the service of notions of intention, message, mimesis and contemporaneity. These concerns were not univalent and could support divergent views, for example in the vexed argument over the radical potential of naturalistic form versus developing approaches to drama-documentary and metafiction. However, the legacy of this agenda in screen studies has been to restrict critical attention to a canon of single television plays, and the dominance of a critical discourse based on authorship, ideology-critique and textual analysis. The alliances formed between socialist television academics and professionals on the basis of the discourses which they share have enabled a productive dialogue to occur between them, but this formation does not include Beckett, whose supposed formalism and abstraction place him outside it.

Critical work on television has recently focused on genres and series rather than one-off programmes, on television audiences rather than authorship, on 'popular' rather than 'elite' programming. In more recent times, academic studies focused on individual programmes but included sitcom, soap opera and popular drama serials as well as single plays (Brandt 1993). Robin Nelson (1997) wrote chapters on critical issues as well as analyses of programmes and included US-produced popular drama and drama series, with relatively few chapters dealing with single television dramas. This process of change derives from the influence of other disciplines than literary studies on the study of television, and from the resulting shifts in the object of study itself. Social science research has situated television in relation to models of the reproduction of social order and the constitution of public (versus private) discourses, the role of broadcasting institutions and their regulation and ownership, and the constitution of audiences. This focus tends to miss television drama since the topic of study is mass communication, in relation to specific audience groups and their reaction to popular genre programming or to kinds of content found in many different programmes (like violence or representations of minority groups). So, in summary, the specific audience formations comprising professional television critics and theorists have not been likely to take an interest in Beckett's work for television, since its aesthetic and institutional forms are distant from their concerns. The less politically engaged tradition of Beckett Studies, however, has begun to analyse the television plays extensively, most often in relation to rarefied theoretical and philosophical debates and not in relation to the historiography of their medium or their actual audiences.

The place of the viewer

Much of the existing criticism of Beckett's television plays has drawn attention to parallels between the structure and form of the plays and philosophical writing. While this has opened up interesting avenues of critical interpretation, too often the plays have been seen as illustrations of concerns with being, subjectivity, vision and transcendence in the philosophical discourses that Beckett himself knew. Because the plays are resistant to interpretation as psychologically realist studies of characters and are characterized by the reduction of narrative, setting and story, they lend themselves to these parallels with European philosophy. However, these arguments based in philosophical illustration may be suggestive of critical interpretation, but they often fail to account for the specifically televisual aspects of the plays' meanings and how these manipulations of television convention affect the viewer's available strategies for interpretation. For example, the use of music in *Ghost Trio* can be connected to the manipulation of visual form in the play. Just as the manipulation of rectangular shapes foregrounds the means of representation and the spatial codes of the performance space and of the television screen, the presence of the tape recorder in *Ghost Trio* may be a reflexive commentary on the use of music in television. The conventional codes for the use of off-screen music in television are similar to those in cinema. Music is used as a mechanism for defining the tone of the programme, for generating signs which direct the viewer how to perceive the pacing, emphasis, emotional register and dramatic turning-points of a play. Music for television is composed after the performance itself and is added to the tape or film during the post-production phase. It is generally used in an 'invisible' manner, subservient to the action of the performers and the rhythms of editing and framing established by the director. Linda Ben-Zvi (1985: 35) regards the music of *Ghost Trio* as a reflexive mechanism to expose 'the artifice of background music'. Certainly, the inclusion of repeated phrases in *Ghost Trio* draws attention not only to the music itself but also to the significance of its use. Whenever the Figure switches on the tape recorder and music is heard, the camera moves closer to him. Rather than being a secondary device to point out significant camera movements or developments in the action, music seems to function as a primary trigger for camera movement. Sound becomes primary, and the manipulation of the television image secondary. Yet despite Ben-Zvi's comments, music in *Ghost Trio* remains significant in terms of tone, reinforcing the Romanticism, nostalgia and loss that are available through the expression, gesture and movement of the Figure, through the Voice's notification that Figure thinks he hears the approach of the absent woman, and through the resignation and lifelessness conveyed by the slow pace of editing and speech and by the greyness of the space as a whole. The music is therefore simultaneously foregrounded and to an extent separate from the other elements of the programme, yet it is also an integrated element of the play which supports the other elements of performance and mise-en-scène. For the viewer, this poses the problem of how to hierarchise the different signifying registers of the piece.

The effect of the separation between the television viewer and the figures in the plays is doubled and reflected in the separation between voice or narrator and the visible figure. Often in Beckett's television plays, a central figure is engaged in a process of reflection, narration or projection that seems to be a component of an on-going process of the realisation of self and the external world through relations established between that self and an external world often represented by an other person. In *Ghost Trio*, Figure several times approaches the mirror in which he might see himself and only finally looks there with an enigmatic smile that does not suggest an achieved self. Joe in *Eh Joe* seems to suffer when repeatedly assaulted by Voice, which is in any case ambiguously posed as an external or internal one. M in *...but the clouds...* strives to unite his self in the present with

W and M1, who appear to represent aspects of his own past. In television adaptations of Beckett's theatre plays, such as *Krapp's Last Tape*, *Not I*, *Rockaby* and *Play*, similar kinds of split subject, confusions between figure and voice, and past and present selves, also occur. The presence of an other is necessary to the sense of self, but the plays dramatise an uncertain boundary between these two. This leads to the incompleteness of both self and other and the inadequacy of representation to resolve this problem, although representation dramatises it and makes it present.

Eckart Voigts-Virchow (2000–1: 124) points to the titles of the plays as indications that they refer to the questioning of being through the questioning of television: 'Significantly, his titles address three metaphors which may be related to precisely the ontological destabilization of TV: images as *ghosts*, as *clouds*, and as *dreams*.' Ghosts, clouds and dreams are not produced under the conscious agency of a subject and are immaterial and intangible. In *Ghost Trio*, Figure thinks he hears an indication of the presence of a woman who does not appear. In *...but the clouds...*, memory and voice seem to conjure up the ghostly presence of a lover. In *Nacht und Träume*, the play seems to dramatise the experience of a dream or vision. As I have argued in other sections of this book, the means of realising these ideas in television form are themselves in dialogue with the assumptions of iconic representation in the medium, supporting those critical interpretations which focus on the plays as metadiscourses about the medium. Inasmuch as the self communicates and stages relations with an other outside itself, it must also be recognisable to itself as an other that another self might communicate with. Similarly, the other must be posed as a potential self with whom the communicating self can establish a relation. Self and other invert and double themselves in the process of communication, and as a precondition for staging that communication (Herren 2007: 16). The verb 'staging' is useful for understanding how this works in the plays, because communication is a spatial process in which position and extension provide the perceptible ground for relations between selves and objects to be proposed. Communication in the television plays 'takes place' even if the act of communication and the significance of what may be communicated are undercut and incomplete. Place and stage demonstrate the specific concrete materiality of the communicative relation, in contrast to the idealisation and abstraction of language and persona that are so often remarked on in Beckett's work.

On this basis, the persistent motif of interpreting Beckett's work in relation to philosophical concerns with identity, language and otherness makes sense, but can be recast as a meditation on the communicative relations which are at stake in broadcasting. Beckett's television dramas divide their personae into two, voice and body, present and past, internal and external. One of the consequences of this is that the personae lack any sense of their own identity as comprising a unity between these two parts. Figure's look at himself in the mirror in *Ghost Trio*, and his failure to realise in the present his desire for the absent loved one signified by the music is an example of this. In a similar way, Joe seems unable to recognise Voice as a part of himself. In *...but the clouds...*, M cannot reconcile himself with M1 and complete a satisfactory narrative connecting his present to the past. At the end of *Film*, E and O do not unite. This separation between self and other, creator and created, inner and outer expresses the fundamental tensions of Western philosophical thought explored variously by Berkeley, Schopenhauer, Husserl, Lyotard, Freud, Lacan and many others.

So while it has been common to discuss Beckett's plays by way of theories of self-consciousness of self, often with a Romantic nostalgia which concludes by restating a lack in being that has a poetic quality, it would be more accurate to discuss the plays as dramatising the unstable boundary between self and other. For both the recognition of the self and the recognition of the other depend upon the possibility of perceiving an otherness within the self, and perceiving an analogous self within the other. This philosophical and ethical structure recalls the work of Levinas, and the structure of invagination, doubling and blurred boundaries, is analogous to the conceptual structure outlined by Derrida. Within these terms, there is no necessity for Romantic nostalgia and negative theology. For the interdependent relation between self and other, inner and outer, representation and the real, object and concept, are constitutive of meaning and do not in themselves possess an ethical or moral value. They are the inescapable terms of Western metaphysics. This conclusion also explains the divide in Beckett's plays between image and sound, body and voice, for this separation works with the possibility that there can be a correspondence between these two media of representation yet also denies their equivalence and translation into each other. Symbolisation, whether in image or language, can be regarded as a form of 'writing' that establishes a constitutive relationship between the real and its representation. Yet this relationship can never be one of equivalence or adequacy. Furthermore, each system of symbolisation has its own particularity as a signifying system and is necessarily untranslatable into another. The apparent parallels between Beckett's drama and these debates in Western metaphysics emerge from the specific forms of symbolisation and communicative relation that broadcasting depends on, inasmuch as it constructs both a necessary relationship and a necessary non-correspondence between the broadcast and its viewer.

Schedules and audiences

One of the key shifts in television production and television criticism is the emphasis on audience, both as a discursive category produced by texts, institutions and technologies, and as a real and specific collection of viewers. In relation to debates over dramatic form and the engagement of audiences, the formal characteristics of Beckett's work demand consideration of these issues because of the primacy of voice and the implication of address to figures and audiences within the work itself as a means of representing the dynamics of viewership. Screening Beckett's plays in the arts programme slots *The Lively Arts* or *Arena* on BBC, or in schools programming blocks on Channel 4 with *Beckett on Film*, are decisions that discipline the ways that audiences will perceive them. Within some programmes, notably *Shades'* enfolding discussion with Martin Esslin and Melvin Bragg, and the introductory remarks preceding SDR's broadcast of Beckett plays in the 1980s, there is explicit guidance as to how the plays should be approached and understood. There is a long and scarcely researched history of this audience positioning practice: for example, the BBC used the scheduling of *The Wednesday Play* (1964–70) between the news and late-evening discussion programmes to produce a discursive context for the plays within the schedule and outside it in press controversy. The aim was both to generate audience interest and to control the lines of audience interpretation (Macmurraugh-Kavanagh 1997b).

Within broadcasting institutions, drama producers construct the audience discursively either as a statistical abstraction or as a foundation on which they can build arguments about the form and function of drama. The television producer Irene Shubik (1975: 179) explained, for instance: 'it has always been the straightforward documentary-type subject which gets the highest audiences, while the more adventurous a play is "stylistically", the smaller its audience is likely to be. One can certainly conclude (if one did not know it already) that the majority of people favour the familiar and expected over the new and unusual.' This comment relates to shifts in policy regarding the audience within the BBC. As Ien Ang (1991) has described, the BBC moved from a conception of a disciplined audience (where programme types, levels of intellectual content, and scheduling patterns would gradually school the audience to listen or watch in a particular way) to a conception of the audience as citizens or consumers exercising a free choice. The introduction of ITV in 1955 forced the BBC to compete against determinedly 'popular' (often American) formats like action drama series and quizzes, and to collect ratings information and aim for minimum audience shares. The conception of British society as a cultural pyramid gave way to a conception of cultural pluralism where the BBC would reflect contemporary society rather than leading it. Hugh Greene (Director General 1960–9) said of BBC output: 'I don't care whether what is reflected in the mirror is bigotry, injustice and intolerance or accomplishment and inspiring achievement. I only want the mirror to be honest, without any curves, and held with as steady a hand as may be' (Briggs 1985: 331). The BBC thus served the audience as intermediary and honest broker and had to appeal to all sectors of society. This suppressed the ideological role of the broadcaster by focusing on the technical means of reflecting society and by stressing professionalism. Such a conception put great power in the hands of producers to determine what should be broadcast, and made clear that their work would be evaluated in terms of their professional competence. This freed producers from external judgements (they were evaluated in the terms of their own peer-group) but also cut them off from the audience, and yet making claims about the audience continued to be a key means of legitimating production decisions. Irene Shubik (1975: 106) defended the BBC's focus on social realism partly by a conception of audience which justified the canon of naturalist and documentary-based drama: 'the characters and situations it describes are portrayed in a readily recognisable "every-day" way and the level of observation of them and their lives is that of good journalism. The writers whose observation plumbs below this level ... are very few, and often disturbing to a mass audience.' The audience was conceived as a collection of diverse and autonomous individuals who the broadcaster cannot discipline in terms of their viewing habits or interests. Broadcasters would not mould their audience but reproduce it in its existing form, on an analogy with the market of autonomous consumers surveyed by empirical market research, and would offer products which related to the audience's needs and preferences. Beckett's work stood out markedly and differently from this set of attitudes to the audience.

Empirical data and contemporary publications reveal how the reception of Beckett's television dramas diverged remarkably between the reactions of generally critical 'ordinary viewers' and more approving professional critics and journalists. Conventionally, the attraction of television drama for the audience has been that it 'offers precisely a "portrait" of individuals and, through such portrayals, the promise of revelation – a sense of insight into the territories of desire and, beyond this, affirmation of the ground of experience in individual identity and personal relationships' (Adams 1998: 149). However, increasingly Beckett's television work became much easier to understand as formalist experimentation rather than stories about people. Elizabeth Klaver (1991: 375) argues that the text of *Quad* is 'a blueprint in which the architecture of the piece is described in diagrams and in mathematical codes which direct the series of permutations' and makes the general point that the later television works are technical instructions rather than dramatic texts in the usual sense (see also Hiebel, 1993). This exacerbated the actual viewing audience's difficulties in understanding or enjoying them. Study of the reception of Beckett's television plays is useful in itself for understanding their significance as cultural interventions, and also reflects back on the relative significance of the television audience's and the press's reactions as legitimating instances that the BBC as an institution could choose to attend to or ignore. In the context of the regard for Beckett and his work at the BBC, reaction to his work from professional critics and ordinary viewers formed a parallel text alongside the plays themselves, a text which could variously challenge or support the institutional validation of Beckett and experimental television drama more generally.

The institutional power of Beckett, his BBC collaborators and the distinguished performers in the plays was at odds with the audience reception of the television plays, which gained very small audiences and unfavourable reactions. Those audiences did not receive the plays as being critical and interesting but thought they were dense and boring. The first available survey of audience reaction to a televised Beckett piece was carried out for the BBC production of *Waiting for Godot*, screened from 9.50 to 11.20 pm on Monday 26 June 1961 (BBC WAC R/9/7/52). The audience was estimated as 5 per cent of the UK population, compared with 22 per cent of the population who were watching the drama *Harpers West One* on ITV at that time. The BBC's Audience Research department recorded the reactions of the 81 members (12 per cent) of their viewing panel who saw the play. The Reaction Index for the play (a measure of appreciation scored out of 100) was 32, well below the average of 66 for plays transmitted from

London in the first quarter of 1961. The BBC report, quoting some of the viewers' answers to researchers' questions, summarised the opinions of the large group giving low marks to the play: 'Their complete bewilderment was occasionally expressed with humility – "the whole thing was much too abstract for my taste" – but more often with frustration coupled with anger – "a lot of fatuous nonsense. I'm not even going to try to decide, as the critics did for months when it first came out, what the author was getting at", and "I'm no Royal Courtier praising the Emperor's new clothes" are comments in point'. A small number of viewers found the play rewarding and engaging, including three or four viewers who found the language compelling to listen to even though they did not understand it, and several viewers praised the acting. But aside from the obvious point that viewers clearly did not regard the play as entertaining television, nor even intriguing as experimental drama, it is the theatre references that are interesting here. At least some viewers were aware of Beckett's significance as a theatre dramatist at this time, and the quotation from a viewer denying that he or she was a 'Royal Courtier' is clearly a reference to the Royal Court Theatre and the burgeoning drama culture in London in the period. The Royal Court was introducing British social realism, and Modernist (sometimes European) drama with influences from Brecht and Artaud, to the stage and building on the contexts of Existentialism, Absurdism and other challenges to naturalism that were becoming the dominant discourses for placing and interpreting Beckett's work. However, there is little sense from the BBC's audience sample that the viewers recognised this dramatic culture as appropriate to television.

This pattern of reaction continued subsequently for both television adaptations and original television plays by Beckett. BBC archives contain internal Audience Research reports on the 13 November 1963 television version of *Krapp's Last Tape* (BBC WAC R9/7/63) and the 1966 *Eh Joe* (BBC WAC T5/1296/1). *Krapp's Last Tape* was directed by Constance Fitzgerald and produced by Peter Luke for the *Festival* strand of theatrical dramas, with Cyril Cusack as Krapp. The audience size was calculated as only 8 per cent of the UK population excluding infants, since only 123 viewers among the 1,100 on the audience panel saw the play. That night in 1963 there were not many people watching television, for while BBC attracted 8 per cent of the population, ITV did not fare much better with 11 per cent of the population. The Reaction Index for the play was 31, close to the very low Reaction Index of 32 for the 1961 BBC production of *Waiting for Godot*. For comparison, the five previous plays in the *Festival* slot had Reaction Indices ranging from 37 to 61, and Indices in the high 50s were the norm. The report noted:

> There was some scattered praise from about a dozen or so viewers who found 'Krapp's Last Tape' an arresting little piece of drama, with an intriguing and moving slant on the theme of lonely old age cherishing the memory of lost chances, but only half regretting the past. Several here spoke highly too, of the technique of presenting this situation by spotlighting ('in pure television style') a decrepit old fellow who is having a session with his collection of recorded tapes.

Appreciative viewers liked the play because they were attracted to its theme, which they understood as old age cherishing the past. A few commented that it was very televisual, enforcing a focus on Krapp by means of lighting that marked him out from the dull surroundings of his room, and using the separate audio track from his tape machine to separate his earlier selves from Cusack's performance as the older man. But the report continued: 'Even so, the point was made that the whole affair had a rather dragging pace, with little variety of action and the play depended entirely on the capabilities of one artist'. Furthermore, 'over two-thirds of those supplying evidence thought the play excruciatingly dull and dreary to watch'. The audience were evidently judging the play according to the conventions of naturalist and psychological drama, and this led to severe criticism of its realisation, and by implication the BBC's decision to produce it at all: 'Krapp's "den" looked too large for his supposed indigence, it was said, and there were many complaints about the detail (the lighting, as "too gloomy" in particular) of the production that viewers, grudgingly for the most part, admitted was in keeping with the mood of the play. One or two thought the management of the "flash-back" sequences (with scenes from Krapp's past appearing to issue from the mirror on the wall) just "plain silly".'

There was an audience research report on the BBC2 broadcast of *Eh Joe* in November 1966 using the same methods. Among the BBC's audience sample, 31 viewers were found to have watched the play, comprising the 3 per cent of the BBC2 viewing panel who saw all or most of it. The overall Reaction Index for the programme was the low figure of 49. One respondent wrote that the play invoked 'the pathetic condition of the isolated human being'. Several viewers liked the use of monologue over silent images, and one viewer wrote: 'Obviously television could be the medium for this sort of thing, and it is a good experiment.' But many viewers thought the play was very depressing, and compelling rather than enjoyable. A third of the sample said it was dull and dreary, with no visual appeal. One viewer wrote: 'I like plays with proper sets, not a bed and a couple of doors hidden by curtains.' This kind of reaction was not confined to Britain, and Julian Garforth (1992: 383) reports that when the SDR channel in Germany showed the version of *Eh Joe* directed there by Beckett in 1966, its late evening screening on the Erstes Programm minority channel achieved a 3 per cent share of the audience. Later, when BBC screened a season of Beckett's dramas for television and television adaptations of his theatre plays in December 1982, they achieved audience sizes too small to be counted, and were therefore not included in the figures produced by the Broadcasters Audience Research Bureau (BARB), the independent audience measurement agency that by then supplied statistical information to British television institutions. Programmes with fewer than 25 individuals reporting their reactions in interviews and by filling in response booklets were not included in the figures, owing to excessive margins of error when multiplied up to produce national figures. None of the Beckett plays had enough viewers in the audience sample to be measured, meaning that they had audiences of less than 0.1

per cent of the UK population.

By 1990, audience rating figures were produced by multiplying up the viewing patterns of people living in about three thousand homes, representative of the demographic profile of Britain as a whole, where television sets were connected to electronic equipment that registered viewing, and viewers also pushed buttons on a handset to show when they were in the room watching. Minute-by-minute viewing figures were produced each week for all programmes on all channels. It was in 1990 that *A Wake for Sam* was shown, the BBC commemoration of Beckett following his death. There were two programmes, on the evening of Saturday 27 January and then on Wednesday 31st. The first evening comprised the Open University's production of *Waiting for Godot*, Act Two, together with readings from Beckett's work, and ran from 7.25 to 8.50 pm on the BBC2 channel. On the sister BBC1 channel, programmes at this time were *The Paul Daniels Magic Show* and *Waterfront Beat* (a police drama). On the Wednesday from 9.25 until 10.20 pm, the compilation included *Krapp's Last Tape* (featuring Patrick Magee) and the 1966 *Eh Joe*. The audience for *A Wake for Sam* on 27 January was 0.4 million (BBC WAC R9/1153/1), whereas the most popular programme that evening was the dating game-show *Blind Date* on ITV, with an audience of 15.5 million. The BBC2 audience fell from the 1.7 million for *Newsview*, the current affairs roundup that preceded *A Wake for Sam*, and rose again after the Beckett tribute to 3.9 million for the entertainment talk show *Saturday Night Clive*. In terms of BBC2's showing in comparison with its competitors from 7.30 to 9.00 pm on 27 January, *A Wake for Sam* got just a 2 per cent share of the available audience watching television at the time of its broadcast.

From the early 1960s to the early 1990s, Beckett's work was frankly disastrous in terms of audience ratings, competitive audience share, or retention of the audience across an evening's broadcasting. Much the same pattern as occurred in Britain applied when the *Beckett on Film* series of television adaptations of Beckett's theatre work was screened on the RTE channel in Ireland in 2001. In the same way as Channel 4's screenings of

the plays in Britain, RTE grouped the plays into blocks, with
the exception of the longer dramas, and their audience sizes
were uniformly disappointing (Saunders 2007: 92). Damien
O'Donnell's *What Where*, Walter Asmus's *Footfalls* and John
Crowley's *Come and Go* were screened as a single programming
block, gaining an audience of 121,000. Patricia Rozema's *Happy
Days* and Conor McPherson's *Endgame* were shown as single
presentations and attracted 87,000 and 92,000 viewers respectively.
The programme featuring Atom Egoyan's *Krapp's Last
Tape*, shown alongside Enda Hughes's *Act Without Words II*, had
the highest rating of any of the programmes at 136,000 viewers
and was the earliest programme in the evening schedule for the
Beckett on Film season, beginning at 9.30 pm. But the audience
size for even these most popular plays compared very poorly to
the much larger audience for the British soap opera *EastEnders*
(460,000 viewers) that evening on RTE, and the subsequent
programme, the Irish-produced soap *Fair City* (743,000 viewers).
Beckett's most famous play, Michael Lindsay Hogg's version of
Waiting for Godot, was screened at 10.30 pm and had a recorded
audience of only 87,000. But clearly, these were not significant
considerations for the BBC or RTE, and any judgement of
Beckett's television work in these terms is bound to condemn it
on grounds that are not appropriate. There were good reasons
for the BBC to persist at least in showing Beckett's plays and in
making programmes about him and his work.

Reviewers and commentators

Neil Taylor (1998: 33) presents an exhaustive analysis of the
theatre writers whose work was shown on television between
1936 and 1994. Beckett's theatre plays were broadcast on only
eighteen occasions, and he ranks as the twenty-ninth most
broadcast twentieth-century dramatist. Television productions
of his work were far outstripped by the three most broadcast
twentieth-century playwrights, George Bernard Shaw, J. B.
Priestley and Noel Coward. When the works of dramatic writers
throughout the span from the ancient classical world to the

present day are considered, Shakespeare, Shaw and Ibsen have their works broadcast most, and Beckett drops down the list to the fortieth most broadcast playwright (Taylor 1998: 34–5). So statistical evidence of the frequency of broadcasts of Beckett's work, and quantitative and qualitative evidence of their reception by British viewers, show that the BBC had no motivation to commission or broadcast Beckett's plays as attractions to its audience. But this did not prevent the BBC from persisting into the 1980s and beyond with television versions of Beckett's theatre plays or his original dramas for television. Clearly, the cultural prestige of Beckett's name and of his work was sufficient to overcome such negative factors. In fact, it was the recognition of Beckett's significance among the powerful but tiny audience of cultural commentators and opinion-formers that legitimated the BBC's continued investment in Beckett's work.

In the 1960s and 1970s it was single plays in high-profile anthology series that were the drama programmes most regularly discussed by reviewers of television in the press (Caughie 1984), although press commentary was very often hostile. Furthermore, institutional support for single plays at the BBC was publicly solid but internally equivocal or even non-existent. Reaction to *Shades* placed Beckett's plays amidst debates about the politics of television form in the 1970s, despite the separation of the plays from the main body of television drama on BBC1 and BBC2. The reviewer Michael Billington (1977), primarily a theatre rather than television critic, called *Ghost Trio* 'a mesmeric piece of painting for TV' in a *Guardian* review and asked 'why naturalism [was] still television drama's dominant mode'. Discussion of the emerging canon of television drama, consisting mainly of plays which were considered in terms of political engagement or formal innovation, focused on critical realism (represented especially by the work of Tony Garnett and Ken Loach) or on aesthetic modernism (especially plays by Dennis Potter). Potter himself, working as a television critic in 1977 and referring to the *Shades* programme, asked in the *Sunday Times*, 'Is this the art which is the response to the despair and pity of our age, or is it made of the kind of futility which helped such desecrations of spirit, such filth of ideologies come into being?' The difference between Potter's and Billington's responses reflects the critical debate of the time over naturalistic political drama versus experimental form. Television work which could be described as innovative, difficult and serious, like Beckett's, has been addressed by discourses originating in literary Modernism, contrasting with the emphasis in Television Studies on social realism. With the important exceptions of a few writers such as David Mercer and Dennis Potter himself, the trajectory of development in British television drama since the 1960s has been away from what has been called (pejoratively) theatrical, literary or self-reflexive work, and toward television versions of cinematic naturalism, with its claims to be socially relevant, contemporary and politically engaged. It is Potter's negative assessment of *Shades*, as irrelevant to contemporary politics and society, which is representative of dominant thinking about television drama, rather than Billington's theatrically influenced, anti-naturalistic understanding of Beckett's work.

By 1972 when a *Radio Times* feature by Ruth Inglis supported a screening of *Krapp's Last Tape* in *Thirty Minute Theatre* on BBC2, the producer Tim Aspinall was quoted uneasily straddling claims for Beckett's power of address to the audience and defensive support for the reach and composition of the viewers: 'We've discovered that 57 per cent of our viewers are working class – whatever that means – but it does suggest that we're not being hopelessly highbrow. But then I'd be hard put to define what is highbrow or lowbrow. All I know is that Beckett writes straight from the heart and the stomach. I don't think you have to understand him intellectually. This play communicates primarily emotionally. Like all the best short plays, it gives you insight.' As part of this claim for the accessibility of Beckett's work, the article recounts that Aspinall spent a day with Beckett in Paris in 1972 and found him very down-to-earth. He was, apparently, talkative, fond of a drink and keen on cars. Although audiences were not drawn to *Krapp's Last Tape* rather than the competing programme on BBC1, *Sportsnight* featuring European Cup football, Aspinall defended the play on the grounds of its potential to move, educate and inspire viewers. Press reaction was important to the BBC because of the legitimacy that praise for demanding programmes granted to it as a Public Service Broadcasting body, and press reactions to Powell's *Lively Arts* programme *Shades* exemplify this.

Sean Day-Lewis reviewed *Shades* for the *Daily Telegraph* (16 April 1977), and wrote: 'Casual viewers who stray into The Lively Arts ... tonight are likely to think that something has gone seriously wrong with their sets ... The shades are all grey, Beckett does not believe in colour television, it seems, just in case too much information is let loose. And then the grey is made as misty as possible so that the characters are dimly perceived. This Tristram Powell production is not to be missed by those of us who are Beckett admirers, but it is uncompromising and may not make converts.' Day-Lewis's comments display an awareness of the problem of finding an audience for the plays while at the same time remaining true to the 'uncompromising' demands associated with Beckett's name by those in the know. Broadsheet newspaper reviews of *Not I*, *Ghost Trio* and *...but the clouds...* in the *Shades* programme were generally very positive, and were larded with references to high-culture producers and works including a comparison between *Not I* and 'Yoko Ono's film collage of backsides' and a description of *Ghost Trio* as 'a sort of minimal oblong of existence shot like a slowed up German Expressionist movie' (*The Observer*, 17 April 1977). Michael Ratcliffe's review for *The Times* on 18 April 1977 argued: 'There is no doubt that the reductionist scale and austerity of Beckett's late work is effective on the small screen, but the dynamics are pitched so low that if the plays were any longer you might well drop off. The timing of *Ghost Trio* was mesmeric, and Donald McWhinnie's direction, in which the camera advanced with tremulous hesitancy on the actor (Ronald Pickup) like a camera in the prehistoric days of moving films, created a world out of time and space.' The discourse of these reviews is fascinating for several reasons. First, Beckett's work was being understood in relation to landmark productions in the spheres of art (Yoko Ono), European cinema (German Expressionism) and silent cinema. This validates the contextual discussion conducted earlier in this book which showed that Beckett was perceived by television professionals as a European Modernist, in an arts culture comprising painting, cinema and sculpture (and not television). There are no comparative remarks in these reviews about Beckett's plays in relation to television drama of whatever kind, though there is brief mention of how the visual aesthetics of *Shades* would seem out of place to viewers and hard to understand. The point here, then, is that the discourse of reviewing acknowledged an imagined reaction by the 'popular' audience but was not bound to it or by it.

Commentary on the German productions of Beckett's plays for television at the SDR channel was similar to the pattern of response in Britain and came mainly from theatre critics (and occasionally arts correspondents or television reviewers) writing for broadsheet newspapers. Reaction to the 1966 German version of *Eh Joe* varied between the familiar poles of some critics appreciating it as an exciting experiment for television while others thought it was depressing and boring (Garforth 1992: 383–6). Reaction to the later *Eh Joe* of 1979 from SDR also included occasional praise for the play as breaking new ground for television, some thirteen years later, in the context of German television's conventional generic programming and hidebound schedule. But some writers were unhappy with the acting in *Eh Joe*, thinking that Klaus Herm's background as a pantomime performer did not equip him with enough subtlety to portray Joe's emotions effectively, and critics also noted with disappointment that some of Nancy Illig's lines (as Voice) were unclear. Among the German critics writing about *Nur noch gewolk* (1977), the German production of *...but the clouds...*, were opinions matching those of British commentators who attempted to locate the drama in terms of plot and character, regarding it as comprehensible since it was about a man waiting for a woman (Garforth 1992: 400–12). By 1981, comments about Beckett's work as a corrective to the norms of television were still being made long after these reactions were first in evidence about *Eh Joe* in the mid-1960s. Peter Iden (1981, trans. Garforth 1992: 632), reviewing *Quadrat* for *Frankfurter Rundschau*, wrote: 'For probably the first time in its history, television has here become the medium of that technique of allegory which indicates the whole world', and 'The broadcast was an event which suddenly showed up the whole management of both television programmes and life itself to be an economy of appearance.' The converse of this view, which was again very familiar in relation to British reactions, was that Beckett's work would be simply incomprehensible to the audience and was inappropriate for broadcast. The unnamed reviewer BNB (1983, trans. Garforth 1992: 635), discussing SDR's *Nacht und Träume* in *Frankfurter Rundschau*, asked, 'What causes an author like Beckett to make use of the language of the medium in such a carelessly amateurish way?' and continued, 'by transmitting the play at midnight, it can be presumed, that as far as the viewers are concerned, a natural selection has taken place.'

By the time of *Quad*'s British screening in 1982, Robert Ottaway's short feature about the forthcoming week's highlights in the *Radio Times* deals consciously with the issue of whether Beckett's work can be assimilated by the television audience. The series of screenings of Beckett's work in an *Arena* season that week (which included *Rockaby*, *Krapp's Last Tape* and *Not I*) were framed by an interest in the performances by Billie Whitelaw featuring in them. Ottoway (1982) admitted: 'There are those who consider that Beckett's minimal attitude to words, recently accentuated, tended towards non-verbal experiment. And so *Quad*, a ballet for four people, will be a test of his ability to communicate without the human voice.' But Ottoway was content to give priority to Beckett's authorial role, as both writer and director, and to think of the audience as a subordinate client for Beckett's communicative intentions, as if set a puzzle by him that viewers would be required to solve: 'But he is directing himself. The meaning will be his, and ours to grasp.' As the documents around Beckett's television work show, the interest in audience reception and the need to engage the audience co-exist with the opportunity to dismiss negative audience responses and small numbers of viewers on the basis of the public service remit of the BBC and SDR in Germany, which was to present 'the best' of arts culture as defined by professional television personnel and an informed reviewing culture in the press, reflecting the invocation of authority discussed in Chapter 3.

The reception of *Film*: author, director and star

With *Film*, the set of audience expectations around Buster Keaton as a star performer established the preconditions both for a spectating position prepared for the 'show' of Keaton's talents, and also a position expecting narrative pleasure. As Richard Dyer (1998: 126) points out, 'audience foreknowledge, the star's name and his/her appearance ... all already signify that condensation of attitudes and values which is the star's image'. Keaton's name, his appearance, and the physical form of comedy which he refined, are attributes of his star image which orient the spectator to and for his films in particular ways. The first audiences of *Film* responded to it as a Keaton short, as I shall explain, and a study of the different discourses around Keaton, his 1920s films and *Film* itself illuminates some of the different and sometimes conflicting insights of critical work on stardom, authorship and audience.

Once *Film* had been made, its early exhibition history reveals that it was Keaton's name around which the film revolved, rather than Beckett's or the director Alan Schneider's. It was difficult to find an audience constituency for *Film*, since Beckett and Schneider lacked any track record in cinema, and the film was clearly not a commercial feature. Schneider (1972: 90) wrote: 'We had difficulty marketing the film. No one wanted it. No one wants shorts anyhow, and this one they didn't want (or understand) with a vengeance.' Its star, however, was extremely well-known, and the film's first notable screening was motivated by an interest in the rediscovered Keaton. From the beginning of *Film*, Keaton can be recognised by his hat, and showing the hat promises the spectator that he will be revealed, though his face is not seen until right at the end. Recognition of Keaton became more valuable than recognition of either the writer, Beckett, or Schneider, the director. Schneider (1972: 90) remembered: 'Then, in the summer of 1965, came an unexpected offer from the New York Film Festival. Amos Vogel had seen a print somewhere and thought it was worth showing – as part of a Keaton revival series. Already the film was becoming Keaton's and not Beckett's. I fought another losing battle to keep it from getting sandwiched in between two Keaton shorts.' This history revolves around the questions of which interpretive frame *Film* might belong in, and whose name is used to organise its meaning. The film was a short, but not a commercial one. It featured Keaton but was not a comedy, a 'Keaton film'. Schneider was promoting it, but as 'Beckett's' film rather than his own creative property. This mismatching of categories is essential to an understanding of the audience's reaction to *Film* at the New York Film Festival. The emphasis on Keaton was perceived by its maker as a misconception of the film, but Keaton's face, his trademark, became fully visible in the final shots, while the first shot was a close-up of his eye which the audience recognised at once and found hilarious. Keaton's face literally frames the film at the beginning and the end, and the only time the audience laughed was when they recognised Keaton at the beginning. Schneider (1972: 93) wrote: 'All through the next twenty-two minutes they sat there, bored, annoyed, baffled, and cheated of the Keaton they had come to see. Who the hell was Beckett?' The audience were then reacting to *Film* as a Keaton film, a short comic movie in black-and-white, which could perhaps be mistaken for a rare short made in his heyday, the 1920s. The audience at a Keaton revival had come with expectations which provided an intertextual frame for *Film*, and the opening of the film reinforced these expectations, though the subsequent unfolding of the film appeared to undercut them completely. Enoch Brater (1975: 173) succinctly remarks: 'Enticed by farce and vaudeville, the audience gets a phenomenology of visual perception instead.' Clearly, the questions of interpretation here relate to whose film *Film* was perceived to be: Keaton's, Beckett's or Schneider's.

However, it seems from the evidence of Beckett's screenplay that it was precisely the intertext of silent comedy which Beckett had wanted to evoke. In particular, as suggested above,

Keaton's film work makes use of the unreality and reflexivity around perception which *Film* remodulates into what Brater calls 'phenomenology'. Beckett's notes on the setting and mood of the film read: 'Climate of film comic and unreal. O should invite laughter throughout by his way of moving. Unreality of street scene' (1972:12). Schneider reports that Keaton misread the script as being in the mode of silent comedy and frequently suggested during shooting that he could make it much funnier if he were allowed to depart from the script and do some comic routines. Keaton had experience as a director himself, as the editor of his own films, and as the scenario writer and ideas-man when being directed by others. One of the reasons that French film critics began to value his work in the late 1950s and early 1960s was that there appeared to be a consistent authorial and directorial signature manifest in them. Lebel (1967: 57) argues that Keaton 'was the real director of his films', and quotes a *Cahiers du Cinéma* interview of 1962 in which Keaton explains 'I was not always the director, or the sole director, of my films. But I worked actively on elaborating the scenarios and selecting the gags and that's why all my films have, I believe, a family resemblance.' The audience of *Film* at the New York Film Festival seem to have believed they found a 'family resemblance' between the opening frames of *Film* and Keaton's silent shorts, but as the film progressed this recognition was increasingly disconfirmed. Andrew Sarris (1969: 43), for example, complained: 'Keaton's metaphorical eye patch and fuzzy vision, his ostentatious awkwardness is a travesty of the alertness and agility that characterized Keaton in his classic period; and it is doubtful that the real Keaton would keep feeling his own pulse even if he had lived to be a hundred in the process [...] Keaton's life force was motion, and to have denied him this even in his old age was to consign him to the scrap heap of film history.' The Keaton of *Film* was sufficiently recognisable to trigger expectations about the film based on his star image, yet sufficiently different in terms of his performance style, action and relationship to point of view and mise-en-scène to open up a disturbing gap between this Keaton and the Keaton of memory whose work was being valued in this period. Recent scholarship on Keaton has shown, in fact, that his work was itself intensely reflexive and intertextual from the beginning of his stage and screen career, and that much of his comedy was rooted in allusive reference to conventional cultural stereotypes and his own fictional personae (King 2007, Krämer 2007, Linville 2007, Sweeney 2007, Wolfe 2007). The 'authentic' Keaton was always already constituted in dialogue with other representations and his own performance of his screen identity, as is his performance in the roles of O and E in *Film*.

An analysis of *Film* in relation to the history and criticism of cinema, as well as in relation to its production history, its problems of spectatorship and information about the response of actual audiences, foregrounds the tension between Beckett and Keaton as the predominant 'stars' whose significance as authorial centres of meaning could function as the key to its reception. An important issue raised by this is the question of institutional context. Seeing Keaton shorts in a film festival context, decades after their first exhibition, and with an audience of film critics, industry figures and aficionados, is clearly different from seeing them in the 1920s in the emergent popular narrative cinema. The audience of *Film*, though knowledgeable, would know Keaton through his films, more than through the media discourses constructing him as a movie star at the times the films were made. As Paul McDonald (1998: 178) has warned, 'overuse of the term "star" to describe any well-known film actor obscures how with most popular film performers, knowledge is limited to the on-screen "personality"'. Different qualifications apply in the case of Samuel Beckett, whose name had become known through media controversies around his plays and whose name identified a set of assumptions about this theatrical work, work which had been actually seen only by a small, educated and cosmopolitan minority. *Waiting for Godot* was first staged in Britain in 1955, directed by Peter Hall, and the play entered popular awareness because of the debates in newspapers, journals and on radio concerning its apparent lack of story or action, and its absurdity. *Endgame* was first staged in Britain in 1957 and became the subject of controversy and public awareness because, at a time of escalating Cold War nuclear tension, it was thought to be set in a post-apocalyptic environment.

Jonathan Kalb (1994: 134–5) writes that *Film* is 'a work of its time, displaying many of the same formal obsessions as the French New Wave, just burgeoning in the early 1960s: a reflexive concern with the staring camera eye, an invocation of Hollywood icons such as Buster Keaton along with a general consciousness of film history, and a resistance to montage in the Bazinian tradition.' These issues of *Film*'s construction, its editing conventions and shot types, raise the question of how the cinema audience might read its film 'language'. *Film* breaks the rules by its lack of wide shots and its absence of shot–reverse–shots until the last minute. The audience is forced to identify with the pursuing camera's point of view almost exclusively, and is deprived of sound or music cues with which to narrativise and understand the scenario. The audience's foremost problem is to understand the 45-degree rule whereby Keaton can be safe from the camera's perception if the camera remains behind him at less than this angle. This rule is alien to the syntax of narrative cinema and appears to allude to the impossibility of seeing oneself in a mirror if positioned beyond 45 degrees to one side. Clas Zilliacus (1976: 186) conducted a survey of audience members at the January 1970 Bleecker Street, New York, screening of *Film*, and his results 'amply confirmed that the two-vision idea did not work'. To clarify the convention, the points of view of the pursuing camera and Keaton were different in visual quality, with a misty 'film' over Keaton's eye, so that the final confrontation between the two would be comprehensible. Because of the scarcity of shot–reverse–shots this special code was needed, but it is certainly questionable whether a viewer who hadn't read the screenplay would understand it, and Ruth Perlmutter (1977: 83) argues that *Film* 'needs to be "read" along with the filmscript, where some details are explained by Beckett.' Perlmutter's invocation of the screenplay of *Film* as a necessary supplement to the film may be sensible, but it does not invalidate the confusion and dissatisfaction among actual spectators who went to see the film, and again makes recourse to Beckett's authority as the writer to stabilise its meaning.

A discussion of Keaton's role in the film, and the audiences' confusion about the film at its early screenings, shows how competing frames of reference, particularly around authorship and the function of the star image, make *Film* difficult to understand, and how interpretations are always particular to a certain kind of spectatorial relation that is dependent on exhibition context and audience expectation and knowledge. Writing about films in which the star image seems to oppose or contradict the use of a certain performer in a particular role, Richard Dyer (1998: 131) explains: 'What analysis is concerned to do is both to discover the nature of the fit between star image and character, and, where the fit is not perfect or selective, to work out where the contradictions are articulated (at what level(s) of signification of character) and to attempt to see what possible sources of "masking" or "pseudo-unification" the film offers (such as the irresistible force of a star image).' *Film* offers a number of 'masking' or 'pseudo-unification' procedures, especially in relation to the image of Keaton, some narrative features of the film which allude to Keaton comedies, and the significance of Beckett's name. But these procedures did not conduce to the production of a satisfactory spectating position for many actual film viewers. Indeed, *Film* alludes to each of these possible forms of spectatorship but leaves the film viewer with the sense that he or she is out of place in each of them.

Audience, form and the politics of television drama

The audience of theorists and students who are spoken to by television theory is not the same as the television audience addressed in Beckett's work. The reason that Beckett's work is potentially so significant is its inclusion of the audience within its own form, by means of direct address to the viewer, and its attempt to represent the processes of viewing and the constitution of the audience for the text. But this concern with audience is necessarily repackaged by some viewers, critics or theorists as a resistance to the work, because they recognise the significance of the work as television experimentation but cannot position themselves for the text as part of the audience which it seems to address. Some viewers have therefore inhabited a dual audience position. They have regarded the plays as important yet unengaging, recognising their aesthetic significance but unwilling to take up the audience-position laid out by the programme for them as television viewers. Television viewers resist the 'preferred readings' of television programmes and the positions that programmes lay out for them, as television theory has repeatedly emphasised (Morley 1992). This resistance can also occur in the decoding of television because of the cultural formations of the writers and viewers who engage in its 'dialogue'. Television hollows out a space for its audiences to occupy, a discursive space that some critics or audiences refuse to accept.

The television plays' form of anti-naturalism is not designed to represent a coherent world, and unlike television naturalistic fiction, further problematises this with narration. Psychological motivations, and conflicts between emotions, are relatively insignificant. Naturalistic form is the one with which the television audience is most familiar, providing a recognisable environment into which characters are placed, and Beckett's avoidance of it means that character is not used as a vehicle for exploring ideas, for its own sake, or for involving the audience in a story. Beckett's plays challenge the audience to decode the play's dramatic form and to relate its concerns to their own experience and ideas. Here, levels of competence are important, and the audiences found it hard to recognise the modality of the plays. The devices of performance, narration, studio 'staginess' and unconventional uses of music, for example, make the position of the television audience mobile and uncertain. Thus the audience can be at any particular time in an excluded position, an aligned or identifying position, or a fully participatory position. The drama is composed of mixed discursive registers. Performativity, the fact of representing in the medium of drama, is foregrounded. The audience would be engaged in a self-conscious process of questioning their own modes of understanding dramatic representation, and questioning their assumptions about what the theatre or television media might be. A high level of competence is required for this kind of drama, and works which undertake to explore it are often those most valued by academic theorists of television drama, and least watched by mass audiences. Beckett's work combines a theatrical mode of performance with reflexivity, in order to separate and comment on performer and role, in ways which potentially foreground the fact of drama as discourse. This reflexive understanding of drama is an important ground for the citation of Beckett's work in Television Studies, for it opens the possibility of self-consciousness about the medium of television performance. Beckett, along with other writers like John McGrath, Troy Kennedy Martin and Dennis Potter, has been concerned with the Modernist exploration of television dramatic form in this sense.

The active agency of the audience is required in order for viewers to constitute themselves as an audience, to take up an orientation to the text which enables a communicative relationship to exist, and for the articulation of experience to become dialogical and productive. The socialist playwright John McGrath, for instance, was articulate about this matter of reception context as well as textual form, and the relationship between them, and wrote in his theoretical text *A Good Night Out* of his desire to specifically engage an active television viewer despite the conditions of reception. His aim was to engage the viewer in a dialogic relationship with television despite its shortcomings (McGrath 1981: 112): 'television-watching is a frame of mind, and the technically sub-standard pictures, the reality of the medium as a piece of furniture, and the inconsequentiality built into it as an experience, all conspire to set severe limits on that frame of mind, on what effort we are prepared to put into, and what depth of reading experience we are expecting to take out of, the time spent watching TV.' In Beckett's formalistic and unconventional television dramas, a similar aim is evident to separate the mass television audience from the imperatives of entertainment and distraction which the forms of mass television broadcasting presuppose. But Beckett's engagement of the audience in a dialogue and production of audience activity rely partly on the creation of a 'new' television form, an experimental formalism which draws on theatrical and cinematic devices as well as television's dramatic forms, blurring the boundaries between them. Two of the interesting consequences of this move are, first, that the Modernist form of Beckett's dramas parallels that of the avant-garde in which no audience or taste grouping currently exists for the work and the work must seek to find such an audience anew. Secondly, following from this, the mixing of forms in contravention of the conventions of genre relies on the existence and familiarity of those conventions. This strategy had already been popularised among television practitioners and intellectuals by John McGrath (1977: 102), who recommended a critical form of drama explored in his 1964 play (written with Troy Kennedy Martin) *Diary of a Young Man*: 'when we come to the more sophisticated devices for putting images together: montage, with soundtrack, creating a story from selected detail, jump-cuts with the urgency of the story linking the elements; moving from news-reader to film to stills – the language of a great deal of television – very few plays, even fewer series, dare speak it.' McGrath's work drew on mixtures of dramatic and factual television techniques with a radically democratic impetus, since both the diversity of voices and the resistance to the orders of genre imply a lessening of hegemonic authority and the fluidity of modes of address and modes of engagement. Beckett's work, in a different use of this mixing of forms and blurring of media boundaries, does not share the same explicit or implicit anti-hegemonic agenda and instead pursues a dialogue with the institutions of the arts in which it participates in them but does not belong in any of them.

Theoretical discourses about television audiences regard the audience either as an object constructed by television or as a subject empowered to interact actively with it. Audience theories can be positioned along a spectrum, whose poles are either considering the audience as passive, positioned and interpolated by the media text or, on the other hand, regarding the audience as active appropriators of meaning amid a complex social and cultural context which permeates both audiences and the media. The first of these positions derives from a broadly textual or 'literary' approach, while the second arises from the concerns of contemporary Cultural Studies. As Valerie Walkerdine (1998) has argued, the textual tradition inherits the concerns of the social theory of the late nineteenth century. The social psychology of that period sought to understand the crowd as a social force, institutionalising the earlier middle-class and governmental fears of the mob or the working class as irrational, illiterate, immoral and violent. The notions of the audience in general in social and media theory inherited this position of the Other, regarded as immoral and suggestible. Frankfurt School theories of the manipulation of masses by modern mechanical and technological media support this set of notions which repudiate 'popular' mass entertainment and its consumers. As Adorno and Horkheimer (1997: 120) wrote: 'Films, radio and magazines make up a system which is uniform as a whole and in every part'. The fact of the mediated mass dissemination of culture determines the media audience as a mass and deprives the audience of both 'authentic' cultural experience and the ability to participate actively in cultural production. The specifics of audience decoding strategies, audience pleasures and differentiations between media and between textualities in the same medium are each relegated to local variations in a monolithic imposition of pre-digested culture from above. Like the notion of children as a suggestible, univalent and homogenous group, the television audience as crowd or mass is the discursive tool which permits blanket denigration of the medium. Beckett critics have argued that his television work is important because it is radically different from this mass culture that surrounds it on television, and it has a productive role in turning the audience from passive to active viewers and in recognising the homogeneity of the majority of television broadcasting. This is a noble aim, but historical evidence shows that it repeatedly failed and that in fact it was support from institutionally powerful television producers and cultural opinion-formers that brought Beckett's dramas to the screen.

The media theorist John Hartley (1992: 17) introduced the terms pedagogy and paedocracy in the mid-1980s in order to describe a struggle for control over television audiences, imagined as vulnerable, unruly and driven by excessive urges: 'there's a struggle between what are presumed to be *paedocratic* audience practices on the one hand (governed *by* childlike qualities), and *pedagogic* discourses on the other (government *over* childish tendencies).' The audience is in the position of the child as a valued but unruly being, not only in the control of the institution (as the child is in the care of a parent) but also perpetually at risk of evading this control. Paedocratic and pedagogic strategies, therefore, enable television institutions to address an audience not only on which they depend but also which they patronise and demean. The pedagogic mode is a strategy of control through which critical and self-reflexive television productions would empower the audience intellectually, and educate and mature the audience. What Hartley describes as pedagogic strategies include the promotion, trailing and reviewing of television, which instruct the audience about what they might watch and how they might watch it. Further pedagogic strategies include the attempts to censor, control or stigmatise programmes or viewing practices in governmental, educational and press contexts. Hartley points out that even though the television audience is perpetually subject to these attempts to control it across a wide range of discourses, the audience is granted an ultimate sovereign power. This is the power not only to switch the television on or off but also to function as the legitimating instance in whose name television is made and to be the economic force which ultimately underwrites the television industry and the television market. The audience is never present to itself, never able to exercise a collective power as a community of subjects which recognises itself as such, but nevertheless the audience is addressed on the assumption that it potentially does have this identity and coherent authority. As Hartley (1992: 108) points out, 'the industry and its regulatory bodies are obliged not only to speak *about* an audience but – crucially, for them – to talk *to* one as well: they need not only to *represent* audiences but also to enter into *relations* with them'. Hartley's argument addresses the othering process through which television institutions and the institutions which represent television (the press, or government) announce the simultaneous disempowerment of the audience and at the same time the value of the audience. Clearly, the pedagogic discourse was sufficiently powerful in the production culture and the executive policy-making echelons of the BBC, SDR and later Channel 4 for Beckett's work to continue to be a legitimate focus of special interest and effort. The distinction between 'mature' and 'childish' audiences was always imaginary: it was and is a matter of discursive construction that enabled a politics of media communication, the legitimation of formal experiment, the valuation of authorship within certain boundaries, and the self-validation of producers and production practices within television institutions. The consequence of such a discursive construction is not only that television audiences are valuable but also that they are feared because they are potentially unruly and ungovernable. Historical and empirical evidence about the audiences of Beckett's television plays (specialist academic and journalist audiences, as well as 'ordinary' viewers) neither necessarily values nor devalues the plays as cultural interventions or as texts. Instead, it historicises and explains how discourses of evaluation based on supposed effects on the audience, on numerical ratings information, or on the sophistication of the plays' engagement with their medium become possible.

6

Afterword: the lessons of history

The specificity of Beckett's work in a Modernist tradition of television drama has important input into debates within Television Studies concerning authorship, institutions, audiences, and the writing of the history of British television. The methodologies and theoretical frameworks of Television Studies are essential research resources for scholars working on Beckett's television plays, and the plays cannot be adequately understood without reference to these contexts. Research into Beckett's television work is important to Beckett Studies because of the different relationships between the aesthetics of this popular mass medium and the media of literature and theatre that have been more familiar to existing critical scholarship on his work. The television plays are also significant to Television Studies (and especially critical historical accounts of British television) because they provide a location to think through several complexly related issues that exist in tension and sometimes in contradiction. A concern for the textual and aesthetic qualities of Beckett's television plays relates them usefully to a European (and not just British) history of Modernist experiment in television as well as in theatre and prose.

The issues of genre, scheduling and audience, and their relationship with Modernism in television, connect the plays to theoretical and historiographic debates that have been important in the history of television criticism. British television drama was initially adduced as an object for critical discourse on an analogy with theatre drama, since television drama began as the re-staging of excerpts from theatre plays, and the relay of performances staged for theatrical exhibition. The emphases produced by methodological frameworks and political agendas in television criticism subsequently determined how criticism shaped the terms in which Beckett's television plays were understood in the decades when they were broadcast. Within the discourses of Television Studies, Beckett's television dramas are currently perceived as marginal (if they are perceived at all) because they do not fit the agendas that the critical discourse has inherited and developed, since the plays have a strong authorial imprint, a theatrical background, were produced in the television studio rather than on film on location, and had comparatively small audiences. Their broadcast on BBC2 and SDR as arts programming rather than drama, and as educational or elite drama on Channel 4 and RTE, gave the plays comparatively small audiences, a perceived elitism, and an apparent lack of relationship with dominant fictional forms in contemporary television. Theoretical work in this book on critical approaches to television drama disputes some of these accepted views, and evaluates the significance of Beckett's plays for Television Studies as part of a rediscovery of a neglected strand of dramatic work for television which engages with the aesthetic and cultural characteristics of the medium. These are television dramas that are self-consciously experimental and distinctive, and which detach themselves from the surrounding flow of programming. The fact that they eschew the 'aesthetic of smooth, almost invisible temporal transition' draws attention to them and to 'the language of television, catching and then holding the "distracted glance"' (Mulvey 2007: 3). Their very peculiarity is what makes them interesting but also easy to overlook in the historiography of television.

The book has placed Beckett's work for television, and to a lesser extent his radio drama and *Film*, in relation to the history and historiography of the period when these productions were created and shown, focusing mainly on British broadcasting. In the future work on Beckett's media drama that will undoubtedly emerge, one direction for analysis should be to develop the historicisation of Beckett's experimentation in these media and the question of the anachronism that I have noted as a textual feature and aesthetic strategy. The pre-history of television amounts to about sixty-five years, from experimentation with picture telegraphy until the early broadcasts of 1936. The period when television became established in Western Europe began in the 1950s, and I have concentrated on historical contexts for Beckett's work from the mid-1960s until the early twenty-first century because this was the epoch when his programmes and film screenplay were made. But expectations about television took some time to form, and looking back before the 1960s would extend the understanding of Beckett's experimentation quite radically because his backward-looking investigation of what the medium could do and could be drew inevitably on discourses about television that were actively developed and contested before his first media productions were conceived. Television's inauguration as a programme medium from the early 1930s, its institutionalisation and the development of scheduling, each offer contexts in which norms were negotiated that could then be experimented with by later programmes such as those that Beckett originated. Beckett's interest in silent cinema, similarly, suggests that the same questions of medium specificity and capability impact on *Film* more profoundly than this book has been able to explore. Beckett criticism has repeatedly taken its bearings from his declarations that speaking, writing and communicating are impossible but inescapable, and this book has argued that his screen dramas stage this communicative relation as a structure, theme and formal template for the audio-visual texts he produced. Television as communication, and television as a mode in which to perform communication and its failures aesthetically, invite further historicization in which Beckett's work constitutes a complex and illuminating example.

A methodology to be avoided, however, is one where a discourse of developmental progression and an invocation of Beckett's authority work to stabilise and unify screen works that are significantly different, and where intertextual reference outwards to other texts and media, as well as intratextual relationships between Beckett's dramas, use these relationships to exaggerate their consistency. For instance, in an otherwise very expert study of Beckett's screen work, Graley Herren (2007: 117) suggests that the three plays in *The Lively Arts: Shades* are the story of the same characters, progressively pared down in the plays until the male figure disappears except as a memory:

> The process of deformation is even more remarkable if one takes the 'prequel' status of *Ghost Trio* into account. Then one can trace the entire male lineage of *Shades*, from the young boy messenger, to the older F, through an older M1 who still retains Clov-like mobility, to the motionless hump of M, reduced to a state of immobility even more complete than Hamm. By the final segment of *Shades* in *Not I*, the male figure is eliminated entirely, retained only as a memory for those spectators who remember that a silent male Auditor once accompanied Mouth in the stage version.

It is this developmental schema, legitimated by a supposed continuity of intention and revision on the part of Beckett as author, that I have tried to resist in this book by discussing the plays and *Film* outside of a chronological structure respecting their dates of writing and screening. As Daniela Caselli (2005: 58) has argued of the repetitions and reworkings of Dante in Beckett's prose, and the reworkings of Beckett's own invocations of Dante, 'Samuel Beckett the author is himself the product of this constant process of incorporation.' To take Beckett's authority and authorship as the ultimate principle of coherence in this oeuvre neglects the ways that the dramas destabilise the boundaries between what is inside and outside the texts and their medium.

The temporal extension of the framework for analysing Beckett's television plays would need to approach questions of development and authority cautiously. Extending the spatial aspect of the investigation would also be useful, to acknowledge more fully the European context of the production of Beckett's screen work and its transnational aesthetic significance. This would introduce a comparative dimension, placing British activity in relation to wider geographical frames. This book has considered the circumstances and realisation of Beckett's television plays in Britain, and very briefly in Germany, drawing attention to the connected assumptions in these countries about the public service functions of broadcasting and the responsibility to support Beckett's television work as an instance of culturally valuable arts broadcasting. In a further international context, work in this study has addressed the US context of the production of *Film* in 1964 and the international circulation of this film in a specific moment of festival exhibition screening and critical discourse around film authorship and stardom. The *Beckett on Film* project, too, crosses national borders and was dependent on economic relationships between different national broadcasters and production companies, as well as cast and production staff whose nationality sometimes impacted on the realization, marketing and reception of the dramas. Beckett is an international figure, and further study of this spatial context could not only illuminate the variant ways in which his persona and work have gained (or failed to gain) cultural visibility but also contribute to the comparative media histories that are just beginning to be written (Bignell and Fickers 2008).

The persistence of Beckett's work on television is linked with the establishment of a cultural and class elite in broadcasting institutions which took Beckett as a totemic figure legitimating their aspirations to take their audience seriously, to raise public taste and to offer what they perceived to be the best in the arts and culture. Television is regarded as the most accessible and central of the broadcasting media, yet despite this, and also because of it, television is at the margins of cultural authority. The requirement to give attention and concentration to programmes such as Beckett's television drama is at odds with the conventional representations in popular and academic discourse of the inattentive and grazing viewer. However, political, institutional and aesthetic pressures to identify with a popular audience, to offer pleasure and to acknowledge resistance to a hegemonic definition of 'quality' are also evident in the material I have presented here. The history of critical discourse on television is itself a short one, and in relation to television drama it has been marked at least since the early 1980s by a nostalgia for a lost Golden Age, as Robin Nelson (1997: 1) has noted: 'A repeated question about TV drama in the 1990s is that of its ability in the future to equal the glories of its past.' George Brandt (1993: 17) had wondered already in the early 1990s whether the best products of TV drama in the 1980s were perhaps 'the golden glow of a setting sun'. Brandt's evaluation was primarily text-based and literary, echoing a set of critical terms displaced by redemptive readings of popular texts (Brundson 1990) and celebrations of popular pleasure which had begun to mark a shift in television criticism from the late 1970s onwards. The complexity of Beckett's role at the BBC is an index of much wider cultural debates within broadcasting and in the arts in general.

So the changing emphases of Television Studies have reinforced the marginalisation of Beckett's television work for three interconnected reasons. First, their strong authorial imprint, theatrical background and studio production associated them with a superseded past. Second, the fact that they were mainly screened on minority channels, in the context of arts programming rather than drama, meant that they attracted comparatively small audiences, were perceived as difficult, and appeared not to relate to dominant television fictional forms of their time. Third, the visual abstraction of the plays, their use of non-naturalistic and non-psychologically realist characters and their apparent lack of relation to a social context meant that critical approaches grounded in gender, class or contemporary social issues apparently had little occasion to discuss them. However, work on Beckett's television plays opens up our understanding of a key tradition in television studio drama against which the location-filmed social realist plays of the British television drama canon reacted. In the context of Television Studies' interest in audience response, data collected by BBC Audience Research reveals interesting information about how the plays were received at the time. Archival work shows how the institutional dynamics of arts programming affected the marketing, presentation and scheduling of Beckett's plays for a certain expected audience. Specialist segments of that audience, spoken for and to by a coterie of experienced reviewers in the broadsheet 'quality' press in Britain and Germany, negotiated a position which recognised the plays' lack of appeal to a mainstream audience but still valued the plays as part of a broad European arts culture. There is a significant tension between Beckett's exploration of medium-specificity in the television plays and the relationships that have been recognised by the plays' producers, reviewers and academic critics with other work in the media of radio, theatre, visual art and prose.

Existing critical work on Beckett's television plays has aimed to value this issue of a televisual aesthetic, regarding it as a salutary corrective to the focus in contemporary television culture on the new, the popular and the spectacular. Graley Herren (2007: 1) has recently argued that 'Beckett approaches the typically frenetic and forward-looking filmed media with a gaze fixed backwards and an ear attuned to echoes from the past', valuing anachronism as a critical strategy. This reading of the screen work has been connected to the thematic concerns of the plays with loss, memory and resurrection, seeing the dramas as 'sites for recollecting and reinventing personal, philosophical, and artistic pasts'. My approach in this book has been to develop similar ideas in relation to the significance of Beckett's work within debates occurring in broadcasting institutions and public discourses about the changing attitudes of creative workers, production institutions and audiences towards television and film. An analysis of these issues shows that television and film have been different in the past and could be different in the future. Historiography is valuable for this reason, since it 'helps to make sense of television's past as well as its current importance; its changing status within the global media economy; its ability to make a social impact, not just in its everyday ubiquitousness but also in relation to key media "events"; and its aesthetic potential for producing programmes that are moving, entertaining, thought-provoking, even beautiful' (Wheatley 2007: 3). In different ways, and often not in obvious ones, Beckett's screen dramas are important to television history, and their analysis is important to the historiography of their medium.

Bibliography

Adamou, C. (2003), 'Screening the unrepresentable: Samuel Beckett's plays for television', unpublished PhD thesis, University of Reading.

Adams, J. (1998), 'Screen play: Elements of a performance aesthetic in television drama', in J. Ridgman (ed.), *Boxed Sets: Television Representations of Theatre*, Luton: John Libbey, 141–57.

Adorno, T. and M. Horkheimer (1997), *Dialectic of Enlightenment*, trans. J. Cumming, London: Verso.

Ang, I. (1991), *Desperately Seeking the Audience*, London: Routledge.

Anonymous (1977), review of *The Lively Arts: Shades*, *The Observer*, 17 April.

Armstrong, T. (1998), *Modernism, Technology and the Body: A Cultural Study*, Cambridge: Cambridge University Press.

Austin, J.L. (1971), *How to Do Things with Words*, Oxford: Oxford University Press.

Bair, D. (1980), *Samuel Beckett: A Biography*, London: Picador.

Bakhtin, M. (1981), *The Dialogic Imagination: Four Essays by M.M. Bakhtin*, ed. M. Holquist, trans. M. Holquist and C. Emerson, Austin: University of Texas Press.

Baudry, J.-L. (1980), 'Ideological effects of the basic cinematic apparatus', in T. Hak Kyung Cha (ed.), *Apparatus*, New York: Tanam Press, 25–40. Also published as 'Ideological effects of the basic cinematic apparatus', trans. A. Williams, *Film Quarterly* 28:2 (1974–75), 39–47.

BBC (1965), *Annual Report and Accounts, 1964–5*, London: HMSO.

BBC WAC RCONT20. Samuel Beckett 1970–79.

BBC WAC R/9/7/52. Audience Research report on *Waiting for Godot*.

BBC WAC R9/7/63. Audience Research report on *Krapp's Last Tape*.

BBC WAC R9/1153/1. TV audience figures: BARB BBC reports 1990.

BBC WAC T5/782/3. Plays Department transmission diary July–

September 1966.
BBC WAC T5/1296/1. *Eh Joe*.
BBC WAC T5/2239/7. TV Drama memos 1964.
BBC WAC T48/74/1. Drama writers file: Samuel Beckett file 1.
BBC WAC T51/350. *The Lively Arts: Shades*.
Beckett, S. (undated a), photocopy of original manuscript of *Eh Joe*, MS1537/1, Beckett International Foundation, University of Reading Library.
Beckett, S. (undated b), photocopy of original typescript of *Eh Joe*, MS1537/3, Beckett International Foundation, University of Reading Library.
Beckett, S. (undated c), photocopy of original typescript of *Eh Joe*, MS1537/4, Beckett International Foundation, University of Reading Library.
Beckett, S. (undated d), photocopy of original typescript of *Eh Joe*, MS1537/5, Beckett International Foundation, University of Reading Library.
Beckett, S. (undated e), photocopy of original typescript of *Eh Joe*, MS1537/6, Beckett International Foundation, University of Reading Library.
Beckett, S. (undated f), holograph copy of *Ghost Trio*, MS1519/1, Beckett International Foundation, University of Reading Library.
Beckett, S. (undated g), untitled holograph draft of *…but the clouds…*, MS 1553/1, Beckett International Foundation, University of Reading Library.
Beckett, S. (undated h), typescript with production notes for *Nacht und Träume*, , MS2465, Beckett International Foundation, University of Reading Library.
Beckett, S. (1957), *Proust*, New York: Grove.
Beckett, S. (1959), *Molloy*, London: John Calder, first published in French 1950.
Beckett, S. (1965), *Proust and Three Dialogues*, London: John Calder.
Beckett, S. (1972), *Film*, London: Faber.
Beckett, S. (1973), *Murphy*, London: Picador.
Beckett, S. (1979), production notebook for the SDR production of *Eh Joe*, MS1730, Beckett International Foundation, University of Reading Library.
Beckett, S. (1983), *Disjecta: Miscellaneous Writings and a Dramatic Fragment*, London: John Calder.
Beckett, S. (1984), *Collected Shorter Plays of Samuel Beckett*, London: Faber.
Beckett, S. (1986), *The Complete Dramatic Works*, London: Faber.

Benjamin, W. (1968), 'The work of art in the age of mechanical reproduction', in *Illuminations*, trans. H. Zohn, New York: Harcourt Brace Jovanovich, 217–52.

Bennett, T., S. Boyd-Bowman, C. Mercer, J. Woollacott (eds) (1981), *Popular Television and Film*, London: BFI / Open University Press.

Ben-Zvi, L. (1985), 'Samuel Beckett's media plays', *Modern Drama* 28:1, 22–37.

Ben-Zvi, L. (ed.) (1992), *Women in Beckett: Performance and Critical Perspectives*, Urbana and Chicago: Chicago University Press.

Bergson, H. (1912), *Matter and Memory*, trans. N. Paul and W. Palmer, New York: Macmillan.

Berkeley, G. (1949), *The Works of George Berkeley, vol. 2 The Principles of Human Knowledge*, ed. T. Jessop, London: Thomas Nelson.

Bignell, J. (1994), 'Trevor Griffiths's political theatre: From *Oi For England* to *The Gulf Between Us*', *New Theatre Quarterly* 10:37, 49–56.

Bignell, J. (1996), 'Method westerns: *The Left-Handed Gun* and *One-Eyed Jacks*', in I. Cameron and D. Pye (eds), *The Movie Book of the Western*, London: Studio Vista, 99–110.

Bignell, J. (1999), 'Questions of authorship: Samuel Beckett and *Film*', in J. Bignell (ed.), *Writing and Cinema*, Harlow and New York: Addison-Wesley Longman, 29–42.

Bignell, J. (2000), *Postmodern Media Culture*, Edinburgh: Edinburgh University Press.

Bignell, J. (2001–2), 'Beckett in television studies', *Journal of Beckett Studies* 10:1–2, 105–18.

Bignell, J. (2002), 'Writing the child in media theory', *Yearbook of English Studies* 32, 127–39.

Bignell, J. (2003), 'Beckett at the BBC: The production and reception of Samuel Beckett's plays for television', in L. Ben-Zvi (ed.), *Drawing on Beckett: Portraits, Performances, and Cultural Contexts*, Tel Aviv: Assaph, 165–82.

Bignell, J. (2005), 'Exemplarity, pedagogy and television history', *New Review of Film and Television Studies* 3:1, 15–32.

Bignell, J. (2006), 'How to watch television: Pedagogy and paedocracy in Beckett's television plays', in M. Buning, M. Engelberts, S. Houppermans, D. van Hulle and D. de Ruyter (eds), *Samuel Beckett Today / Aujourd'hui* 15, 'Historicising Beckett / Issues of performance, Beckett dans l'histoire / En jouant Beckett', 281–93.

Bignell, J. and A. Fickers (eds) (2008), *A European Television History*, New York: Blackwell.

Bignell, J. and S. Lacey (eds) (2005), *Popular Television Drama: Critical Perspectives*, Manchester: Manchester University Press.

Bignell, J., S. Lacey and M. Macmurraugh-Kavanagh (eds) (2000a), 'Editors' introduction to Part II' in *British Television Drama: Past, Present and Future*, Basingstoke: Palgrave, 81–92.

Bignell, J., S. Lacey and M. Macmurraugh-Kavanagh (eds) (2000b), *British Television Drama: Past, Present and Future*, Basingstoke: Palgrave.

Billington, M. (1977), review of *The Lively Arts: Shades*, *The Guardian*, 19 April.

Bishop, C. (1958a), 'The great stone face', *Film Quarterly* 12, 10–15.

Bishop, C. (1958b), 'An interview with Buster Keaton' *Film Quarterly* 12, 15–22.

Bishop, T. (1987), 'Beckett transposing, Beckett transposed: Plays on television', in A. W. Freedman *et al.* (eds), *Beckett Translating / Translating Beckett*, University Park: Pennsylvania University Press, 167–73.

Blanchot, M. and Derrida, J. (2000), *The Instant of My Death / Demeure: Fiction and Testimony*, trans. E. Rottenberg, Palo Alto: Stanford University Press.

BNB (unnamed reviewer) (1983), 'Der Kritik meint', *Frankfurter Rundschau*, no. 118, 24 May, 20.

Bradby, D. (2001), *Waiting for Godot*, Cambridge: Cambridge University Press.

Brandt, G. (ed.) (1981), *British Television Drama*, Cambridge: Cambridge University Press.

Brandt, G. (ed.) (1993), *British Television Drama in the 1980s*, Cambridge: Cambridge University Press.

Brater, E. (1975), 'The thinking eye in Beckett's *Film*', *Modern Language Quarterly* 36:2, 169–71.

Brater, E. (1985), 'Towards a poetics of television technology: Beckett's *Nacht und Träume* and *Quad*.' *Modern Drama* 28:1, 48–54.

Brater, E. (ed.) (1986), *Beckett at 80 / Beckett in Context*, Oxford: Oxford University Press.

Brater, E. (1987), *Beyond Minimalism: Beckett's Late Style in the Theater*, New York and Oxford: Oxford University Press.

Briggs, A. (1985), *The BBC: The First Fifty Years*, Oxford: Oxford University Press.

Brundson, C. (1990), 'Problems with quality', *Screen* 31:1, 67–90.

Brundson, C. (1990), 'Television: Aesthetics and audiences', in P. Mellencamp (ed.) *Logics of Television: Essays in Cultural Criticism*, Bloomington: Indiana University Press, 59–72.

Brundson, C, (1998), 'What is the "television" of television studies?' in C. Geraghty and D. Lusted (eds), *The Television Studies Book*, London: Arnold, 95–113.

Brundson, C., J. D'Acci and L. Spigel (eds) (1997), *Feminist Television Criticism: A Reader*, Oxford: Oxford University Press.

Bryden, M. (1995), '*Quad*: Dancing genders', in C. Wulf (ed.), 'The Savage Eye / L'oeil fauve: New Essays on Beckett's Television Plays', *Samuel Beckett Today / Aujourd'hui*, 4, Amsterdam: Rodopi, 109–22.

Buckingham, D. (1993a), *Children Talking Television: The Making of Television Literacy*, London: Falmer.

Buckingham, D. (ed.) (1993b), *Reading Audiences: Young People and the Media*, Manchester: Manchester University Press.

Buckingham, D. (1996), *Moving Images: Understanding Children's Emotional Responses to Television*, Manchester: Manchester University Press.

Bull, J. (1984) *New British Political Dramatists*, Basingstoke: Macmillan.

Buning, M. and L. Oppenheim (eds) (1993), 'Beckett in the 1990s', *Samuel Beckett Today / Aujourd'hui* 2, Amsterdam: Rodopi.

Bürger, P. (1984), *Theory of the Avant-Garde*, trans. J. Schulte-Sasse, Minnesota: University of Minnesota Press.

Burman, E. (2007), *Deconstructing Developmental Psychology*, second ed., London: Routledge.

Butler, J. (1990), *Gender Trouble: Feminism and the Subversion of Identity*, London: Routledge.

Cardwell, S. (2002), *Adaptation Revisited: Television and the Classic Novel*, Manchester: Manchester University Press.

Carey, P. (1988), 'The *Quad* pieces: A screen for the unseeable', in R. J. Davis and L. St.John Butler (eds), *Make Sense Who May: Essays on Samuel Beckett's Later Works* Gerrards Cross: Colin Smythe, 145–50.

Carson, B., and M. Llewellyn-Jones (eds) (2000), *Frames and Fictions on Television: The Politics of Identity within Drama*, Exeter: Intellect.

Caselli, D. (2005), *Beckett's Dantes: Intertextuality in the Fiction and Criticism*, Manchester: Manchester University Press.

Caughie, J. (1984), 'Television criticism: A discourse in search of an object', *Screen* 25: 4–5, 109–20.

Caughie, J. (1991), 'Before the golden age: Early television drama', in J. Corner (ed.), *Popular Television in Britain*, London: BFI, 22–41.

Caughie, J. (2000), *Television Drama: Realism, Modernism and British Culture*, Oxford: Oxford University Press.

Cooke, L. (2003), *British Television Drama: A History*, London, BFI.
Cooke, L. (2007), 'An experiment in television drama: John McGrath's *The Adventures of Frank*', in L. Mulvey and J. Sexton (eds), *Experimental British Television*, Manchester: Manchester University Press, 106–19.
Corner, J. (1995), *Television Form and Public Address*, London: Edward Arnold.
Coward, R. (1987), 'Dennis Potter and the question of the television author', *Critical Quarterly* 29:4, 79–87.
Crary, J. (1992), *Techniques of the Observer: On Vision and Modernity in the 19th Century*, Cambridge: MIT Press.
Dardis, T. (1979), *Keaton: The Man who Wouldn't Lie Down*, Harmondsworth: Penguin.
Davis, A. (1967), 'For me – drama without padding', *TV Times* southern region ed., 13–19 May, 8.
Day-Lewis, S. (1977), review of *The Lively Arts: Shades*, *Daily Telegraph*, 16 April.
Day-Lewis, S. (ed.) (1998), *Talk of Drama: Views of the Television Dramatist Now and Then*, Luton: University of Luton Press.
Deinst, R. (1994), *Still Life in Real Time: Theory after Television*, Durham: Duke University Press.
Deleuze, G. (1993), 'Le plus grand film Irlandais ("Film" de Beckett)', *Critique et Clinique*, Paris: Minuit, 36–9.
Deleuze, G. (1996), 'The exhausted', trans. C. Kerslake, *parallax* 3, 113–35. First published as 'l'Epuisé' in *Quad et autres pièces pour la télévision*, Paris: Minuit, 1992.
Derrida, J. (1976), *Of Grammatology*, trans. G. Spivak, Baltimore: Johns Hopkins University Press.
Docherty, T. (ed.) (1993), *Postmodernism: A Reader*, London: Harvester Wheatsheaf.
Dodsworth, M. (1975), '*Film* and the religion of art', in K. Worth (ed.), *Beckett the Shape Changer*, London: Routledge and Kegan Paul, 161–82.
Dyer, R. (1998), *Stars*, London: BFI.
Edmands, R. and M. Hewitt (1968), 'Just a face looking', *Torchlight* 15 November, 9.
Ellis, J. (1982), *Visible Fictions: Cinema, Television, Video*, London: Routledge and Kegan Paul.
Ellis, J. (2000), *Seeing Things: Television in the Age of Uncertainty*, London: I. B. Tauris.
Esslin, M. (1975), 'Samuel Beckett and the art of broadcasting', *Encounter* 45, 38–46; reprinted in Esslin, *Mediations: Essays on*

Brecht, Beckett and the Media, New York: Grove, 1982, 125–54.

Esslin, M. (1982), *Mediations: Essays on Brecht, Beckett and the Media*. New York: Grove.

Esslin, M. (1983), 'Visions of absence: Beckett's *Footfalls*, *Ghost Trio* and *...but the clouds...*', in I. Donaldson (ed.), *Transformation in Modern European Drama*, Atlantic Highlands: Humanities Press, 119–29.

Esslin, M. (1987), 'A poetry of moving images', in A. W. Freedman *et al.* (eds), *Beckett Translating / Translating Beckett*, University Park: Pennsylvania University Press, 65–76.

Esslin, M. (1991), *Theatre of the Absurd*, Harmondsworth: Penguin.

Fehsenfeld, M. (1982), 'Beckett's late works: An appraisal', *Modern Drama* 25:3, 355–62.

Feshbach, S. (1999), 'Unswamping a backwater: On Samuel Beckett's *Film*', in L. Oppenheimer (ed.), *Samuel Beckett and the Arts: Music, Visual Arts, and Non-print Media*, New York: Garland, 333–63.

Feuer, J. (1983), 'The concept of live television: Ontology as ideology', in E.A. Kaplan, *Regarding Television: Critical Approaches – An Anthology*, Los Angeles: University Publications of America, 12–22.

Fiske, J. (1987), *Television Culture*, London: Methuen.

Fletcher, J. and J. Spurling (1978), *Samuel Beckett: A Study of his Plays*, London: Eyre Methuen.

Fletcher, J. and J. Spurling (1985), *Beckett the Playwright*, rev. ed., New York: Hill and Wang.

Friedberg, A. (1993), *Window Shopping: Cinema and the Postmodern*, Berkeley: University of California Press.

Freud, S. (1957), *A General Selection from the Works of Sigmund Freud*, New York: Liveright.

Freund, P. (1998), 'The eye in the object: Identification and surveillance in Samuel Beckett's screen dramas', *Journal of Film and Video* 50:1, 42–9.

Frost, E. (1991), 'Fundamental sounds: Recording Samuel Beckett's radio plays', *Theatre Journal* 43:3, 361–76.

Frost, E. and A. McMullan (2003), 'The Blue Angel *Beckett on Film* project: Questions of adaptation, aesthetics, and audience in filming Samuel Beckett's theatrical canon', in L. Ben-Zvi (ed.), *Drawing on Beckett: Portraits, Performances and Cultural Contexts*, Tel Aviv: Assaph, 215–38.

Fry, T. (ed.) (1993), *RUATV?: Heidegger and the Televisual*, Sydney: Power Institute.

Gale, S. H. (2001), *The Films of Harold Pinter*, Albany: New York State

University Press.
Garforth, J. (1992), 'Samuel Beckett in Germany: His work in the German theatre', unpublished PhD thesis, University of Birmingham.
Genette, G. (1997), *Paratexts: Thresholds of Interpretation*, trans. J. Lewin, Cambridge: Cambridge University Press.
Gernsheim, H. and A. (1955), *The History of Photography*, London: London University Press.
Gidal, P. (1992), 'Beckett and sexuality (terribly short version)', in L. Ben-Zvi (ed.), *Women in Beckett: Performance and Critical Perspectives*, Urbana: University of Illinois Press, 187–9.
Gilbert, W. S. (1980), 'The television play: Outside the consensus', *Screen Education* 35, 35–44.
Gombrich, E. (1960), *Art and Illusion*, London and New York: Phaidon.
Greenhalgh, S. (1998), '*The Mysteries* at the National Theatre and Channel 4: Popular theatre into popular television', in J. Ridgman (ed.), *Boxed Sets: Television Representations of Theatre*, Luton: John Libbey, 63–88.
Gontarski, S.E. (1983), 'The anatomy of Beckett's *Eh Joe*', *Modern Drama* 26:4, 425–34.
Gontarski, S.E. (1986), '"Quad" and "Catastrophe"' in S.E. Gontarski (ed.), *On Beckett: Essays and Criticism*, New York: Grove.
Hallam, J. and M. Marshment (1995), 'Framing experience: Case studies in the reception of *Oranges Are Not the Only Fruit*', *Screen* 36:1, 1–15.
Hannah, J. (1997), 'Tracing the development of Beckett's "perceptual" screen work', unpublished MA thesis, University of Reading.
Hansen, M. (1991), *Babel and Babylon: Spectatorship in American Silent Cinema*, Cambridge: Harvard University Press.
Harmon, M. (ed.) (1998), *No Author Better Served: The Correspondence of Samuel Beckett and Alan Schneider*, Cambridge: Harvard University Press.
Hartley, J. (1992), *Tele-ology: Studies in Television*, London: Routledge.
Heath, S. (1990), 'Representing television', in P. Mellencamp (ed.), *Logics of Television: Essays in Cultural Criticism*, Bloomington: Indiana University Press, 267–302.
Heath, S. and G. Skirrow (1977), 'Television: A world in action', *Screen* 18:2, 7–59.
Henning, S. Debevec (1982), '*Film*: A dialogue between Beckett and Berkeley', *Journal of Beckett Studies* 7, 89–99.
Herren, G. (1998), 'Unfamiliar chambers: Power and pattern in Samuel Beckett's *Ghost Trio*', *Journal of Beckett Studies* 8:1, 73–100.
Herren, G. (2000), 'Splitting images: Samuel Beckett's *Nacht und*

Träume', *Modern Drama* 43, 182–91.
Herren, G. (2001), 'Nacht und Träume as Beckett's *Agony in the Garden*', *Journal of Beckett Studies* 11:1, 54–70.
Herren, G. (2007), *Samuel Beckett's Plays on Film and Television*, New York and Basingstoke: Palgrave Macmillan.
Hiebel, H. (1993), 'Quadrat 1+2 as television play', in M. Buning and L. Oppenheim (eds), 'Beckett in the 1990s', *Samuel Beckett Today / Aujourd'hui* 2, Amsterdam: Rodopi, 335–43.
Hill, J. (2007), '"Creative in its own right": The Langham Group and the search for a new television drama', in L. Mulvey and J. Sexton (eds), *Experimental British Television*, Manchester: Manchester University Press, 17–30.
Hill, L. (1996), '"Fuck life": *Rockaby*, sex, and the body', in L. Oppenheim and M. Buning (eds), *Beckett On and On...*, Madison: Farleigh Dickinson, 19–26.
Hird, A. (2005), '"Plain murder"? The death of the author in *Beckett on Film*', unpublished MA dissertation, University of Reading.
Hodge, B. and D. Tripp (1986), *Children and Television: A Semiotic Approach*, Cambridge: Polity.
Homan, S. (1992), *Filming Beckett's Television Plays: A Director's Experience*, Lewisburg: Bucknell University Press.
Hudson, R. (1972), 'Television in Britain: Description and dissent. Interviews with Tony Garnett and John Gould', *Theatre Quarterly* 2:6, 18–25.
Iden, P. (1981), 'Solange es geht', *Frankfurter Rundschau*, no. 235, 10 October, 6.
Inglis, R. (1972), 'Why Beckett's boxes became tins', *Radio Times*, 23 November, 13–15.
Jacobs, J. (1998), 'No respect: Shot and scene in early television drama', in J. Ridgman (ed.), *Boxed Sets: Television Representations of Theatre*, Luton: John Libbey, 39–61.
Jacobs, J. (2000), *The Intimate Screen: Early British Television Drama*, Oxford: Oxford University Press.
Kalb, J. (1989), *Beckett in Performance*, Cambridge: Cambridge University Press.
Kalb, J. (1994), 'The mediated Quixote: The radio and television plays, and *Film*', in J. Pilling (ed.), *The Cambridge Companion to Beckett*, Cambridge: Cambridge University Press, 124–44.
Katz, D. (1995), 'Mirror resembling screens: Yeats, Beckett and *...but the clouds...*', in C. Wulf (ed.), 'The Savage Eye / L'oeil fauve: New Essays on Beckett's Television Plays', *Samuel Beckett Today / Aujourd'hui*, 4, Amsterdam: Rodopi, 83–92.

Kennedy Martin, T. (1964), 'Nats go home: First statement of a new drama for television', *Encore* 48, 21–33.

King, R. (2007), 'Slapstick and mis-remembrance: Buster Keaton's Columbia shorts', *New Review of Film and Television Studies* 5:3, 333–52.

Kirkley, R. B. (1992), 'A catch in the breath: Language and consciousness in Samuel Beckett's ...*but the clouds*...', *Modern Drama* 35:4, 607–16.

Klaver, E. (1991), 'Samuel Beckett's *Ohio Impromptu*, *Quad*, and *What Where*: How it is in the matrix of text and television', *Contemporary Literature* 32:3, 366–82.

Knowlson, J. (1986), '*Ghost Trio / Geister Trio*', in E. Brater (ed.), *Beckett at 80 / Beckett in Context*, Oxford: Oxford University Press, 193–207.

Knowlson, J. (1996), *Damned to Fame: The Life of Samuel Beckett*, London: Bloomsbury.

Krämer, P. (2007), 'Battered child: Buster Keaton's stage performance and vaudeville stardom in the early 1900s', *New Review of Film and Television Studies* 5:3, 253–68.

Lamont, R. (1990), 'Beckett's *Eh Joe*: Lending an ear to the anima', in L. Ben-Zvi (ed.), *Women in Beckett: Performance and Critical Prespectives*, Urbana: University of Illinois Press, 228–35.

Latham, A. (1971), *Crazy Sundays: F. Scott Fitzgerald in Hollywood*, New York: Viking.

Lawley, P. (1983), 'Counterpoint, absence and the medium in Beckett's *Not I*', *Modern Drama* 26:4, 408–12.

Lawley, P. (1984), 'Beckett's dramatic counterpoint: A reading of *Play*', *Journal of Beckett Studies* 9, 25–41.

Laws, C. (2003), 'Beethoven's haunting of Beckett's *Ghost Trio*', in L. Ben-Zvi (ed,), *Drawing on Beckett: Portraits, Performances, and Cultural Contexts*, Tel Aviv: Assaph, 197–213.

Lebel, J.-P. (1967), *Buster Keaton*, trans. P.D. Stovin, London: Zwemmer and Barnes, first published Paris: Editions Universitaires, 1964.

Linville, S. (2007), 'Black face / white face: Keaton and comic doubling', *New Review of Film and Television Studies* 5:3, 269–84.

Lyotard, J-F. (1971), *Discours, Figure*, Paris: Klinckseick.

Lyotard, J-F. (1984), 'The sublime and the avant-garde', *Artforum*, 22:8, 36–43.

Lyotard, J-F. (1991), *The Inhuman: Reflections on Time*, trans G. Bennington and R. Bowlby, Cambridge: Polity.

Lyotard, J-F. (1993), 'Answering the question: What is postmodernism?', in T. Docherty (ed.), *Postmodernism: A Reader*, London: Harvester

Wheatsheaf, 38–46.

MacDonald, S. (1993), *Avant-Garde Film: Motion Studies*, Cambridge: Cambridge University Press.

Macmurraugh-Kavanagh, M. (1997a), 'The BBC and the birth of "The Wednesday Play", 1962–66: Institutional containment versus "agitational contempoaraneity"', *Historical Journal of Film, Radio and Television* 17:3, 367–81.

Macmurraugh-Kavanagh, M. (1997b), '"Drama" into "news": Strategies of intervention in The Wednesday Play', *Screen* 38:3, 247–59.

Marculescu, I. (1989), 'Beckett and the temptation of solipsism', *Journal of Beckett Studies* 11/12, 89–99.

Marshall, S. (1990), 'Video installation in Britain – the early years', in C. Iles, *Signs of the Times: A Decade of Video, Film and Slide-Tape Installation in Britain, 1980–1990*, Oxford: Museum of Modern Art, 12–17.

Marx, K. (1990), *Capital*, vol. 1, trans. B. Fowkes, Harmondsworth: Penguin.

McCaffrey, D. W. (1968), *Four Great Comedians: Chaplin, Lloyd, Keaton, Langdon*, London: Zwemmer and Barnes.

McDonald, P. (1998), 'Supplementary chapter: Reconceptualising stardom', in R. Dyer, *Stars*, London: BFI, 175–200.

McGrath, J. (1977), 'TV drama: The case against naturalism', *Sight and Sound* 36:2, 100–5.

McGrath, J. (1981), *A Good Night Out: Popular Theatre, Audience, Class and Form*, London: Methuen.

McLuhan, M. (1987), *Understanding Media: The Extensions of Man*, London: Ark [first published 1964].

McMullan, A. (1993), *Theatre on Trial: Samuel Beckett's Later Drama*, London: Routledge.

McMullan, A. (1997), 'Versions of embodiment / visions of the body in Beckett's ... *but the clouds* ...', in M. Buning, M. Engelberts and S. Houppermans (eds), 'Samuel Beckett: Crossroads and borderlines. L'Oeuvre-carrefour / L'Oeuvre limite', *Samuel Beckett Today / Aujourd'hui* 6, Amsterdam: Rodopi, 353–64.

Mepham, J. (1990), 'The ethics of quality in television', in G. Mulgan (ed.), *The Question of Quality*, London: BFI, 56–72.

Mercier, V. (1977), *Beckett / Beckett*, Oxford: Oxford University Press.

Metz, C. (1982), *The Imaginary Signifier: Psychoanalysis and the Cinema*, trans. B. Brewster, Bloomington: Indiana University Press.

Miller, T. (2000), 'Beckett's political technology: Expression, confession, and torture in the later drama', in M. Buning, M. Engelberts and O.

Kosters (eds), 'Beckett and religion, Beckett / aesthetics and politics', *Samuel Beckett Today / Aujourd'hui* 9, Amsterdam: Rodopi, 255–78.

Millington, B. and R. Nelson (1986), *Boys from the Blackstuff: The Making of TV Drama*, London: Comedia.

Moorjani, A. (1996), 'Mourning Schopenhauer, and Beckett's art of shadows', in L. Oppenheim and M. Buning (eds), *Beckett On and On*, Madison: Farleigh Dickinson University Press, 83–101.

Morley, D. (1992), *Television, Audiences and Cultural Studies*, London: Routledge.

Mulvey, L. (2007), 'Introduction: Experimental British television', in L. Mulvey and J. Sexton (eds), *Experimental British Television*, Manchester: Manchester University Press, 1–16.

Murdoch, G. (1980), 'Authorship and organisation', *Screen Education* 35, 19–34.

Murphy, V. (1975), 'Being and perception: Beckett's *Film*', *Modern Drama* 18:1, 43–8.

Neale, S. (1985), *Cinema and Technology: Image, Sound, Colour*, Basingstoke: Macmillan.

Nelson, R. (1997), *TV Drama in Transition: Forms, Values and Cultural Change*, Basingstoke: Macmillan.

Newcomb, H. (1974), *TV: The Most Popular Art*, New York: Anchor.

Oldham, G. (1996), *Keaton's Silent Shorts: Beyond the Laughter*, Carbondale: Southern Illinois University Press.

Oppenheim, L. (ed.) (1999), *Samuel Beckett and the Arts: Music, Visual Arts, and Non-print Media*, New York: Garland.

Oppenheim, L. (2000), *The Painted Word: Samuel Beckett's Dialogue with Art*, Ann Arbor: University of Michigan Press.

Ottaway, R. (1982), 'Say it again, Sam. Again', *Radio Times* 11–17 December 1982, 21.

Parker, A. and E. Kosofsky Sedgwick (1995), *Peformativity and Performance*, London: Routledge.

Perlmutter, R. (1977), 'Beckett's *Film* and Beckett and film', *Journal of Modern Literature* 6:1, 83–94.

Pike, F. (ed.) (1982), *Ah! Mischief: The Writer and Television*, London: Faber.

Potter, D. (1977), review of *The Lively Arts: Shades*, *Sunday Times*, 24 April.

Prinz, J. (1999), 'Resonant images: Beckett and German Expressionism', in L. Oppenheim (ed.), *Samuel Beckett and the Arts: Music, Visual Arts, and Non-print Media*, New York: Garland, 153–71.

Ratcliffe, M. (1977), review of *The Lively Arts: Shades*, *The Times*, 18

April.

Rees, A. L. (2007), 'Experimenting on air: UK artists' film on television', in L. Mulvey and J. Sexton (eds), *Experimental British Television*, Manchester: Manchester University Press, 146–65.

Ridgman, J. (ed.) (1998), *Boxed Sets: Television Representations of Theatre*, Luton: John Libbey.

Russell, C. (1989), 'The figure in the monitor: Beckett, Lacan, and Video', *Cinema Journal* 28:4, 20–37.

Sarris, A. (1969), 'Buster Keaton and Samuel Beckett', *Columbia University Forum* 12:4, 42–3.

Saunders, G. (2007), 'Reclaiming Sam for Ireland: The *Beckett on Film* project', in R. Cave and B. Levitas (eds), *Irish Theatre in England*, Dublin: Carysfort, 79–96.

Schneider, A. (1972), 'On directing *Film*', in S. Beckett, *Film*, London: Faber, 63–94.

Schopenhauer, A. (1966), *The World as Will and Representation*, trans. E. Payne, New York: Dover.

Shubik, I. (1975), *Play for Today: The Evolution of Television Drama*, London; Davis-Poynter.

Sierz, A. (undated), Interview with Alan Moloney, Beckett on Film website (www.channel4.com/culture/microsites/B/beckett/maloney_interview.html).

Singleton-Turner, R. (1994), *Television and Children*, London: BBC.

Sweeney, K. (2007), '*Three Ages*: Keaton's burlesque of the "mythic ages" genre', *New Review of Film and Television Studies* 5:3, 285–98.

Taylor, N. (1998), 'A history of the stage play on BBC television', in J. Ridgman (ed.), *Boxed Sets: Television Representations of Theatre*, Luton: John Libbey, 23–37.

Thomas, H. (1959), *The Armchair Theatre*, London: Weidenfeld and Nicholson.

Tulloch, J. (1990), *Television Drama: Agency, Audience and Myth*, London: Routledge.

Tulloch, J. and M. Alvarado (1983), *Doctor Who: The Unfolding Text*, Basingstoke: Macmillan.

Voigts-Virchow, E. (1998), 'Exhausted cameras: Beckett in the TV-zoo', in J. Jeffers (ed.), *Samuel Beckett: A Casebook*, New York: Garland, 225–49.

Voigts-Virchow, E. (2000–1), 'Face values: Beckett Inc., the camera plays and cultural liminality', *Journal of Beckett Studies* 10:1/2, 119–35.

Walker, J. A. (1993), *Arts TV: A History of Arts Television in Britain*,

London: John Libbey.

Walkerdine, V. (1998), 'Children in cyberspace: A new frontier', in K. Lesnik-Oberstein (ed.), *Children in Culture: Approaches to Childhood*, Basingstoke: Macmillan, 231–47.

Wees, W. (1992), *Light Moving in Time: Studies in the Visual Aesthetics of Avant-garde Film*, Berkeley: University of California Press.

Weiss, K. (2002), 'Modernization and mechanization: Technology in the works of Samuel Beckett', unpublished PhD thesis, University of Reading.

West, T. (2000), 'CODA: Timothy West discusses "Acting on stage: acting on screen", followed by extracts from the discussion after his and John Caughie's presentations', in J. Bignell, S. Lacey and M. Macmurraugh-Kavanagh (eds), *British Television Drama: Past, Present and Future*, Basingstoke: Palgrave, 170–3.

Wheatley, H. (2007), 'Introduction: Re-viewing television histories', in H. Wheatley (ed.), *Re-viewing Television History: Critical Issues in Television Historiography*, London: I. B. Tauris, 1–12.

Wheldon, Sir H. (1976), The British experience in television', *The Listener* 95:2447, 4 March, 265–7.

Williams, L. (1981), *Figures of Desire: A Theory and Analysis of Surrealist Film*, Berkeley: University of California Press.

Williams, R. (1968), *Drama in Performance*, London: C.A. Watts.

Williams, R. (1981), *Culture*, London: Fontana.

Williams, R. (1990), *Television, Technology and Cultural Form*, London: Fontana [first published 1974].

Wolfe, C. (2007), 'Western unsettlement: Transcontinental journeys, comic plotting and Keaton's *Go West*', *New Review of Film and Television Studies* 5:3, 299–316.

Worth, K. (1992), 'Women in Beckett's radio and television plays', in L. Ben-Zvi (ed.), *Women in Beckett: Performance and Critical Perspectives*, Urbana: University of Illinois Press, 236–42.

Zettl, H. (1978), 'The rare case of television aesthetics', *Journal of the University Film Association* 30:2, 1–12.

Zilliacus, C. (1976), *Beckett and Broadcasting: A Study of the works of Samuel Beckett for and in Radio and Television*, Åbo: Åbo Academie.

Zinman, T. (1995), '*Eh Joe* and the peephole aesthetic', in C. Wulf (ed.), 'The Savage Eye/L'oeil fauve: New Essays on Beckett's Television Plays', *Samuel Beckett Today/Aujourd'hui*, 4, Amsterdam: Rodopi, 53–64.

Index

Beckett's works are entered individually by title; works not by Beckett give the originator's name.

absence 113–14, 165, 175
Act Without Words I & II 73, 86, 87, 122, 184
Adamou, Christina 98
Adams, John 146–7
adaptations of stage plays 14–15, 19, 100, 123, 184–5
    production methods 32–41
    Public Service Broadcasting 76–82
Adorno, Theodor 199
adverts in Beckett productions 166–7
aesthetics of television 18–19, 25, 102–3, 208
    digital technology 36–7
    production of Beckett's plays 38–9, 40–1
agency 91–2, 114–15, 147, 197–8
All That Fall 62, 106, 108, 112
anachronism 10, 12, 53, 128, 203–4, 207, 208
    production methods 25, 38–9, 42–3
Ang, Ien 177
anthology drama series 37, 39, 42–3, 53–4, 55–6, 104, 106
    television criticism 169–70, 185
Arena (BBC series) 59, 61, 65–6, 78, 189
Arikha, Avigdor 149
Armstrong, Tim 112
Arnheim, Rudolf 131
art: and Beckett's work 126, 138–51, 159–61
    perception 151–2, 160–1
    television 141–3
arts programming 8, 10–11, 14, 59–62, 127

    on Channel 4 121–2
    European co-productions 78–9
    scheduling of plays 52, 58–9, 77, 108, 121–2, 176–7, 189, 203, 207
    television criticism 169–70
    video art 65–6
Asmus, Walter 86
Aspinall, Tim 186–7
Attenborough, David 61
audience: and agency 197–8
    broadcasting and conceptions of 165–8, 186, 189–90
    camerawork in *Eh Joe* 21, 22, 48
    competence 196–8
    critical constructions 198–9
    critical evaluation 164, 168–8, 172–6, 195–6, 207–8
    expectations and *Film* 191, 192, 193
    identification and *Play* 33–4
    paedocratic and pedagogic strategies 154–6, 159, 168, 199–201
    perception 151–63, 191, 193
    ratings and reception of plays 179–84, 199
    scheduling 87, 176–84
    Television Studies 5
    types of audience and forms of television 195–201
    voice and mediation with viewer 152–3, 168, 173–4, 176
    see also spectatorship
audience research 10–11, 16, 179–84, 207
'auteur theory' 117
authorship: and Beckett's work 13–14,

88–124, 189
Film 190–1, 193, 194–5
television critical canon 171
avant-garde 198
cinema 13, 52, 66–76, 114, 131–3
television 9–10, 17, 18–19, 53, 67

Baker, Richard 66
Bakewell, Michael 62, 103, 106
Baudry, Jean-Louis 68–9
BBC: audience and scheduling 177–8
cultivation of Beckett as author 88–9, 99–111, 129–31, 185, 207
overseas sales of programmes 78–9
production technologies and *Eh Joe* 19–27
see also Public Service Broadcasting *and individual plays*
BBC Audience Research 10, 16, 164, 179–80, 207
BBC Radio 13, 52, 62, 77, 88–9, 105, 106, 108
BBC Written Archives Centre 10–11
BBC2 channel 77, 78, 81
Beckett, John 62
Beckett, Samuel: and adaptation of stage plays 32–3, 107, 109
audience reception 183–4, 199
authorial control 44–5, 89, 100, 103–4, 106–11, 123–4, 189
authorship and signatures in *Film* 115–19
collaboration with actors and directors 107, 118–19
cultural significance and value 79–80, 101–2, 185, 205–6
Ealing studios 39
on *Film* 70–2, 93
interest in art 144–5, 160–1
photographic images of 119
public awareness of 193–4
published screenplays 82–3, 89
refusal to be interviewed 108–9
see also individual works
Beckett at 80 (BBC documentary) 119
Beckett on Film series (Channel 4/RTE, 2001) 1, 4–5, 15, 101–2, 206
audience 167
broadcasting context 83–7, 119–21
DVD of series 87, 119
Irish context 84–6
mise-en-scène 73–4

production technologies 31–7
Beckett Studies 2–3, 171–6, 199
Television Studies 11, 16, 202
Ben-Zvi, Linda 18, 95, 128, 153, 155, 173
Benjamin, Walter 111, 141, 142–3
Bergson, Henri 28
Berkeley, Bishop George 71
Bignell, Jonathan 38, 40
billing of plays 57–8, 62, 122, 186–7
Billington, Michael 185, 186
black-and-white *see* monochrome productions
Blin, Roger 130, 132
bodily representation 146–51
Boorman, John 61
Bradby, David 68, 72
Bragg, Melvyn 59, 61–2, 119, 130
Brandt, George 207
Brater, Enoch 24–5, 98, 128, 131, 191
Bray, Barbara 62
Breath 78, 86
broadcasting contexts 12–13, 52–87, 103–4, 105–6, 127–8
audience 165–8, 176–7, 179–84, 189–90, 195–6
historiography 16, 203–4, 208
Modernism 128–33, 158–9, 188, 197, 202–3
socialist criticism 170–1
Brown, Warren 107, 109
Bryden, Mary 98
Buckingham, David 154–5
Buñuel, Luis 131–2
Bürger, Peter 67
Burton, Humphrey 59
…but the clouds… (BBC TV, 1977) 70, 108
absence 113, 114
artistic composition 138, 139
Beckett's authorial control 109–10
broadcasting context 59
critics' responses 187, 188
framing effects 153
identity in 112, 175
production 32, 38, 39–40, 41, 49–50
setting 144, 162
title 162, 174
voice in 90, 97, 173–4
Butler, Judith 113–14

Cahiers du Cinéma (journal) 117–18, 192

camerawork: and aesthetics of television
  40–1
 artistic composition 139–41
 avant-garde film and Beckett's work
  131–2
 critics' reviews 187
 Eh Joe 20–2, 23–4, 25–6, 40, 45,
  47–8, 90–1, 112, 146–7, 157
 Film 91–4, 194
 Ghost Trio 45, 157
 media literacy 157–8
 Play 33–4, 35, 75–6
 Quad 29–31
 in stage adaptations 23–4, 37
 voices 44–5, 146–7
Carey, Phyllis 98, 99
Cascando 62
Caselli, Daniela 123, 126–7, 205
Catastrophe 86
Caughie, John 67, 72
Channel 4 66, 119–22, 123
 see also Beckett on Film series
Chien Andalou, Un (Buñuel) 67, 72,
  131–2
children: perception of media 152,
  154–8, 158–9
 see also paedocracy
cinema: audience and spectatorship 166
 avant-garde 13, 52, 66–76, 114,
  131–2
 'cinematic' production style 17, 31,
  32, 34–6, 39–41, 102, 164, 186
 cultural production 143
 Modernism 129, 131–3
 see also film
cinematography *see* camerawork
 lighting
Clark, Sir Kenneth 61
class and arts programming 60, 186
close-up shots 54, 131–2, 147–8
 Eh Joe 21–2, 23, 112, 114, 146–7, 148
Cocteau, Jean 132
Colgan, Michael 83, 84
colour productions 30–1, 41–4, 99
Come and Go 86–7, 122, 184
communication and plays 174–5, 204
context *see* broadcasting contexts; European context
Cooke, Lez 24
co-productions 78–9, 85
Coward, Ros 88, 89
Craig, (Edward) Gordon 68

critical evaluation 15–16, 164–201,
  206–7
 TV critics' reviews 185–6, 187–90,
  207–8
 TV drama 3–4, 16, 52, 100, 102,
  168–72, 184–90, 195–6, 202–3,
  207–8
Crowley, John 86–7
Cultural Studies 3–4, 154–5, 170–1, 199

Day-Lewis, Sean 187
Deinst, Richard 28–9
Deren, Maya 67–8
Derrida, Jacques 175
developmental psychology 155, 156–7
digital technology 36–7
directors as 'auteurs' 117
Docherty, Thomas 72
domestic settings 143–4, 145–6, 162
Duthuit, Georges 160–1
Dyer, Richard 135, 190, 195

Ealing film studios 39
editing 17, 23–4, 26, 92
education: pedagogic presentation
  154–6, 159, 168, 199–201
 schools programming 122
Egoyan, Atom 86
Eh Joe (BBC TV, 1966) 13, 81
 absence 113
 agency and authorship 97–8
 audience response 180, 182, 183
 Beckett's authorial control 103
 broadcasting context 52, 57–8, 106
 close-up shots 21–2, 23, 112, 114,
  146–7, 148
 critical responses 188
 eye and voyeurism in 91
 German production 182, 188
 portraiture 146, 148
 production methods 17, 19–27, 40,
  41, 44–8, 157
 role of voice/Voice 44–8, 90, 91, 146,
  173, 175
 setting 144, 145
 sound and identity in 112, 175
 title 162
Eisenstein, Sergei 131, 151
Elliot, John 104
Elliott, Nick 61
Ellis, John 3, 170
Embers 62, 106

Endgame 62, 86, 184, 193–4
episodic serials 54–5
Esslin, Martin 44, 62–3, 80, 101, 105, 144
    Shades 58, 59, 61–2, 106, 108, 119, 130
European context 85, 205–6
    Beckett's cultural value 79–80, 130, 205–6
    co-productions 78–9
    European Modernism 128–33, 187–8
evaluation *see* critical evaluation
experimental programming: radio drama 13
    television 9–10, 12, 72, 81, 82, 186, 203–4
    see also avant-garde
Expressionist films 75, 187
Exton, Clive 19
eye as theme 67–8, 91–2, 115, 131–2
Eyre, Richard 86

Fable (Hopkins) 55–6
Fehsenfeld, Martha 98, 99, 139, 160
feminist theory and television 5
Feshbach, Sidney 149
Festival (BBC series) 104, 130, 180–1
Feuer, Jane 28
film: as physical format 17, 27, 28–9, 31–7, 102
    see also cinema; *Film*
Film (short film, 1964, 1979) 1, 10, 90, 97, 206
    audience expectations 191, 192, 193, 195
    authorship and agency 114–19
    avant-garde cinema 67–72, 75
    camerawork and agency in 91–4
    critical reception 11, 190–5
    intertextuality 149, 191
    Keaton and silent cinema tradition 133–8, 191–3, 195, 204
    Modernist cinema 131–3
    production 19–20, 33, 40, 45, 47
    self and other 175
    setting 145
First Night (BBC series) 37, 104
Fitzgerald, Constance 180
Fletcher, John 23, 44
Footfalls 86, 99, 122, 148, 184
Ford, John 117

framing effects 153
Frankfurt School 199
Freund, Peter 96
Friedberg, Anne 72
Futurism 75, 149

Gale, Steven 82
Garforth, Julian 112, 182, 188–9
Garnett, Tony 56, 102, 104, 185
Garrad, Charles 86
Gate Theatre, Dublin 32, 83–4, 85–6
gender identity 113–14
geometric forms in plays 139
German television productions 206
German TV productions: audience ratings 182, 189
    co-productions with BBC 78–9
    critical reception 188–9
    mise-en-scène 73–4
    production technologies 17, 23, 25, 39, 43–4, 45, 49
    Public Service Broadcasting 1, 166–7, 189–90
    see also Süddeutscher Rundfunk
Ghost Trio (*Tryst*) (BBC TV, 1977) 107–8, 165
    absence 113, 175
    abstract form in 162–3
    artistic composition 138, 139
    broadcasting context 59
    critics' response 185, 187–8
    framing effects 153
    music in 48–9, 172–3
    production 32, 38, 39–40, 41–2, 45
    role of voice/Voice 90, 94–7, 152–3, 155, 168, 173
    setting 145–6, 162–3
    title 162, 174
Gibson, Alan 57
Gilbert, W. Stephen 39
Gombrich, Ernst 151–2
Gontarski, Stan 19–20, 46, 47, 97–8, 128, 149
Greene, Hugh 177–8
Grossaert, Jan 148

Hall, David 64–6
Hansen, Miriam 133–4
Happy Days 72, 85, 86, 167, 184
Harris, Lionel 104
Hartley, John 199–201
Hawks, Howard 117

Hayden, Henri 130
Herren, Graley 2, 28, 205, 208
　on art and Beckett 142, 143, 144–5, 148, 163
　on audience and spectatorship 166, 167
　on *Ghost Trio* 94–5, 97
Hill, Leslie 111
Hiller, Susan 65
Hirst, Damien 86
historiography of television 16, 203–4, 208
Hitchcock, Alfred 117, 129
Hoey, Brian 64
Hopkins, John 55–6, 56, 106
Horkheimer, Max 199
Horror of Darkness (Hopkins) 56
Hughes, Enda 86

Iden, Peter 188–9
identification 33–4
identity 111–12, 175
　gender identity 113–14
Inglis, Ruth 186
institutions 13–14
　audience 177–8, 189, 199–201
　authority 189–90
　authorship 88–124, 189
　avant-garde 132–3
　pedagogic discourse 154–6, 159, 168, 199–201
　TV drama 5–6, 67, 178, 185, 206–7
intertextual relationships 14, 125–63, 191, 204–5
Ionesco, Eugène 131

Jacobs, Jason 38
J.M. Mime 99
Jordan, Neil 86

Kalb, Jonathan 70, 138, 146, 148, 155, 194
Kaufman, Boris 93
Keaton, Buster 68, 70, 117–18, 133–8, 190–5
Kirkley, Richard Bruce 112
Klaver, Elizabeth 179
Kleist, Heinrich von 68, 95
Knowlson, James 72, 81, 95, 96
Krapp's Last Tape 112, 161, 174
　audience 180–2, 186–7
　BBC productions 47, 53, 91, 104, 106, 107, 130, 180–2, 183
　Beckett on Film 86, 87, 184
Kustow, Michael 120

Langham Group 18–19
Late Night Line-up (BBC series) 103
Lawley, Paul 34–5
Lebel, Jean-Patrick 136–7, 192
Lefevre, Robin 86
Levinas, Emmanuel 175
Lewis, Jim 43
lighting 22–3, 43–5
Lindsay-Hogg, Michael 86, 184
Lively Arts, The (BBC series) 52, 78, 107, 108
　see also Shades programme
'liveness' of productions 27–9, 31–2, 165–6
Loach, Ken 56, 102, 185
long-take shots 20–1, 25–6, 29–30, 31–2, 40, 73, 93–4
Lost Ones, The 161
Luke, Peter 104, 180
Lyotard, Jean-François 36–7, 72

McDonald, Paul 193
McDonald, Scott 67
MacGowran, Jack 22–3, 24, 26, 57–8, 101, 106
McGrath, John 47, 197, 198
MacGreevy, Thomas 145
McLuhan, Marshall 64, 158–9, 160
McMullan, Anna 35, 74, 128
McPherson, Conor 86
MacTaggart, James 19, 55, 56, 104
McWhinnie, Donald 53, 62, 105, 106, 130, 187
　Beckett's authority 103, 107–8, 109
Magee, Patrick 57
Mamet, David 86
Marks, Stephany 109–10
Martin, Troy Kennedy 19, 54, 197, 198
masking and star image 195
Mason, Ronald 63
mass culture 199
media literacy 154, 156–8, 158–9
Mercer, David 3, 186
Mercier, Vivien 46–7
Metz, Christian 33–4
Midgley, Robin 63
Minghella, Anthony 33, 35, 36, 75, 86
minimalism 125, 132–3, 187

Mitchell, Katie 86
Modernism: and bodily representation
    149–51
  European context 128–33, 180,
    187–8, 198
  perception of art 151–2, 153, 158–9
  television 9–10, 25, 72, 101, 127–8,
    158–9, 186, 197
  video art 64
Molloy 20
Moloney, Alan 84
Monitor (BBC series) 59, 61
monochrome productions 30–1, 41–4,
    99, 113, 187
Moore, Harry 78
Morahan, Christopher 55
Morris, John 108
Mulvey, Laura 12, 203
Murphy 161
music in *Ghost Trio* 48–9, 172–3
Myers, Sidney 93

Nacht und Träume (SDR production)
    24–5, 49, 90, 113
  critics' response 189
  intertextuality 132, 139–40, 145, 148
  title 162, 174
naturalism in TV drama 15, 129, 143–4,
    145–6, 147–8, 162, 164, 178, 185
  anti-naturalism of Beckett plays 14,
    22, 38, 40, 47, 186, 196–7, 207
Nauman, Bruce 25, 101, 150–1
Nelson, Robin 171, 207
New Wave cinema 17, 19, 116, 194
New York Film Festival and *Film* 191,
    192
Newcomb, Horace 169
Newman, Sydney 104
Not I 148, 174
  BBC productions 32, 41, 59, 107,
    147, 187
  Beckett on Film 86, 147
Nyman, Michael 66

O'Connor, James 56
O'Donnell, Damien 74, 86
Ohio Impromptu 86
Old Tune, The 62, 112
Ono, Yoko 67, 187
Open University *Godot* production 183
Oppenheim, Lois 160
otherness 96, 200–1

self and other 173–4, 175–6
Ottaway, Robert 189
Out of the Unknown (BBC series) 57
Owen, Alun 19, 24, 53–4
Oxtoby, David 101

paedocracy 54–5, 158, 159, 199–200
Page, Anthony 56
painting *see* art
pedagogic strategies 154–6, 159, 168,
    199–201
perception 28
  camerawork in *Film* 194
  viewers' experience 151–63, 191,
    193
performativity 113, 114
Perlmutter, Ruth 194
Phillips, Sian 58
philosophical interpretations 172–6
photography 69–70, 90–1, 111, 119
Piece of Monologue, A 63, 86
Pinget, Robert: *La Manivelle* 62
Pinter, Harold 130, 131
Plater, Alan 54
Play 174
  BBC productions 62–3, 107, 109
  Beckett on Film 32–7, 45, 75–6, 86
Play for Today (BBC series) 53, 55, 100
Play of the Month (BBC series) 104, 106
Playhouse, The (Keaton short) 134,
    135–6
politics and TV plays 5–7, 100, 170–1,
    186
popular culture 199
postmodernism 72, 149
post-structuralism 149
Potter, Dennis 48, 55, 185–6, 197
Powell, Tristram 58, 78, 106, 107, 108,
    109, 130, 187
press reviews 185–6, 187–90, 207–8
production technologies 12, 17–51
Proust, Marcel 111, 161
pseudo-unification and star image 195
Public Service Broadcasting 6, 72, 100,
    127, 167–8
  BBC productions 76–82, 123, 166–7,
    187, 189–90
  Channel 4 119–20, 122, 123
  German productions 1, 166–7,
    189–90
Pudovkin, Vsevolov 131

Quad (*Quadrat I & II*, 1981) (SDR production) 113, 139, 157, 160, 179
    authorship and agency 98–9, 189
    BBC presentation (1982) 41, 63–4, 80, 81–2, 189
    broadcasting context 81–2
    critics' responses 188–9
    framing effects 153
    as postmodernist work 149
    production 24–5, 29–31, 41, 43–4
    title 162

radio *see* BBC Radio
Radio Times 57–8, 62, 63–4, 122, 186–7, 189
ratings for Beckett plays 179–84, 189
realism and TV drama 3, 17, 102, 162
    and Beckett's work 112–13
    and critical evaluation 100, 164, 185, 186
    see also social realism in TV drama
reflexivity 128, 129, 153, 172–3, 197
Reiner Moritz (German TV company) 79
Reisz, Karel 86
repetition 35–7
Review (BBC series) 78
Ridley, Anna 65, 66
Rockaby 20, 73, 86, 174
Rosenthal, Jack 101
Rosset, Barney 131
Rough for Radio 63, 106
Rough for Theatre I & II 85–6
Royal Court Theatre, London 101, 180
Rozema, Patricia 86
RTE (Irish channel) 85, 183–4
    see also Beckett on Film series
Ruskin, John 151–2
Russell, Catherine 18, 128
Russell, Ken 61

Sarris, Andrew 192
Saunders, Graham 84
scheduling 57, 58, 77, 108, 189, 203, 207
    advertising breaks 167
    audiences 87, 176–84
    Beckett on Film 121–2
    contexts for *Film* 191
Schiller Theatre, Berlin 32
Schlesinger, John 61
Schneider, Alan 32, 70–2, 93, 118–19, 134, 190–1

schools slot for *Beckett on Film* 122
Schopenhauer, Artur 71
screenplays 82–3, 89, 194
SDR *see* Süddeutscher Rundfunk
Second House (BBC series) 107
Seddon, Peter 103
self and other 173–4, 175–6
settings 143–4, 145–6, 162–3
Shades programme (*Lively Arts* series, 1977) 4, 13, 119, 130, 205
    authenticity and realism 113–14
    authorial control 107–10
    broadcasting context 52, 58, 59–60, 106, 176–7
    critical reception 185–6, 187–8
    as European co-production 78–9
    production 39–40, 41–2, 49
    see also …but the clouds…; Ghost Trio; Not I
Sherlock Junior (Keaton film) 133–4, 134–5
shots *see* camerawork
Shubik, Irene 177, 178
silent cinema and *Film* 133–8, 191–3, 195, 204
simulacra and digital technology 36, 37
single camera filming 23–4, 29–30, 67, 157
single TV plays 4, 8, 55, 169–71, 185–6
Singleton-Turner, Roger 156–7
social class and arts programmes 60, 186
social issues and TV drama 56
social realism in TV drama 12, 17, 31, 178–9, 185, 186, 207
social science 171
socialist criticism 170–1
sound 26, 44–51, 111–12
South Bank Show, The (ITV series) 59, 61
space 73–4, 95–6, 97
    visual space and intertextuality 125–6, 138–9, 145–6, 153
spectatorship 125, 126, 133–8, 166–7, 191–3, 195
    see also audience
Spurling, John 23
star image and film characters 195
studio recordings 18, 31, 32, 34, 37–41
Sturridge, Charles 86
Süddeutscher Rundfunk (SDR) 29, 39, 43–4, 167, 177, 182, 188,
    see also Nacht und Träume; Quad;

Was Wo
Surrealist film 67, 75–6, 112, 131–2
Sutton, Shaun 104

Taylor, Neil 80–1, 184–5
television drama: and audience 195–201
　as context for Beckett's work 6–8, 55, 56–7, 103–4, 105–6
　critical evaluation 3–4, 16, 52, 100, 102, 164, 168–72, 184–90, 202–3, 206–8
　cultivation of authors 89, 99–104, 105–11, 129–31, 185, 206
　domestic settings 143–4, 145–6, 162
　forms of 53–7
　Modernism 128–9, 197, 202
　Public Service Broadcasting ethos 77–82, 100, 123, *see also* adaptations of stage plays; anthology drama series; avant-garde: television; production technologies; single TV plays
Television Studies 197
　audience 5, 195
　Beckett Studies 11, 16, 202
　Beckett's audio-visual works 3, 9, 203, 207
　Modernist context 202–3
　television criticism and Beckett 168–9, 186
temporality 29, 99
　'liveness' 27–9, 30–1, 165–6
That Time 86
theatre: Beckett's theatre work 14–15
　dramatists' work on television 184–5
　'theatrical' production style 17, 23–4, 32, 37–41, 102, 164, 197, 207
　see also adaptations of stage plays
Théâtre Récamier, Paris 84–5
Theatre 625 (BBC series) 37, 104, 106
Third Programme (BBC radio channel) 52, 77, 88–9, 108
Thirty Minute Theatre (BBC series) 53–4, 104, 186
This Quarter (journal) 132
titles of TV plays 162, 174

Velde, Bram van 161
Vertov, Dziga 151
video art 64–6, 149–51

videotape production 17, 19, 25, 26–9
viewers *see* audience
visual meaning theories 15, 125
visual space and intertextuality 125–6, 138–9, 145–6, 153
Vogel, Amos 191
voice: agency and author's voice 90–9, 147
　mediation with viewer 152–3, 168, 173–4, 176
　production methods 44–8, 49–50, 146–7
Voigts-Virchow, Eckart 52–3, 102, 132–3, 157, 174
voyeurism 91, 95, 97

Waiting for Godot 32, 72, 96, 193
　audience reception 183, 184
　BBC radio 63
　BBC TV production 103–4, 129, 179–80, 183
　Beckett on Film 85, 86, 167
Wake for Sam, A (BBC documentary) 119, 183
Walkerdine, Valerie 199
Walsh, Kieron 86
Was Wo (SDR production) 73–4, 112
Wednesday Play, The (BBC series) 42–3, 53, 55, 57, 177
Wees, William 67
Weiss, Katherine 111
West, Timothy 77
What Where 73–4, 86, 112, 122, 184
Wheatley, Helen 208
Wheldon, Huw 59, 61, 100–1
Whitelaw, Billie 107, 109, 189
Williams, Linda 75
Williams, Raymond 3, 143–4, 169, 170
witnessing in TV drama 48
women: gender and absence 113–14
Wood, Peter 63
Words and Music 62, 106

Yentob, Alan 61

Zettl, Herbert 28
Zilliacus, Clas 91, 194
Zinman, Toby 91

EU authorised representative for GPSR:
Easy Access System Europe, Mustamäe tee 50,
10621 Tallinn, Estonia
gpsr.requests@easproject.com

www.ingramcontent.com/pod-product-compliance
Lightning Source LLC
Chambersburg PA
CBHW070941230426
43666CB00011B/2512